The People of the
NORTHERN HIGHLANDS AND ISLES
1800 - 1850

By
David Dobson

Published for Clearfield Company by
Genealogical Publishing Company
Baltimore, Maryland
2021

ISBN 9780806359328

INTRODUCTION

This book contains references to people in the Northern Highlands of Scotland and the Northern Isles, at home and abroad, between 1800 and 1850. The counties concerned in the Northern Highlands are Ross and Cromarty, Sutherland and Caithness; and in the Northern Isles, the counties of Orkney and of Shetland. Most of the persons named were derived from primary sources such as court records, contemporary newspapers and journals, monumental inscriptions, and documents located in archives in the United Kingdom. Most entries bring together emigrants, their destinations, especially in North America and Australasia, and their kin who remained in Scotland.

The late eighteenth and early nineteenth century in Scotland marked the time of the notorious Highland Clearances, when landowners evicted their tenants to establish large sheep farms that were more profitable than collecting rent. The worst evictions were in Sutherland, particularly in Kildonan by Patrick Sellar, factor for the Marquis of Stafford, later Duke of Sutherland. Some landlords promoted re-settlement in coastal crofts, some encouraged emigration or fishing, but the evictions in Sutherland were particularly harsh. Donald Sage, who witnessed the evictions at Achness, wrote *'they gave the inmates an hour to pack up and carry off their furniture and then set the cottages on fire. To this plan they ruthlessly adhered. The roofs and rafters were lighted up into one red blaze'*. By 1811 around 15,000 tenants had been evicted off the Sutherland estates. Thomas Douglas, Earl of Selkirk, alleviated the problem by organising emigration from the area to the Canadian Maritimes and to the Red River in what now is Manitoba.

During this period of poverty and famine, various landowners attempted to export consignments of foodstuffs, mainly grain, from ports such as Wick in Caithness. Various Highlanders who opposed the exportation of grain—which led to riots and subsequent trials in some cases--are listed in the book. For example, in 1792 the ringleaders of a group resisting the growth of sheep herding were tried and sentenced to transportation to the colonies. Fortuitously, the Hudson's Bay Company absorbed some of the displaced Northerners, as it was an important recruiter of workers, mainly from Orkney but also Shetland and Caithness, most of whom were employed around Hudson Bay in Canada.

David Dobson, Dundee, Scotland, 2021.

REFERENCES

ANY St Andrew's Society of New York

AR Acadian Recorder, series

AJ Aberdeen Journal, series

AMC Annals of Megantic County, Quebec

BM Blackwood's Magazine, series

DPCA Dundee, Perth & Cupar Advertiser, series

EA Edinburgh Advertiser, series

EC Edinburgh Courant, series

EEC Edinburgh Evening Courant, series

F Fasti Ecclesiae Scoticanae, series

GM Gentleman's Magazine, series

HBCA Hudson Bay Company Archives

HBRS Hudson Bay Record Society

HOM History of the Mathesons, Stirling

IJ Inverness Journal, series

KCA King's College, Aberdeen

MCA Marischal College, Aberdeen

MG Montreal Gazette, series

NARA National Archives, Records Administration

NCSA North Carolina State Archives

NEHGS New England Historic Genealogical Society

NLS National Library of Scotland

NRS National Records of Scotland

OA Orkney Archives

OL Orkney Library

OM Orkney Miscellany, series

PAC Public Archives of Canada

PAPEI Public Archives, Prince Edward Island

S The Scotsman, series

SA Shetland Archives

SCA South Carolina Archives

SCS Scots Charitable Society of Boston

SG Scottish Guardian, series

SHR Scottish Historical Review, series

SHS Scottish History Society

SM Scots Magazine, series

W The Witness, series

ZFH Zetland Family Histories

"JOHN O' GROAT'S."

A REAL "SCOTTISH GRIEVANCE."

DUNCAN.—"[illegible] but my mother is frail, and can't be sent out of the country in that ship; will you not let *Flora and her* [illegible]
FACTOR.—[illegible] "[illegible] with the old woman; she will not be here in the way of his *Lordship's* [illegible]"

PEOPLE OF THE NORTHERN HIGHLANDS AND ISLES, 1800-1850

ADAM, ALEXANDER, a tanner in Halkirk, Caithness, in 1801. [NRS.CS271.6.96]

ADAMSON, JOHN, and Agnes Duncan, adulterers in Burroland, Sandwick, Shetland, a petition for their separation in 1806. [SA.12.6.1806.44]

ADAMSON, WILLIAM, born in Tingwall, Shetland, an employee of the Hudson Bay Company from 1842 to 1850. [HBRS.16.352]

ADAMSON, WILLIAM, in Whaligoe, Caithness, died 4 November 1856, father of Peter Adamson a farmer in Bayfield, Canada. [NRS.S/H.1863]

AIRD, ALEXANDER, a merchant in Invergordon, Ross and Cromarty, dead by 1850, father of John Mackenzie Aird in Grenada. [NRS.S/H.1850]

AIRD, GUSTAVUS, Moderator of the Free Presbytery of Dornoch, Sutherland, a letter in 1845. [NRS.GD112.51.71]

ALLAN, DONALD, born 1812 in Ross-shire, educated at King's College, Aberdeen, 1829, a minister in Ontario from 1838 to 1874, died in December 1884. [F.7.624]

ALLAN, JAMES, emigrated via Cromarty or Thurso aboard the Lady Grey bound for Pictou, Nova Scotia, in June 1841. [NRS.RH1.2.908]

ANDERSON, ALEXANDER ROSE MUNRO, son of John Anderson, [1789-1840], and his wife Mary Ross, [1806-1871], died in Broken Hill, Australia. [Ardgay, Ross-shire, gravestone]

ANDERSON, ARTHUR, tenant in East Burrafirth, Aithsting, Shetland, versus Gideon Gifford of Busta, Aithsting, in 1801. [SA.SC12.6.1801.18]

ANDERSON, BARBARA, wife of William Gow in Wester Wick, Caithness, accused of resisting an officer of the law in 1821. [NRS.AD14.21.97]

ANDERSON, DAVINA LUCY MURRAY, born 19 July 1850 in Walls and Flotta, daughter of Reverend William Anderson and his wife Lucy Hay Murray, married Gerard Affleck Scott a physician in Australia. [F.7.256]

ANDERSON, EDWARD, in Hudson Bay Company Service, husband of Christian Anderson in Lerwick, Shetland, a letter, 1857. [HBCA.PAM.A10/42.557]

ANDERSON, or MORRISON, GEORGE, unemployed in Wick, Caithness, accused of prison breaking in 1813. [NRS.AD14.3.86]

ANDERSON, HUGH, a wright in Edderton, Ross-shire, accused of cutting and stealing timber in 1817. [NRS.JC26.1817.60]

ANDERSON, JAMES, jr., in Rispond, Durness, Sutherland, draft substitution of Admiralty in 1800. [NRS.GD84.2.76]

ANDERSON, JAMES, born 1797 in Cromarty, son of James Anderson a farmer, was educated at Marischal College, Aberdeen, in 1829, a minister in Ontario from 1835, died in Ormston on 6 April 1864. [F.7.625]

ANDERSON, JAMES, born in Wick, Caithness, died near Georgetown, South Carolina, on 31 December 1820. [Prince George, Winyah, gravestone]

ANDERSON, JOHN, a merchant in Leith, a sasine, 1791. [NRS.RS.Caithness.211]

ANDERSON, JOHN, son of James Anderson a farmer, in Kilcoy, Killearnan, Ross-shire, was accused of murder in 1835. [NRS.JC26.1835.126]

ANDERSON, MAGNUS, in Hovesta, Bressay, Shetland, a summons of removal, 1800. [SA.SC12.6.1800.59]

ANDERSON, MARY, daughter of James Anderson of Rispond, Sutherland, married James Hall from Jamaica, on 13 September 1854. [EEC.22634]

ANDERSON, ROBERT MUNRO, son of John Anderson, [1789-1840], and his wife Mary Ross, [1806-1871], died in New York. [Ardgay gravestone]

ANDERSON, WILLIAM, kenner of fishing, tenant in Easter Doll of Brora, parish of Clyne, Sutherland, in 1811. [SHS.8.90]

ANGUS, ANDREW, a mariner in Stromness, a sasine, 1806. [NRS.R.S.Orkney.692]

ANGUS, JOHN, in Toft, Delting, Shetland, versus Magnus Jameson, servant of Robert Scollay, a case re the restoration of a cow, 1795. [SA.SC12.6.1795.40]

ANGUS, JOHN, a merchant in Delting, Shetland, was accused of plundering a Norwegian shipwreck in 1803. [SA.SC12.6.1803.47]

ANGUS, JOHN, third son of David Angus from Thurso, Caithness, but residing in Edinburgh, married Annie Williams, only daughter of Thomas Williams in Hartford, Connecticut, there on 22 February 1874. [S.9547]

ANGUS, THOMAS, born 1778, from Stromness, Orkney, emigrated via Stornaway on the Prince of Wales to the Hudson Bay Company settlement on the Red River in 1811. [PAC.M155.145]

ANGUS, WILLIAM, a joiner in Wick, Caithness, was accused of mobbing and rioting in 1827. [NRS.AD14.27.218]

ARCUS, MARGARET, born 12 September 1832, died 16 November 1893, wife of Peter Morrison. [Lerwick gravestone, Shetland]

ANGUS, WILLIAM, in Lerwick, Shetland, a victim of theft in 1837. [SA.AD14.37.342]

ARMSTRONG, DONALD, born 1866, son of Thomas Armstrong, died in Blackall, Queensland, Australia, on 14 June 1899. [Kildonan gravestone, Sutherland]

ARMSTRONG, WILLIAM, born 1853, son of Thomas Armstrong, died in Waikawa, New Zealand, on 8 December 1898. [Kildonan gravestone, Sutherland]

ARTHUR, JAMES INNES, born 22 July 1785 in Resolis, Ross and Cromarty, son of Reverend Robert Arthur and his wife Anne Munro, settled in Demerara, died on 20 August 1816. [F.7.19]

ARTHUR, ROBERT, late in Berbice, fifth son of Reverend Robert Arthur of Resolis, died in Cromarty on 3 July 1829. [S.994]

ATKINSON and MARSHALL, tenants of the Great Sheep Tenement in Lairg, Sutherland, in 1808. [SHS.8.228]

BAIGRIE, Captain, ROBERT, and his heirs, tenants of Midgarty, Sutherland, in 1808, 1811. [SHS.8.101/230]

BAIKIE, JAMES, in Seaton, Stromness, Orkney, versus William Scott in Edinburgh, 1818. [NRS.CS42.16.31]

BAIKIE, JAMES, in Kirkwall, a letter to Samuel Laing of Pabdale, Orkney, 1821. [NRS.GD31.497]

BAIKIE, JOHN, born 1817 in Orkney, a labourer in Hudson Bay Company Service, died in Victoria, British Columbia, on 16 February 1866. [Ross Bay gravestone, B.C.]

BAIKIE, MAGNUS, born 1774, a carpenter in Wick, Caithness, died 19 December 1858, husband of Charlotte Baikie, born 1774, died 1825. [Wick gravestone, Caithness]

BAIKIE, ROBERT, of Tankerness, a heritor of St Ola, Orkney, a memorandum in 1815. [NRS.GD31.489]

BAILLIE, ADAM, born 1770, a farmer, with his wife and ten children, in Wester Culmaily, Sutherland, in 1810. [SHS.1.14/15]

BAILLIE, DONALD, born 1770, with his wife and four children, in Sallichtown, Culmaily, Sutherland, in 1810. [SHS.1.14/15]

BAILLIE, DONALD, born 1794 in Sutherland, died 13 September 1875, husband of Espie, born 1816, died 1910. [Baillie cemetery, Lovat, Pictou, Nova Scotia]

BAILLIE, DONALD, with his mother and two sisters, emigrated from Kilbraur, Strathbrora, Sutherland, emigrated to Nova Scotia in 1820.

BAILLIE, GEORGE, born 1775, with family, from Sutherland, emigrated via Cromarty aboard the Ossian bound for Pictou, Nova Scotia, on 25 June 1821. [Inverness Journal.29 June 1821]

BAILLIE, GEORGE, born 1784 in Clyne, Sutherland, died 27 December 1855, his wife Catherine ....., born 1780 in Clyne, died 1 June 1826. [Stewart cemetery, Pictou, NS]

BAILLIE, JOHN, born 1780, a servant of Colonel Sutherland and his wife in Wester Culmaily, Sutherland, in 1810. [SHS.1.14/15]

BAILLIE, JOHN, born 1805 in Clyne, Sutherland, died 7 December 1881, his wife Margaret ....., born 1796 in Clyne, died 3 September 1869. [Baillie cemetery, Pictou, Nova Scotia]

BAILLIE, MARGARET, born 1766, a widow, with her family of nine, from Sutherland, emigrated via Cromarty aboard the Ossian bound for Pictou, Nova Scotia, on 25 June 1821. [Inverness Journal.29 June 1821]

BAILLIE, ROBERT, born 1757 in Clyne, Sutherland, settled in Nova Scotia in 1814, a petition for a land grant on 6 October 1814, died 19 August 1832. [NSARM. RG20.series A][Baillie cemetery, Pictou, NS]

BAILLIE, WILLIAM, born 1801 in Clyne, Sutherland, died 14 September 1875, husband of Janet ....., born 1809 in Clyne, died 5 October 1881. [Baillie cemetery, Pictou, Nova Scotia]

BAILLIE, WILLIAM, with his wife and four children, emigrated from Scottarie in Strathbrora, to Nova Scotia in 1820.

BAIN, DONALD, born 1774 in Thurso, Caithness, a surgeon who died in St Jago, Savanna, Clarendon, Jamaica, in June 1801. [GM.72.83[

BAIN, GEORGE, in Bienachelt, Latheron, Caithness, a victim of rioting in 1829. [NRS.AD14.29.350]

BAIN, JOHN, and his wife Jane Durran, [1844-1901] in Dunbeath Mains, parents of Christina Bain, born 1873, died in Brownwood, Texas, on 21 September 1899. [Dunbeath gravestone, Caithness]

BAIN, PETER, born 1801, a farmer in Murkle, died 31 August 1878, husband of Georgina Campbell, born 1805, died 5 March 1877, parents of Peter Bain, born 1833, died in Maryborough, Australia, on 17 April 1907. [Olrig gravestone, Caithness]

BAIN, WILLIAM WATT, a writer in Kirkwall, Orkney, versus Reverend William Grant in Cross and Burness parish, Sanday, in 1825. [OA.SC11.5.125.29]

BALFOUR, DAVID, in Trenaby, Westray, Orkney, versus James Yorston in Rammany, Graemsay, a summons, 1850. [OA.SC11.5.1850.14]

BALLENDEN, JAMES, a mariner in Stromness, Orkney, a sasine, 1802. [NRS.R.S.Orkney.531]

BALLENDEN, JOHN, born 1810 in Stromness, Orkney, of the Hudson Bay Company from 1829 to 7 December 1856. [HBRS.3.427]

BALLENTYNE, WILLIAM, formerly a weaver or shoemaker in Thurso, Caithness, later a missionary, was accused of conducting a clandestine marriage, case dismissed on 23 September 1799. [NRS.JC11.44]

BANKS, CHARLES, born in Cadboll, Ross-shire, a merchant in Charleston, South Carolina, died in Philadelphia on 24 May 1813, his wife had died there on 14 May 1813. [GM.83.592]

BANKS, M., of Letterewe, Wester Ross, papers, 1848. [NRS.HD21.43]

BANNERMAN, CHRISTIAN, born 1793, from Sutherland, emigrated via Stromness on the Prince of Wales to the Hudson Bay Company settlement at York Fort on 23 June 1815, landed there on 26 August 1815. [PAC.M1659/61] [MG19.E4.1.165/8]

BANNERMAN, DONALD, born 1761, [he died on 24 September 1813], his wife Christian born 1767, son William born 1795, son Donald born 1805, daughter Christian born 1797, from Badflinch, emigrated via Stromness, Orkney, on the Prince of Wales to the Hudson Bay Company settlement at Fort Churchill on 29 June 1813. [PAC.M155.165-8]

BANNERMAN, DONALD, joint tenant in Balblair, Golspie, Sutherland, in 1815. [SHS.8.226]

BANNERMAN, DONALD, emigrated from Cromarty or Thurso aboard the Lady Grey bound for Pictou, Nova Scotia, in June 1841. [NRS.RH1.2.908]

BANNERMAN, GEORGE, born 1791, from Kildonan, Sutherland, emigrated via Stromness, Orkney, on the Prince of Wales to the Hudson Bay Company settlement at Fort Churchill on 29 June 1813. [PAC.M155.165-8]

BANNERMAN, HUGH, born 1795, his sister Elizabeth born 1793, and Mary Bannerman, Alexander born 1794, sister Christian born 1796, from Dalhalmy, Kildonan, Sutherland, emigrated via Stromness on the Prince of Wales to Fort Churchill on 29 June 1813. [PAC.M155.165-8]

BANNERMAN, JOHN, born 1760, wife Catherine McKay born 1787, son Alexander Bannerman born 1814, from Sutherland, emigrated via Stromness on the Prince of Wales to York Fort on 23 June 1815, landed there on 26 August 1815. [PAC.M1659/61] [MG19.E4.1.165/8]

BANNERMAN, JOHN, born 1794, died in January 1814, with sister Christian born 1796, from Dalhalmy, Sutherland, emigrated via Stromness on the Prince of Wales to the Hudson Bay Company settlement at Fort Churchill on 29 June 1813. [PAC.M155.165-8]

BANNERMAN, alias MCDAVY, JOHN, a tenant in Ulbster, Kildonan, Sutherland, was accused of rioting, resulting from the removal or eviction of tenants in Kildonan in 1813. [NRS.AD14.13.9; SC9.7.64] [SHS.8.136]

BANNERMAN, JOHN, a weaver, emigrated from Cromarty or Thurso aboard the Lady Grey bound for Pictou, Nova Scotia, in June 1841. [NRS.RH1.2.908]

BANNERMAN, WILLIAM, born 1760, a labourer, wife Barbara Gunn born 1765, son William born 1799 a shoemaker, son Alexander born 1801, son Donald born 1807, son George born, emigrated via Stromness on the Prince of Wales to the Hudson Bay Company settlement at York Fort on 23 June 1815, landed there on 26 August 1815. [PAC.M1659/61] [MG19.E4.1.165/8]

BANNERMAN, WILLIAM, emigrated from Cromarty or Thurso aboard the Lady Grey bound for Pictou, Nova Scotia, in June 1841. [NRS.RH1.2.908]

BARCLAY, JAMES, a shoemaker in Dornoch, Sutherland, dead by 1830, father of John Barclay a mason in America. [NRS.S/H.1830]

BARCLAY, JOHN, tenant in Croftmeadick, Dornoch, Sutherland, in 1811. [SHS.8.61]

BARNETSON, ALEXANDER, a writer and messenger at arms in Thurso, Caithness, versus David Clyne a Solicitor of the Supreme Court, in 1829. [NRS.228.B.15.23]

BARNIE, JOHN, born, born 1801, died 16 April 1876, husband of Jane Campbell Sinclair, born 1819, died in Lybster on 11 August 1899. [Canisbay gravestone, Caithness]

BARRIE, ROBERT, in Kirkwall, Orkney, a Lieutenant of the Royal Navy, versus Ann Arnot in Glasgow, re aliment, 1819. [NRS.CS228.A8.28]

BAUCHOPE, ALEXANDER LOCKHART, of Easter Brora, Clyne, Sutherland, was a victim of theft in Edinburgh in 1848. [NRS.AD14.48.361]

BAYNE, Reverend CHARLES, in Fodderty, Ross-shire, letters, 1828. [NRS.GD46.12.11]

BEATON, DAVID, in Clovgarth, Stromness, Orkney, and his spouse Catherine Brown, versus Peter Gaudie, son of the late George Gaudie, in Newsheal, Marwick, Birsay, in 1826. [NRS.CS228.B16.39]

BEATTIE, JOHN, born 24 March 1844 in Evie and Rendall parish, Orkney, son of Reverend William Beattie and his wife Isabella Rankin, a merchant in Montreal. [F.7.216]

BEATON, DAVID, in Clovigarth, Stromness, Orkney, and his wife Catherine Brown, versus Peter Gaudie, son of the deceased George Gaudie in Nethersheal, Marwick, Orkney, 1826. [NRS.CS228.B16.39]

BEATON, HUGH, emigrated from Cromarty or Thurso aboard the Lady Grey bound for Pictou, Nova Scotia, in June 1841. [NRS.RH1.2.908]

BEATTON, JOHN, in Stromness, Orkney, father of John William Clark, a clerk, who died at Rio Grande do Sol, Brazil, on 1 November 1878. [EC.29393]; testament, 1879. [NRS.SC70.1.195/1]

BEATSON, MAGNUS, a skipper in Stromness, husband of Elizabeth Loutit, parents of Peter and John, a sasine, 1806. [NRS.R.S.Orkney.684]

BEATTIE, ELIZABETH HARVEY, daughter of Alexander Beattie of the Royal Academy in Tain, Ross and Cromarty, married Robert Ridley, a merchant, in Peterborough, Upper Canada, on 12 May 1842. [AJ.4928]

BEGG, ISABELLA, born 1822 in Kirkwall, Orkney, died in Victoria, British Columbia, on 29 August 1867. [Ross Bay gravestone, B.C.]

BEGG, MATTHEW, in Insista, Bressay, Shetland, a summons of removal, 1800. [SA.SC12.6.1800.59]

BETHUNE, ALEXANDER, born 11 February 1847, son of Roderick Bethune and his wife Ann Bremner, died in Queensland, Australia, on 21 November 1867. [Avoch gravestone, Ross and Cromarty]

BETHUNE, BETH, born 1792, from Uig, Ross-shire, emigrated via Stornaway on the Prince of Wales to the Hudson Bay Company settlement on the Red River in 1811. [PAC.M155.145]

BETHUNE, DAVID, born 1771 in Dingwall, emigrated to Tobago, moved to New York in 1792, a merchant, died in 1824. [ANY.I.318]

BETHUNE, DONALD, and his wife Ann Anderson, both born in Sutherland, emigrated to Nova Scotia in 1822. [Lansdowne gravestone, Pictou, NS]

BETHUNE, HUGH, youngest son of Reverend Bethune in Alness, Ross and Cromarty, died in Berbice on 18 October 1821. [AJ.3861]

BETHUNE, JOHN, born 2 October 1774 in Alness, Ross and Cromarty, son of Reverend Angus Bethune and his wife Catherine Munro, settled in Berbice, died 18 April 1819. [F.7.27]

BETHUNE, Reverend JOHN, tenant of Auchiroch, Dornoch, Sutherland, in 1811, tenant in Knockglass, Dornoch, in 1815. [SHS.8.59/222]

BETHUNE, JOHN, second son of Reverend John Bethune in Dornoch, Sutherland, died in Berbice in August 1804. [SM.66.885]

BETHUNE, W. MACDONALD, born in Ross-shire, a Customs Collector, married Sarah Edwards Channing, eldest daughter of Thomas Channing a merchant, in Carbona, Newfoundland, on 1 June 1848. [AJ.5245][SG.1733]

BEWS, DAVID, in Pabdale, St Ola, Orkney, a testament, 1822. [NRS.GD31.501]

BEWS, MARGARET, in Kirkwall, Orkney, versus Peter Sabiston a servant in Crantit, St Ola, Orkney, re aliment, 1822. [OA.SC11.5.1822.50]

BINSTON, JAMES, a shoemaker at St Margaret's Hope, South Ronaldsay, Orkney, versus James Laird in Burray in 1804. [OA.SC11.5.1804.37]

BISSET, WILLIAM, a shoemaker in Jemimaville, Resolis, Cromarty, accused of mobbing and prison breaking in 1844. [NRS.AD14.44.443]

BOGLE, Reverend COLIN, minister of Walls, Sandness, Papa and Foula, Shetland, versus Lillias Sinclair, wife of Andrew Sinclair a tenant in Gord, Walls, the said Andrew Sinclair, and her father in law Jacob Sinclair in 1830. [SA.SC12.6.1830.83]

BOLT and NICOLSON, merchants in Lerwick, Shetland, tacksmen of Fetlar, versus George Clunes in Aith, Fetlar in 1792. [SA.SC12.6.1792.26]

BOOG, JAMES, tenant in Skelbo, Dornoch, Sutherland, in 1815. [SHS.8.222]

BOOG, Mrs, a tenant in Skelbo, Dornoch, Sutherland, in 1811. [SHS.8.65]

BRABNER, JEAN, daughter of Robert Brabner a mariner in Kirkwall, Orkney, versus her spouse William Laughton a messenger in Kirkwall, a process of separation and aliment in 1804. [NRS.CS8.6.1190]

BRANDER, JAMES, a writer in Golspie, Sutherland, and William Sutherland a writer in Dornoch, versus Elizabeth McKenzie, widow of James Scott a feuar in Brora, Sutherland, 1828. [NRS.CS228.B.17.31]; trustee of John McKenzie, a cattle dealer in Ledbeg, Assynt, Sutherland, in 1832. [NRS.CS96.4262]

BRECHIN, or ANDERSON, JEAN, in Kilcoy, Killearnan, Ross-shire, was murdered in 1835. [NRS.JC26.1835.126]

BREMNER, DAVID, born 1798, in East Murkle, died 15 April 1851, husband of Catherine Bremner, born 1801, died 26 February 1886, parents of James in Sydney, New South Wales, Australia. [Olrig gravestone, Caithness]

BREMNER, HUGH, writer in Thurso, versus William Wilson agent of the Caithness Banking Company in Thurso, 1818. [NRS.CS228.B.15.22]

BREMNER, JAMES, a carpenter and shipbuilder in Pultneytown, Caithness, accused of mobbing and rioting in 1827. [NRS.AD14.27.218]

BREMNER, Reverend JAMES, minister of the united parish of Walls and Flotta, Orkney,1828. [OA.CS228.B17.36]

BREMNER, JAMES, in Pultneytown, Caithness, father of Alexander Bremner in Sydney, Australia, 1857. [NRS.S/H]

BREMNER, JOHN, born 1837, fleet paymaster of the Royal Navy, died in Hong Kong on 30 September 1896. [Canisbay gravestone, Caithness]

BREMNER, WALTER, versus Hugh Bremner a writer in Thurso, Caithness,1818. [NRS.CS42.20.13]

BRIMS, DONALD, a fisherman in Thurso, Caithness, father of Helen Brims, dead by 1857. [NRS.S/H]

BROTCHIE, GEORGE, a merchant in Kirkwall, Orkney, versus Reverend William Grant in Cross and Burness, Sanday, re debt in 1825. [OA.SC11.5.1825.64]

BROCHTIE, Reverend JAMES, in Westray, Orkney, versus Thomas Traill in Holland, Papa Westray, in 1849. [OA.SC11.5.1849.14]

BROCK, GEORGE, of West Greenland farm, Dunnet, Caithness, the victim of sheep stealing in 1847. [NRS.AD14.47.128]

BROCK, JANET, daughter of Alexander Brock in Wester Wick, Caïthness, accused of resisting an officer of the law in 1821. [NRS.AD14.21.97]

BROCK, MARGARET, daughter of Ann Farquhar a widow in Wester Wick, Caithness, accused of resisting an officer of the law in 1821. [NRS.AD14.21.97]

BROOMFIELD, ELIZABETH, born 1825, daughter of George Broomfield and his wife Ann Brander, wife of James Armstrong, died in Australia on 30 March 1858. [Clyne, Kirkton, gravestone, Sutherland]

BROTCHIE, GEORGE, a merchant in Kirkwall, Orkney, versus Reverend William Grant in Cross and Burness parish, Sanday, in 1825. [OA.SC11.5.125.66]

BROUGH, CHRISTIAN, in Binbister, Harray, versus Peter Sinclair in Sandaiken, Deerness, Orkney, re alimony in 1841. [OA.SC11.5.1841.60]

BROWN, JESSIE SCOTT, born 1829 in Stromness, Orkney, died in Victoria, British Columbia, on 2 October 1896. [Ross Bay gravestone, B.C.]

BROWN, JOHN, a tenant farmer at Uyeasound, Aithsting, Shetland, was accused of theft from a stranded ship in 1816. [NRS.AD14.16.26]

BROWN, ROBERT, born 1756, a tenant farmer at Uyeasound, Aithsting, Shetland, was accused of theft from a stranded ship in 1816. [NRS.AD14.16.26]

BROWN, ROBERT, born 1803 in Caithness, died 4 July 1861. [Caledonia gravestone, Pictou, Nova Scotia]

BROWN, WILLIAM H., born 1830 in Stromness, Orkney, died in Victoria, British Columbia, on 20 January 1898. [Ross Bay gravestone, B.C.]

BRUCE, ALEXANDER, tenant in Toftkemp, Caithness, versus William Sinclair of Freswick, 1803. [NRS.CS271.624]

BRUCE, or FARQUHAR, HELEN, wife of John Farquhar tenant in Wester Wick, Caithness, accused of resisting an officer of the law in 1821. [NRS.AD14.21.97]

BRUCE, JAMES, a tailor in Stromness, Orkney, father of Suetonious Bruce who died in Ottawa on 19 July 1874. [S.9696]

BRUCE, JOHN, born 1753, from Aultsmoral, Clyne, Sutherland, emigrated via Stromness on the Prince of Wales to the Hudson Bay Company settlement at Fort Churchill on 29 June 1813. [PAC.M155.165-8]

BRUCE, JOHN, of Catfirth in Shetland, versus his tenants in Catfirth and Nesting, a summons of removal in 1803. [SA.SC12.6.1803.13]

BRUCE, JOHN WILLIAM, was accused of falsehood, fraud and wilful imposition at Golspie Post Office, Sutherland, trial papers, 1824, outlawed. [NRS.JC26.1824.197]

BRUCE, ROBERT, a tenant in Lirribul, Kildonan, Sutherland, was accused of rioting, resulting from the removal or eviction of tenants in Kildonan in 1813. [NRS.AD14.13.9; SC9.7.64]

BRUCE, WILLIAM, of Simbuster, Shetland, a summons for the removal of his tenants in Nesting, Whalsay, etc. in 1800. [SA.SC12.6.1800.26]

BRUCE, WILLIAM, born 1828, son of Robert Bruce and his wife Betsy Mackay, died in Donald, Victoria, Australia, on 17 April 1894. [Clyne, Kirkton, gravestone, Sutherland]

BRUDE, JOHN, tenant in the Bog, Caithness, versus William Sinclair of Freswick, 1803. [NRS.CS271.624]

BUDGE, JAMES, born 1797, a farmer in Bigtown, Shetland, died in Olrig on 27 November 1867, husband of Margaret Robertson, born 1798, died 28 December 1878. [Olrig gravestone, Caithness]

BUDGE, JAMES, a miller in Dunnet, Caithness, in 1816. [NRS.GD136.868]

BUDGE, ROBERT, a merchant in Thurso, Caithness, versus William Levach a merchant in Thurso, 1800. [NRS.CS271.475.8]

BUDGE, ROBERT FORBES, a merchant in Valparaiso, Chile, later a surgeon in Lerwick, Shetland, 20 December 1841. [NRS.RGS.225.29]

BUDGE, THOMAS, born 1821 in Halkirk, Caithness, died 14 January 1862. [Anglican cemetery, East St John, New Brunswick]

BURGESS, COLIN, born 1797 in Dingwall, Ross and Cromarty, died in Toronto on 19 January 1841. [AJ.4866]

CALDER, DAVID, from Caithness, married Maria Caldwell from Halifax, Nova Scotia, there on 2 March 1839. [Acadian Recorder, 9.3.1839]

CALDER, EAVENDER, born 1808 in Sutherland, was drowned at Southampton, York County, New Brunswick. [Weekly Observer, 9.7.1833]

CALDER, EMILIA, in Watten, Caithness, versus John Wright, a merchant and innkeeper in Stromness, Orkney, in 1832. [OA.SC11.5.1832.116]

CALDER, JAMES, son of Reverend John Calder in Roskeen, Ross-shire, died in Nassau, New Providence, on 27 February 1818. [AJ.3687][S.2.85]

CAMERON, or DOUNE, ALEXANDER, in Auchlunachan, Loch Broom, Wester Ross, was accused of wilful fire-raising in 1828. [NRS.AD14.28.392]

CAMERON, ALLAN, of the Bengal Horse Artillery, son of Alexander Cameron in Culcraigie, Ross-shire, died in Mhow, East Indies, on 28 September 1821. [AJ.3878]

CAMERON, ANGUS, in Drumbuy, Lochalsh and Plockton District, to emigrate to America around 1850. [NRS.HD.21.53]

CAMERON, ARCHIBALD, a road-maker of Rosehall, Creich, Sutherland, was accused of rioting in 1821. [NRS.AD14.21.93]

CAMERON, DONALD, in Nigg, versus Donald McLean in Brae, Resolis, Cromarty, in 1830. [NRS.SC24.10.95]

CAMERON, JOHN, born in Dingwall, Ross and Cromarty, emigrated to South Carolina in 1802, settled in Sumter, S.C., applied for naturalisation there on 3 March 1804. [SCA; Citizenship book.49]

CAMERON, or CASTLE, JOHN, a fisher in Ullapool, Wester Ross, was accused of rioting in 1833. [NRS.AD14.33.117]

CAMERON, JOHN, born 1814 in Strathpeffer, Ross and Cromarty, son of William and Mary Cameron, died at Brass River, Africa, on 5 January 1847. [AJ.5187][Fodderty gravestone]

CAMERON, MURDOCH, son of Alexander Cameron, [1784-1872], a farmer in Achlonachan, and his wife Margaret Ross, [1787-1843], settled in Victoria, Australia. [Loch Broom, Wester Ross, gravestone]

CAMERON, RODERICK, joint tenant of Clyne Milnton, parish of Clyne, Sutherland, in 1811. [SHS.8.95]

CAMERON, RODERICK, a fisher in Ullapool, Wester Ross, was accused of rioting in 1833. [NRS.AD14.33.117]

CAMPBELL, AENEAS, born 1839, son of Donald Campbell and his wife Christine, died in Benin, Africa, on 10 September 1863. [Dornoch gravestone, Sutherland]

CAMPBELL, ALEXANDER, born 1780, with his mother, brother and sister, in Sergeant Gordon's croft, Rhiorn, Culmaily, Sutherland, in 1810. [SHS.1.14/15]

CAMPBELL, ALEXANDER, emigrated from Cromarty or Thurso aboard the Lady Grey bound for Pictou, Nova Scotia, in June 1841. [NRS.RH1.2.908]

CAMPBELL, or MCIVER, ALLAN, born 1802, a fisher in Ullapool, Wester Ross, was accused of rioting in 1833. [NRS.AD14.33.117]

CAMPBELL, ANGUS, son of Donald Campbell a shepherd, a tenant in Clunel of Gruids, Lairg, Sutherland, was accused of rioting in 1821. [NRS.AD14.21.93]

CAMPBELL, ANN, born 1780, emigrated via Thurso, Caithness, on the Elizabeth and Ann bound for Prince Edward Island on 8 November 1806. [PAPEI]

CAMPBELL, BARBARA, born 1747 in Caithness, died on 4 May 1840. [New Brunswick Courier, 9.5.1840]

CAMPBELL, DONALD, born 1777 in Clyne, Sutherland, died 24 December 1835, husband of Jane McKay, born 1803, died 1894. [Stewart cemetery, Pictou, NS]

CAMPBELL, DONALD, born 1847, son of Charles Campbell and his wife Ann, died in America in 1874. [Balnakeil, Durness, gravestone, Sutherland]

CAMPBELL, GEORGE, born 1788, his wife Helen born 1793, and daughter Belle born 1812, from Auchraigh, Creich, Sutherland, emigrated via Stromness on the Prince of Wales to Fort Churchill on 29 June 1813. [PAC.M155.165-8]

CAMPBELL, Captain JOHN, in Carsgo, versus Captain John McDonald in Thurso, Caithness, in 1811. [NRS.CS36.2.19]

CAMPBELL, JOHN, joint tenant in Eiden, Rogart, Sutherland, in 1815. [SHS.8.231]

CAMPBELL, JOHN, schoolmaster at Lochalsh, Wester Ross, a petition, 1825. [NRS.GD112.11.9.7-8]

CAMPBELL, JOHN, emigrated from Cromarty or Thurso aboard the Lady Grey bound for Pictou, Nova Scotia, in June 1841. [NRS.RH1.2.908]

CAMPBELL, MURDOCH, born 1782 in Ross-shire, emigrated to Nova Scotia in 1803, died 1819. [Caledonia gravestone, Pictou, NS]

CAMPBELL, NORMAN, born 1783 in Gairloch, Wester Ross, sometime of Brooklyn, New York, died in Dingwall on 4 December 1868, husband of Ann McIver, born 1795, died in Brooklyn on 5 May 1860, buried there, parents of Colin C. Campbell in Brooklyn. [St Clement's gravestone, Dingwall, Ross and Cromarty]

CAMPBELL, WILLIAM, born 1853, son of Charles Campbell and his wife Ann, died in Canada on 2 November 1906. [Balnakeil, Durness, gravestone, Sutherland]

CAMPBELL, Mrs, born 1750, in Coulnacraig, Culmaily, Sutherland, with a married daughter, in 1810. [SHS.1.14/15]

CAMPBELL, Mrs, born 1750, with her sister, born 1760, and two children, near the Colonel's stables, in Wester Culmaily, Sutherland, in 1810. [SHS.1.14/15]

CARMACK, JAMES, in the Manse of Thurso, Caithness, a victim of theft in 1830. [NRS.JC26.1830.90]

CARNABY, BENJAMIN, a shipowner in Thurso, Caithness, 1822. [NRS.CS230.SEQN.C.1.42]

CHALMERS, WILLIAM, tacksman of Rousay, versus David Mowat in Rousay, Orkney, summons of removal in 1801. [OA.SC11.5.1801.11]

CHAMBERS, JOHN, born 1792, from Walls, Orkney, emigrated via Stornaway on the Prince of Wales to the Hudson Bay Company settlement on the Red River in 1811. [PAC.M155.145]

CHAPPY, ROBERT, a sailor in Hogan, son of Henry Chappy of Nesbuster, a sasine, 1807. [NRS.R.S.Shetland.525]

CHISHOLM, ALEXANDER, from Ross-shire, married Eliza Mills from Hampshire, in Georgetown, Demerara on 5 September 1840. [AJ.3844]

CHISHOLM, ALEXANDER, from Ross-shire, married Janet Fordyce, second daughter of Alexander Dingwall Fordyce, in Lescraigie, Fergus, Upper Canada, on 1 October1840. [AJ.3846]

CHISHOLM, DAVID, born in Altopkin, Nigg, Ross-shire, the editor of the 'Montreal Gazette', died in Montreal in 1842. [AJ.4949]

CHISHOLM, or MCLEAN, HELEN, in Parkhill, Ross-shire, died 4 December 1857, mother of Robert McLean a merchant in Mobile, Alabama. [NRS.S/H]

CHISHOLM, RODERICK, born 1799, son of Alexander Chisholm, a tenant in Tolly, Fodderty, Ross-shire, 1822. [NRS.AD14.22.136]

CHISHOLM, WILLIAM, emigrated from Cromarty or Thurso aboard the Lady Grey bound for Pictou, Nova Scotia, in June 1841. [NRS.RH1.2.908]

CHISHOLM, WILLIAM, born 1843, died in Boston, Massachusetts, on 26 January 1911. [Creich gravestone, Sutherland]

CHRISTENSEN, Mrs MARY, born 1847 in Orkney, wife of Captain James Christensen, died in Victoria, British Columbia, on 2 June 1895. [Ross Bay gravestone]

CHRISTIE, GEORGE, born 1821, a clerk to John and James Christie agents for the Aberdeen Town and Country Bank in Golspie, Sutherland, in 1840. [NRS.AD14.40.447]

CHRISTIE, JAMES, sheriff officer in Dornoch, Sutherland, 1840. [NRS.AD14.40.447]

CHRISTIE, JAMES, a partner of the Helmsdale Distillery, Sutherland, in 1840. [NRS.AD14.40.447]

CHRISTIE, THOMAS, a tenant in Gardie, Mid Yell, Shetland, summons of removal, 1800. [SA.SC12.6.1800.17]

CHRISTIE, PETER, in Unifirth, Aithsling, Shetland, summons of removal in 1807, [SA.SC12.6.1807.6]

CLARK, HUGH's heirs, tenants of Coulkein Drumbaig, Assynt, Sutherland, in 1811. [SHS.8.52]

CLARKE, JOHN, tenant in Eriboll, Sutherland, and his sons Dr James Clarke and Alexander Clarke, a bond in 1828. [NRS.GD84.1.112]

CLARK, ROBERT, tenant of the Park, Dornoch, Sutherland, in 1811. [SHS.8.63]

CLARK, ROBERT, a butcher in Dornoch, Sutherland, accused of assault in 1843. [NRS.AD14.43.25]

CLARK, THOMAS MCLEOD, from Tain, Ross and Cromarty, a merchant in New York, married Jessie McKay, daughter of Thomas McKay, at Rideau Hall near Bytown, Canada West, on 6 June 1854. [W.XV.1563]

CLOUSTON, ANNE ROSE, daughter of Edward Clouston in Stromness, Orkney, married Augustus E. Pelly at York Factory, Hudson Bay, on 28 August 1849. [AJ.5314]

CLOUSTON, EDWARD, born 27 September 1787, son of Reverend William Clouston of Kingshouse and his wife Isabella Traill, a planter in Jamaica, a sasine in Orkney in 1834, died in 1866. [SA.R.S.Orkney.173] [F.7.253]

CLOUSTON, JAMES, in Stromness, Orkney, a labourer in the service of the Hudson Bay Company from 1842. [HBRS.16.354]

CLOUSTON, JOSEPH, son of Robert Clouston, a carpenter and sailor in Stromness, Orkney, a sasine, 1793. [NRS.R.S.Orkney.293]

CLOUSTON, ROBERT, a skipper in Stromness, Orkney, a sasine, 1798. [NRS.R.S.Orkney.422/820]

CLOUSTON, ROBERT, a merchant in Stromness, Orkney, versus Benjamin Smith a fish curer in Burray, 1827. [OA.SC11.5.1827.6]

CLOUSTON, ROBERT, Chief Trader in Hudson Bay Company Service, eldest son of Edward Clouston the HBC agent in Orkney, died at sea between Honolulu and San Francisco on 14 August 1858. [W.XIX.2026]

CLOUSTON, THOMAS, a skipper in Newberry, New England, son of Robert Clouston a carpenter and sailor in Stromness, Orkney, sasines, 1776, 1787. [NRS.R.S.Orkney.133]

CLOUSTOUN, WILLIAM, born 1794 in Orkney, an employee of the Hudson Bay Company from 1812 to 1843. [HBRS.3.431]

CLOUSTON, WILLIAM, born 22 December 1839 in Sandwick, died in India on 9 May 1869. [F.7.249]

CLUNAS, Captain GORDON, tenant in the parish of Kildonan, Sutherland, in 1811. [SHS.8.102]

CLUNIS, JAMES, in Aith, Fetlar, Shetland, was accused of assaulting William Danielson in Littleland, Fetlar, in 1821. [SA.SC12.6.1821.47]

CLUNAS, or MCKENZIE, Mrs, tenant in Kintraid, Rogart, Sutherland, 1811. [SHS.8.69]

CLUNAS, Major, tenant in Torrish, Kildonan, Sutherland, in 1815. [SHS.8.227]

CLYNE, CATHERINE, eldest daughter of Alexander Clyne in Scarmalet, married Reverend Alexander Campbell a Free Church missionary in Nova Scotia, at Bower, Caithness, on 8 September 1845. [W.610]

COGHILL, DAVID, teacher in the village subscription school, was given a recommendation signed by parents and the minister of Latheron, Caithness, in 1837. [NRS.GD136.755]

COOPER, DAVID, son of Alexander Cooper and his wife Barbara Henderson in Caithness, died in California on 6 September 1857. [Latheron gravestone, Caithness]

COOPER, JAMES, born 1792, son of William Cooper, [1746-1836], and his wife Janet Nicholson, 1755-1835], Colour Sergeant of the 73rd Regiment, died 4 May 1849. [Old Latheron gravestone, Caithness]

COOPER, JAMES, born 25 December 1810 in Janetstown, son of Alexander Cooper and his wife Barbara Henderson in Caithness, died in California on 6 September 1857. [Latheron gravestone, Caithness]

COOPER, JOHN, born 1792, from Sanda, Orkney, emigrated via Stornaway on the Prince of Wales to the Hudson Bay Company settlement on the Red River in 1811. [PAC.M155.145]

COPELAND, WILLIAM, a merchant in Lerwick, Shetland, in 1841. [NRS.CS280.27.17]

COPLAND, JAMES, born 1751, died 24 March 1832, husband of Jane Pottinger, born 1763, died 13 December 1852. [Lerwick gravestone, Shetland]

CORBET, WILLIAM, a labourer in Pultneytown, Caithness, accused of mobbing and rioting in 1827. [NRS.AD14.27.2]

CORIE, PATRICK, son of Patrick Corie, a merchant in Kirkwall, and his wife Elizabeth Drevar, was lost at the Cape of Good Hope, South Africa, in September 1864. [St Magnus gravestone, Kirkwall, Orkney]

CORMACK, ALEXANDER, a skipper in Wick, a sasine, 1801. [NRS.R.S.Caithness.387]; born 1760, died 12 May 1826. [Wick gravestone]

CORMACK, ALEXANDER, born 1799, died 11 March 1879, husband of Ann Nicolson, born 1802, died 18 May 1873, parents of James born 1829, died 7 April 1906. [Canisbay gravestone, Caithness]

CORMACK, ANN, in Thurso, dead by 1851, sister of William Cormack a merchant in Montreal. [NRS.S/H]

CORMACK, CHRISTIAN, sister of Euphemia Cormack in Louisburgh, Wick, Caithness, accused of resisting an officer of the law in 1821. [NRS.AD14.21.97]

CORMACK, ENEAS, in Montreal, Quebec, tenant of Samuel Forbes the tacksman of Bankhead of Wick, Caithness, testament, 15 January 1814. [NRS.CC4.5.1.298]

CORMACK, or DICKSON, EUPHEMIA, daughter of John Dickson in Louisburgh, Wick, Caithness, accused of resisting an officer of the law in 1821. [NRS.AD14.21.97]

CORMACK, JAMES, a merchant in Montreal later in Tongue, Sutherland, dead by 1851, brother of William Cormack a merchant in Montreal. [NRS.S/H]

CORMACK, WILLIAM, son of James Cormack a farmer in Tain, Ross and Cromarty, was educated at Marischal College, Aberdeen, in 1846, later a minister of the Dutch Reformed Church at Burghersdorf, Cape of Good Hope, South Africa. [MCA.II.534]

CORRIGAL, ADAM, in Burray, Orkney, versus James Sutherland the principal tacksman on Burray, in 1800. [OA.SC11.5.1800.10]

CORRIGILL, JOHN, a seaman aboard the Nassau, son of John Corrigill tenant in Mirbister, a sasine, 1799. [NRS.R.S.Orkney.433]

CORRIGAL, JOHN, from Orphir, Orkney, a Hudson Bay Company employee from 1837 until 1848 when he settled at the Red River, married Elizabeth Firth in 1848, parents of Eliza and William Charles. [HBRS.16.355]

COUTS, ANDREW, in Aith, Fetlar, Shetland, versus James Johnson there in 1800. [SA.SC12.6.1800.75]

COVIE, PATRICK, a merchant in Kirkwall, husband of Elizabeth Drever, parents of Patrick Covie who was lost off the Cape of Good Hope, South Africa, in September 1864. [St Magnus gravestone, Kirkwall]

CRAIG JAMES, born 1835, son of John Craig and his wife Catherine Weir, died in the West Indies on 6 October 1876. [Bower gravestone, Caithness]

CRAIGIE, GEORGE, from Orkney, settled in Portsmouth, New Hampshire, dead by 1836. [NRS.NRAS.0627.5.7]

CRAIGIE, THOMAS, born 1830 in Orkney, a labourer in Hudson Bay Company Service, died in Victoria, British Columbia, on 18 June 1882. [Ross Bay gravestone, B.C.]

CRAMOND, WILLIAM, son of Jane Cramond in Tain, Ross and Cromarty, a merchant in Philadelphia by 1785, died on 26 October 1843. [ANY.I.200]

CRAIG, JAMES, born 1835, son of John Craig and his wife Catherine Weir, died in the West Indies on 6 October 1876. [Bower gravestone, Caithness]

CRAIGIE, HUGH, emigrated via Scrabster, Caithness, on board the Superior of Peterhead bound for Pictou, Nova Scotia, landed there in June 1842. [Pictou Observer, 21.6.1842]

CRAMOND, JAMES, son of Jane Cramond in Tain, a merchant in Philadelphia and New York, died in N.Y. on 29 September 1799. [ANY.I.200]

CRAMOND, WILLIAM, son of Jane Cramond in Tain, emigrated to America before 1779, a merchant in Philadelphia in 1785, died on 26 October 1843. [ANY.I.200]

CROMARTY, JAMES, a farmer in Mossaquoy, Deerness, Orkney, versus Gilbert Skea a farmer in Northouse, Deerness, and his wife ..... Cromarty, in 1849. [OA.SC11.5.1849.39]

CROMARTY, WILLIAM, born 1 May 1731 on South Ronaldsay, Orkney, settled on South River, North Carolina, in 1758, died 21 September 1807. [Cromarty gravestone, Bladen County, NC]

CROOKSHANK, ANDREW, a mariner, son of Robert Cruickshank a skipper in Stromness, Orkney, a sasine, 1810. [NRS.R.S.Orkney.792-793]

CUNNINGHAM, MATTHEW, in Burghead, versus Alexander Gordon, fish curer, late in Burghead, Cromarty, in 1829. [NRS.CS44.174.44]

CURSITTER, CATHERINE, and Elizabeth Cursitter, heirs to their grandfather James Cursitter in Kirkbuster, Stromness, Orkney, 1826. [NRS.CS228.B16.39.5]

CURSITTER, JOHN, at Burness Firth, Orkney, a petition as he had moved from the lands of Goe without thatching the farmhouse in 1804. [OA.SC11.5.1804.48]

DALLAS, JAMES, a saddler in Dornoch and in Golspie, Sutherland, financial records from 1812 to 1817. [NRS.CS96.1540-1544]; tenant in Golspie, Sutherland, in 1815. [SHS.8.225]

DALLAS, JOHN, in Teanahaun, Ross-shire, a victim of crime in 1835. [NRS.AD14.35.3]

DANIELSON, LILIAS, in Hillswick, Northmavine, Shetland, was accused of fornicating with Arthur Brown in Uyea, Northmavine, in 1801. [SA.SC12.6.1801.5]

DARG, ROBERT, in Kirkwall, versus Andrew Wilson, a fishcurer on Stronsay, Orkney, 1832. [OA.SC11.5.1832.111]

DAVIDSON, AGNES ELIZABETH, relict of John Gifford a surgeon in Urafirth, Northmavine, Shetland, versus Andrew Robertson of Eastness, Northmavine, in 1814. [SA.SC12.6.1814.44]

DAVIDSON, AGNES, third daughter of William Davidson a merchant in Wick, Caithness, married E. S. Babcock a merchant in Madison, Indiana, on 28 May 1844. [AJ.5044][EEC.21080]

DAVIDSON, ALEXANDER, depute Sheriff Clerk of Sutherland from 1836 to 1848, also depute town clerk of Dornoch in 1844. [NRS.GD347.41]

DAVIDSON, COLIN, born 1808, a tailor in Jemimaville, Resolis, Cromarty, accused of mobbing and prison breaking in 1844. [NRS.AD14.44.443]

DAVIDSON, DONALD, in Thurso, Caithness, a victim of theft in 1830. [NRS.JC26.1830.90]

DAVIDSON, GEORGE, minister of Latheron Free Church, Dunbeath, Caithness, a petition, 1845. [NRS.GD1.2.51.178]

DAVIDSON, HELEN, daughter of John Davidson in Wester, Wick, Caithness, accused of resisting an officer of the law in 1821. [NRS.AD14.21.97]

DAVIDSON, ISABELLA, second daughter of William Davidson a merchant in Wick, Caithness, married John Ingle of Evansville, in Madison, Indiana, on 29 November 1842. [AJ.4958]

DAVIDSON, JAMES ANDREW, born 1845, son of Reverend George Moir Davidson in Watten, Caithness, a veterinary surgeon who died in Whitby, Ontario, on 8 June 1871. [S.8709]

DAVIDSON, JANET, daughter of William Davidson in Wester Wick, Caithness, accused of resisting an officer of the law in 1821. [NRS.AD14.21.97]

DAVIDSON, JOHN, a sub-tenant in Wick, Caithness, accused of resisting an officer of the law in 1821. [NRS.AD14.21.97]

DAVIDSON, KENNETH, born 1774 in Ross-shire, died 24 1. November 1874, husband of Isabella Fraser, born 1806 died 1881. [Hill gravestone, Pictou, NS]

DAVIDSON, MARJORY, daughter of Charles Davidson a tenant, in Wester Killimster, Caithness, accused of resisting an officer of the law in 1821. [NRS.AD14.21.97]

DAVIDSON, ROBERT, born 1815, second son of William Davidson a merchant in Wick, Caithness, was drowned in the River Ohio, near Louisville, Kentucky, on 22 June 1840. [EEC.20088]

DAVIDSON, WILLIAM, a fish-curer in Wick, Caithness, father of William Davidson, MD, in Madison, Indiana, 1863. [NRS.SC20.34.46.267-271; S/H.1864; RS27.83.275]

DELDAY, JANE, in Thieveshall, Deerness, Orkney, versus John Aitken in Duncan's House, Deerness, re alimony in 1848. [OA.SC11.5.1848.24]

DEMPSTER, JOHN HAMILTON, Captain of the Honourable East India ship Rose, a sasine, 1792. [NRS.R.S.Sutherland.99-100]

DEMPSTER, Mrs SOPER's heirs, tenants of Langwall, Rogart, Sutherland, in 1811. [SHS.8.73]

DEMPSTER, W.S., tenant of Skibo, Dornoch, Sutherland, in 1811. [SHS.8.60]

DENNISON, JAMES, a mariner from Orkney, was naturalised in South Carolina on 12 December 1796. [NARA.M1183.1]

DENNISON, JAMES, [1806-1875], and his wife Margaret Wallace, [1798-1874], in Sandwick, Orkney, parents of Robert Scarth Dennison, born 1841, who settled in Winsted, Connecticut. [St Magnus gravestone, Kirkwall] [Lady gravestone, Stronsay, Orkney]

DEYELL, JOHN, a tenant farmer in Aith, Aithsting, Shetland, was accused of theft from a stranded ship in 1816. [NRS.AD14.16.26]

DICK, D., in Glenshiel by Lochalsh, Wester Ross, a letter re Murdoch MacRa tenant at Shiel Bridge, Invershiel, in 1832. [NRS.GD46.1.240]

DICKSON, JAMES, born 1778, from Harra, Orkney, emigrated via Stornaway on the Prince of Wales to the Hudson Bay Company settlement on the Red River in 1811. [PAC.M155.145]

DICKSON, JOHN, in Dornoch, Sutherland, a decreet in October 1834. [NRS.CS46.1834.10/10]

DINGWALL, JAMES, born 1821, son of Murdo Dingwall, [1783-1861], and his wife Charlotte Sutherland, [1778-1866], died in Dunedin, New Zealand, on 28 February 1914. [Clyne, Kirkton, Sutherland, gravestone]

DISHINGTON, Reverend ANDREW, transferred from Yell, Shetland, to Stronsay in 1803, [SA.CH2.1071.62]; minister of Stronsay and Eday, Orkney, versus Margaret Izatt or Anderson in Stronsay, 1804. [NRS.SC11.2.1804.54]

DONALDSON, GILBERT, a tenant in Raefirth, Mid Yell, Shetland, summons of removal, 1800. [SA.SC12.6.1800.17]

DONALDSON, JOHN, born 1820 in Shetland, died 10 October 1877. [Anglican cemetery, Eastern Passage, Halifax, NS]

DOUGLAS, DONALD, born 1773, died 21 May 1818, his wife Margaret Grant, born 1775, died 26 January 1838, both from Sutherland, emigrated to Nova Scotia in 1803. [Millbrook gravestone, Pictou, NS]

DOUGLAS, DONALD, born 1791, with family, from Sutherland, emigrated via Cromarty aboard the Ossian bound for Pictou, Nova Scotia, on 25 June 1821. [Inverness Journal.29 June 1821]

DOUGLAS, JAMES, joint tenant in Achunoluechrach, Rogart, Sutherland, in 1815. [SHS.8.232]

DOUGLAS, NORMAN, born 1803, with family, from Sutherland, emigrated via Cromarty aboard the Ossian bound for Pictou, Nova Scotia, on 25 June 1821. [Inverness Journal.29 June 1821]

DOUL, PETER, in Aithsting, Shetland, 1803. [NRS.SC12.6.1803.6]

DREVER, DAVID, sr., in Sanday, Orkney, disposed of property in Kirkwall, Orkney, to Elizabeth Fotheringham, his wife, in 1802. [NRS.GD31.448]

DUFF, HECTOR ROSS, son of Hugo Ross a farmer in Edderton, Ross-shire, was educated at Marischal College, Aberdeen, in 1844. [MCA]

DUFF, JOHN, son of Hugo Ross a farmer in Edderton, Ross-shire, was educated at Marischal College, Aberdeen, in 1844, graduated MD from King's College, Aberdeen, in 1848, became a Surgeon Major of the Royal Artillery. [MCA][KCA]

DUFF, WALTER ROSS, son of Hugo Ross a farmer in Edderton, Ross-shire, was educated at Marischal College, Aberdeen, in 1840, later was a planter in Ceylon. [MCA]

DUNBAR, GEORGE, born 1773, a midshipman who died aboard the man o'war Champion in Cromarty Harbour on 20 March 1789. [Cromarty gravestone]

DUNCAN, JAMES, tenant of Glen, Golspie Tower and Golspie Inn, Kildonan, Sutherland, in 1808, 1811, 1815. [SGS.8.86/87/226/227]

DUNCAN, JAMES, in Golspie and Cyderhall, Sutherland, deceased, a sequestration petition, 1847. [NRS.CS278.2.61]

DUNNET, GEORGE, born 1845, son of James Dunnet, [1800-1884], and his wife Barbara Brotchie, [1812-1893], died in Boston, Massachusetts, on 7 May 1891. [Canisbay gravestone, Caithness]

DUNNET, JOHN, a skipper in Thurso, son of George Dunnet a merchant in Thurso, a sasine, 1800. [NRS.R.S.Caithness.341]

DUNNET, THOMAS, a saddler in Wick, Caithness, father of Lizzie Dunnet who married Alexander William Roberts of the Free Church Training College in Lovedale, in Port Elizabeth, South Africa on 16 June 1884. [S.12797]

DURRAN, GEORGE, in Hillhead of Dunnet, Caithness, a letter from Morison Snody in Dunnet in 1829. [NRS.GD136.567]

DYKER, WILLIAM MURRAY, with a wife and three children, in Loanafrishillock, Culmaily, Sutherland, in 1810. [SHS.1.14/15]

EDMONDSON, Dr ARTHUR, a physician in Lerwick, versus William Hay and the other partners of the Shetland Banking Company in 1828. [NRS.CS44.141.52]

EDMONSTON, BIOT, son of Laurence Edmonston MD in Unst, Shetland, was educated at Marischal College, Aberdeen, in 1846, later was a minister. [MCA]

EDMONSTON, ARTHUR, MD, born 10 November 1775, died in February 1811. [Lerwick gravestone, Shetland]

EDMONSTON, CHARLES, born 20 June 1782 in Lerwick in the Shetland Islands, son of Laurence Edmonston a surgeon, emigrated to Charleston, South Carolina, in 1799, a merchant, was naturalised in South Carolina on 26 March 1810. [NARA.M1183.1] [ZFH]

EDMONSTON, THOMAS, son of Laurence Edmonston MD at Balta Sound, Shetland, was educated at Marischal College, Aberdeen, in 1843, later was Professor of Botany at Anderson's College, in Glasgow. [MCA]

ELRICK, HAY, a clock and watchmaker in Kirkwall, Orkney, versus the Magistrates of Kirkwall in 1829. [NRS.CS44.174.65]

ERASMUSON, JOHN, in Houll, Quarff, Shetland, summons of removal in 1804. [SA.SC12.6.1804.22]

ERICKSON, ELIZABETH, daughter of Erick Adamson in Blosta, Cunningsburgh, Shetland, was accused of carrying off cattle in 1827. [SA.SC12.6.1827.72]

ERSKINE, DAVID, in Kirkwall, Orkney, versus Robert Pringle in 1817. [NRS.CS40.25.111]

EUNSON, DAVID, innkeeper in Kirkwall, Orkney, versus James Garrioch merchant in Littlehouse, a decreet, 1816. [NRS.CS42.16.73]

FALCONER, COSMO, tenant in Golspie muir, parish of Golspie, Sutherland, in 1811, 1815. [SHS.8.85/226]

FARQUHAR, ANN, sister of John Farquhar, and widow of Hugh Brock in Wester Wick, Caithness, accused of resisting an officer of the law in 1821. [NRS.AD14.21.97]

FARQUHARSON, ALEXANDER, an innkeeper in Wick, Caithness, sederunt books 1835-1840. [NRS.CS96.4079-4081]

FEA, JAMES, a skipper n Lerwick, son of Magnus Fea, a sasine, 1799. [NRS.R.S.Shetland.386]

FEA, THOMAS, born 1767, died 1 November 1841, husband of Jane Green, born 1770, died 23 October 1838. [Lerwick gravestone, Shetland]

FERGUSON, GEORGE, a tenant in Kilfedarmore, Strathborn, Clyne, Sutherland, was accused of rioting, resulting from the removal or eviction of tenants in Kildonan in 1813. [NRS.AD14.13.9; SC9.7.64]

FERGUSON, HUGH W., born in Rogart, Sutherland, was naturalised in South Carolina on 22 February 1822. [S.C. Circuit Court Journal.9.220]

FERGUSON, JAMES, an Excise officer in Thurso, Caithness, dead by 1860. [NRS.S/H]

FERGUSON, JOHN, born 1787 in Sutherland, a tailor in Charleston, South Carolina, was naturalised there on 17 November 1813. [NARA.M1183.1]

FERGUSON, ROBERT, emigrated from Cromarty or Thurso aboard the Lady Grey bound for Pictou, Nova Scotia, in June 1841. [NRS.RH1.2.908]

FERGUSON, W. and I., tenants of Longuish, Golspie, Sutherland, in 1811. [SHS.8.89]

FINDLATOR, WILLIAM, minister of the Free Church in Durness, Sutherland, a petition, 1845. [NRS.GD112.51.192]

FINLAY, HUGH, a shipmaster in Cottascarth, Orkney, died in January 1838, father of William Loutit Finlay, a railway clerk in Galt, North America. [NRS.S/H]

FINLAY, WILLIAM, from Stromness, Orkney, emigrated via Stornaway on the Prince of Wales to the Hudson Bay Company settlement on the Red River in 1811. [PAC.M155.145]

FINLAYSON, ALEXANDER, in Aronisk, Lochalsh and Plockton district, to emigrate to America around 1850. [NRS.HD21.53]

FINLAYSON, DUNCAN, in Inverein, Contin, Ross-shire, accused of assaulting Revenue officers in 1818, was outlawed. [NRS.JC11.59]

FINLAYSON, DUNCAN, born 1800, died 1875, his wife Christy MacAulay, born 1808, died 1901, from Lochalsh, Wester Ross, emigrated aboard the Pallas to Nova Scotia on 28 August 1821. [Grand River Presbyterian gravestone, Richmond County, NS]

FINLAYSON, DUNCAN, in Aronisk, Lochalsh and Plockton district, Wester Ross, to emigrate to America around 1850. [NRS.HD21.53]

FINLAYSON, DUNCAN, in Ardelvie, Lochalsh and Plockton district, Wester Ross, to emigrate to America around 1850. [NRS.HD21.53]

FINLAYSON, FINLAY, in Erbsaig, Lochalsh and Plockton district, Wester Ross, to emigrate to America around 1850. [NRS.HD21.53]

FINLAYSON, JOHN ADAM, born 1833 in Dingwall, Ross and Cromarty, grandson of Roderick Finlayson, [1812-1889], and his wife Catherine McKenzie, [182-1902], died in Buenos Ayres, Argentina, in 1907. [Dingwall gravestone]

FINLAYSON, JOHN, born 1825, a weaver, son of Andrew Finlayson a weaver, in Cromarty, accused of mobbing and prison breaking in 1844. [NRS.AD14.44.443]

FINLAYSON, JOHN, in Kirkton of Lochalsh, Lochalsh and Plockton district, Wester Ross, to emigrate to America around 1850. [NRS.HD21.53]

FINLAYSON, JOHN HOYES, born 1820, son of Reverend John Finlayson in Cromarty, died in Kingston, Jamaica, on 2 December 1849. [AJ.5324]

FINLAYSON, JOHN BAIN in Erbsaig, Lochalsh and Plockton district, Wester Ross, to emigrate to America around 1850. [NRS.HD21.53]

FINLAYSON, MALCOLM, born 1797, died 19 March 1871, first wife Mary McKenzie, born 1797, died in June 1831. [Lochcarron gravestone, Ross and Cromarty]

FINLAYSON, ROBERT, minister at Lochs, Lewis, in 1830, [NRS.GD46.12.39]; a letter, 1831. [NRS.GD46.12.42]

FINLAYSON, RORY, in Aronisk, Lochalsh and Plockton district, Wester Ross, to emigrate to America around 1850. [NRS.HD21.53]

FLETT, BETSY, born 1847 in Orkney, died in Victoria, British Columbia, on 17 August 1916. [Ross Bay gravestone, B.C.]

FLETT, GEORGE, born 1775 in Firth, Orkney, an employee of the Hudson Bay Company from 1796 to 1823, from Stromness to York Factory in 1796, died at Red River on 10 June 1850. [HBRS.2.213][OL.ms21.5]

FLETTE, GEORGE, born 1803 on Birsay, an employee of the Hudson Bay Company from 1833 until he drowned near York Factory on 15 October 1849. [HBRS.16.357]

FLETT, JAMES, born 1839 on Birsay, Orkney, settled in Victoria, British Columbia, in 1871, died there on 12 January 1901. [Ross Bay gravestone, B.C.]

FLETT, JOHN, born 1809 in Orkney, died in Victoria, British Columbia, on 18 August 1881. [Ross Bay gravestone, B.C.]

FLETT, JOHN, born 1816 in Kirkwall, a watchmaker in Brora, Sutherland, formerly in Wick, Caithness, accused of housebreaking and theft in 1836. [NRS.AD14.36.4]

FLETT, JOHN, born 1828 in Stromness, Orkney, a cooper in Hudson Bay Company Service, died in Victoria, British Columbia, on 4 February 1886. [Ross Bay gravestone, B.C.]

FLETT, MARGARET, daughter of Robert Flett, from Kirkwall, Orkney, married James S. Sloane, a printer in Toronto, there on 28 January 1857. [EEC.21042]

FLETT, WILLIAM, from Orkney, died in Rupert's Land, Canada, on 11 November 1823, testament, 1826. [NRS.SC70.1.34]

FOLSETTER, WILLIAM, tacksman of North Strynzie, Stronsay, Orkney, versus Richard Maxwell in the House of Goar in 1806. [OA.SC11.5.1806.82/105]

FOLSTAR, JOHN, from Firth, Orkney, a Hudson Bay Company employee from 1838 to 1844. [HBRS. 16.357]

FORBES, BETTY, in Howland, Burness, versus George Muir a wright in Scar, Orkney, in 1804. [OA.SC11.5.1804.62]

FORBES, ELIZABETH, relict of Reverend George McCulloch in Loth, tenant in Kilmote, parish of Loth, Sutherland, 1811. [SHS.8.100]

FORBES, FLORA, youngest daughter of Major Forbes in Ribigal, Sutherland, married Mitchell Scobie in Melbourne, Australia, on 13 August 1845. [AJ.4338]

FORBES, ROBERT, miller at Inverlael, Loch Broom, Wester Ross, was accused of wilful fire-raising in 1828. [NRS.AD14.28.392]

FORBES, SCOTT, a merchant in Delting, Shetland, was accused of plundering a Norwegian shipwreck in 1803. [SA.SC12.6.1803.47]

FOTHERINGHAM, ANNE, wife of Thomas Traill of Westove, died 13 March 1828, buried at St Martin's Church, Vevey, Switzerland. [NRS.NRAS.01.0110.43]

FOTHERINGHAM, PATRICK, a writer in Kirkwall, Orkney, a bond, 1801. [NRS.CS97.111.134/1]; versus James Sinclair, a mason in Kirkwall, and John Delday in Gairth, Deerness, in 1800. [OA.SC11.5.1800.5]

FOUBISTER, JOHN, a tacksman, and John Ritch in North Keigar, versus Francis Barnet in Backie, Deerness, Orkney 1806. [OA.SC11.5.1806.92]

FOWLER, ANDREW, born 1755, died in Trelawney, Jamaica, in June 1796, brother of James Fowler of Grange and Raddery. [Rosemarkie plaque, Ross and Cromarty]

FOWLER, JAMES, in Jamaica, a deed dated 21 April 1802; later, in Rosemarkie, 1829. [NRS.RD4.271.842; CS17.1.46.384]

FOWLER, JOHN, in Trelawney, Jamaica, father of Sarah Fowler, wife of George Budge a Lieutenant of the Ross-shire Militia in 1816. [NRS.PS3.16.281]; John Fowler, born in 1754, of Friendship Estate, Trelawney, died in June 1792, 'commander of the Leeward Troop of Trelawney Horse', brother of James Fowler of Grange and Raddery. [Rosemarkie plaque, Ross and Cromarty]

FOWLER, SARAH WILLIAMS, daughter of John Fowler of Trelawney, Jamaica, and widow of Lieutenant George Budge of the Ross-shire Militia, died in June 1816. [NRS.PS3.16.281]

FRASER, ADAM, a tenant farmer and cattle dealer in Clyne Milton, Sutherland, was banished for seven years in 1801. [NRS.JC11.45]

FRASER, ALEXANDER, [1825-1904], and his wife Janet Gordon, [1825-1891], parents of William Fraser, born 1860, a blacksmith, who died in Ipswich, Queensland, Australia, on 30 October 1890. [Dornoch gravestone, Sutherland]

FRASER, ALEXANDER, and his wife Isobel McDougall in Invergordon, Ross and Cromarty, were parents of Donald Fraser, born 3 February 1864, was educated at Aberdeen University in 1886, a minister in New South Wales, Australia, from 1893. [F.7.588]

FRASER, ANGUS, tenant of Dean's House, Laroch, Dornoch, and Pitgrudy, Sutherland, in 1811. [SHS.8.59]

FRAZER, ANGUS, tenant in Pitgrudy, Dornoch, Sutherland, in 1808, and in 1815. [SHS.8.220/221]

FRASER, ANN, daughter of Margaret Johnston in Gargarton, Killearnan, Ross-shire, accused of assaulting a Revenue officer in 1816. [NRS.JC26.1816.39]

FRASER, Captain CHARLES, born 1823 in Cromarty, son of William Fraser, died in Maitland Street, Dunedin, Otago, New Zealand, on 8 February 1885. [S.13029]

FRASER, COLLIN MACKENZIE, born 1801 in Ross-shire, was educated at King's College, Aberdeen, from 1816 to 1822, a minister of the Dutch Reformed Church in Beaufort West, South Africa, died in 1870. [F.7.561]

FRASER, DONALD, a forrester, formerly a fox-hunter and fisher, at Little Struig, Glen Strathfarrar, Wester Ross, was accused of wilful fire-raising in 1828. [NRS.AD14.28.392]

FRASER, DONALD, born 1797, agent of the British Society for the Encouragement of the Fisheries, in Ullapool, Wester Ross, was accused of rioting in 1833. [NRS.AD14.33.117]

FRASER, ELIZABETH, born 1783, from Borrobal, Kildonan, Sutherland, emigrated via Stromness on the Prince of Wales to the Hudson Bay Company settlement at Fort Churchill on 29 June 1813. [PAC.M155.165-8]

FRASER, GEORGE, and his wife Mary McIntyre, parents of Alick Fraser, born 1861, died in Murraysburg, South Africa, on 1 December 1897. [Gairloch gravestone, Ross and Cromarty]

FRASER, GEORGE, a baker from Munlochy, Ross-shire, married Catherine Ross, daughter of David Ross in Invergordon, in Hoboken, New Jersey, on 6 December 1867, settled in Chicago, Illinois, before 1869. [S.7617/8014/8398]

FRASER, HUGH, emigrated from Cromarty or Thurso aboard the Lady Grey bound for Pictou, Nova Scotia, in June 1841. [NRS.RH1.2.908]

FRASER, ISABELLA, in Geanean, Cromarty, victim of theft and fraud in 1836. [NRS.AD14.36.2]

FRASER, JAMES, born 1800 in Foddarty, Ross-shire, was educated at King's College, Aberdeen, in 1822, a missionary on Cape Breton from 1837, died there on 8 April 1874. [F.7.607]

FRASER, JANE, born 1831 in Stromness, Orkney, married William Spence in Stromness on 27 February 1851, died in Victoria, British Columbia, on 13 September 1875. [Ross Bay gravestone, BC]

FRASER, JEAN, with family, emigrated from Achrinsdale, Rogart, Sutherland, to Canada in 1829. [NLS.313.878]

FRASER, JOANNA, daughter of Donald Fraser and his wife Mary Joyner in Invergordon, Ross and Cromarty, wife of Roderick Mackenzie in Wisconsin in 1871. [NRS.S/H]

FRASER, JOHN, born 1789 in Sutherland, emigrated to Pictou, Nova Scotia, in 1818, died on 30 April 1861. [New Lairg gravestone, N.S.]

FRASER, JOHN, born 1789, died 30 April 1861, his wife Christina Sutherland, born 1794, died 18 December 1857, both natives of Sutherland, emigrated to Pictou, Nova Scotia, in 1818. [Landsdowne gravestone, Pictou, NS]

FRASER, JOHN, a tenant in Gardie, Mid Yell, Shetland, summons of removal, 1800. [SA.SC12.6.1800.17]

FRASER, JOHN, born 1792 in Ross-shire, died 26 April 1874. [Knox Presbyterian cemetery, Baddeck, Victoria County, NS]

FRASER, JOHN, born 1827, a painter in Dornoch, Ross and Cromarty, was accused of theft in 1850. [NRS.AD14.50.552]

FRASER, OLIVER, joint tenant in Kerrow of Kinbrace, Lairg, Sutherland, in 1808. [SHS.8.229]

FRASER, PETER, born 17 February 1834 in Dingwall, Ross and Cromarty, son of John Fraser, [1809-1878], and his wife Jane McGregor, [1809-1865], died in San Francisco, California, on 11 May 1862. [Greenock gravestone, Renfrewshire]

FRASER, THOMAS, manager of the Cromarty Wine Company, versus John Cockburn Ross in 1811. [NRS.CS42.2.37]

FRASER, THOMAS, schoolmaster in Golspie, Sutherland, a letter, 1851. [NRS.GD248.571.5]

FREW, THOMAS MCNAUGHTON, [1829-1900], and his wife Christina Rose, [1835-1924], parents of Duncan John Frew, born 1862, died in Salt Lake City, Utah, on 29 March 1923. [St Clement's gravestone, Dingwall, Ross and Cromarty]

GADIE, LAURENCE, Peter Gadie, and John Gadie tenants in Croon, Nesting, Shetland, summons of removal in 1803. [SA.SC12.6.1803.13]

GADIE, LAURENCE, Peter Gadie, and John Gadie tenants in Catfirth, Nesting, Shetland, summons of removal in 1803. [SA.SC12.6.1803.13]

GADOE, PETER, tenant in Croon, Nesting, Shetland, summons of removal in 1803. [SA.SC12.6.1803.13]

GAIR, Captain, from Fortrose, Ross and Cromarty, married Barbara McIver, third daughter of William McIver from Jamaica, in Inverness on 11 August 1821. [SM.88.293]

GALLIE, HECTOR, a farmer in Easter Rarichie, Ross-shire, dead by 1859. [NRS.S/H]

GALLIE, RODERICK, a merchant in Invergordon, Ross and Cromarty, dead by 1847, uncle of James Boggs Gallie in Nova Scotia. [NRS.S/H]

GARDEN, THOMAS, in Golspie, Sutherland, a letter re the Achness rioters, 1821. [NRS.SC9.79.12]

GARIOCH, BENJAMIN, a skipper on South Ronaldsay, a sasine, 1803. [NRS.R.S.Orkney.572]

GARIOCH, WILLIAM, a skipper in Stromness, Orkney, a sasine, 1801. [NRS.R.S.Orkney.495]

GARSON, DAVID, from Orkney, a steersman employed by the Hudson Bay Company around 1817. [OL.ms21.5]

GEARIE, or MCKAY, JANET, a prisoner in Dornoch Tolbooth, Ross and Cromarty, applied for temporary liberation to have her baby, in 1835. [NRS.SC9.78.5]

GEDDES, GEORGE, a mariner in Stromness, husband of Anna Beaton, a sasine, 1790. [NRS.R.S.Orkney.218]

GEDDES, ROBERT, a mason and weaver in Wick, Caithness, accused of mobbing and rioting in 1827. [NRS.AD14.27.218]

GEORGESON, JAMES, born 1841, a blacksmith from Thrumster, Caithness, died in South Africa on 8 April 1890, husband of Helen Donaldson, born 1836, died at Heather Inn on 14 November 1891. [Ulbster gravestone, Caithness]

GIBSON, JAMES, born 1835 in Orkney, settled in Victoria, British Columbia, in 1862, died there on 17 February 1900. [Ross Bay gravestone, B.C.]

GIBSON, JOHN, a skipper in Orkney, a sasine, 1800. [NRS.R.S.Orkney.455]

GIBSON, JOHN, in Corse, St Ola, Orkney, versus Alexander Linklater in Ireland, St Ola, in 1801. [OA.SC11.5.1801.34]

GIFFORD, ARTHUR, of Busta, versus Reverend John Morrison minister of Delting, Shetland, in 1817. [NRS.CS271.62009]

GIFFORD, GIDEON, of Busta, Aithsling, Shetland, versus Arthur Anderson, tenant of East Burrafirth, Aithsling, in 1801. [SA.SC12.6.1801.18]; versus Andrew Herculeson tenant in Grobesness, Delting, re trespassing in 1801. [SA.SC12.6.1801.16]; versus George Cheyne, schoolmaster of Brunthammersland, Tingwall, in 1801. [SA.SC12.6.1801.8]

GILBERTSON, THOMAS, born 1796, a merchant in Lerwick, died 1868, husband of Bessie Coutts, born 1798, died 1871. [Knab Rod gravestone, Lerwick, Shetland]

GILCHRIST, DONALD, with family, emigrated from Achrinsale, Clyne, Sutherland, to Canada in 1829. [NLS.313.878]

GILCHRIST, GEORGE, born 1854, son of William Gilchrist and his wife Annie Polson, died in Indiana on 30 September 1896. [Loth, Brora, gravestone, Sutherland]

GILCHRIST, JOHN, and family, from West Helmsdale, Loth, Sutherland, emigrated to Canada in 1829. [NLS.313.878]

GILCHRIST, JOHN, and family, from Culgower, Loth, Sutherland, emigrated to Canada in 1829. [NLS.313.878]

GILCHRIST, WILLIAM, born 1847, son of William Gilchrist and his wife Annie Polson, drowned off Sydney, Australia, on 26 October 1881. [Loth, Brora, gravestone]

GILLANDERS, ALEXANDER, son of Lachlan Gillanders, [1769-1844], a farmer in Kishorn, and his wife Margaret Mackenzie, [1783-1832], settled in Canada West. [Kishorn gravestone, Ross and Cromarty]

GILLANDERS, THOMAS, born 1802, second son of George Gillanders in Lewis, was drowned off Buenos Ayres, Argentina, in December 1831. [AJ.4411]

GILLIES, JAMES, born 1800 in Stromness, Orkney, emigrated to Bonaventure County, Quebec, in 1825. [SG.32.2.61]

GOAR, JESSIE, born 1821 in Eday, Orkney, wife of ..... Irvine, settled in Victoria, British Columbia, in 1851, died there on 18 March 1907. [Ross Bay gravestone, BC]

GOAR, PATRICK, in Warsetter, Sanday, Orkney, versus John Gourlie a rabbit catcher on Sanday, re rent due for rabbit lines in 1801. [OA.SC11.5.1801.58]

GOODLAD, ELIZABETH, versus Thomas Bettie and Hay Balance in Gairdings of Nation, Delting, Shetland, a petition for ejection, 1803. [SA.SC12.6.1803.11]

GOODLAD, SCOTT, in Trusta, Aithsting, Shetland, a victim of sheep-stealing in 1837. [NRS.AD14.37.471; JC26.1837.534]

GORDON, ADAM, a tenant in Grimachkary, Lairg, Sutherland, in 1808. [SHS.8.229]

GORDON, ALEXANDER, born 1775, a farmer with wife and four children, in Rhiorn, Culmaily, Golspie, Sutherland, in 1808 and 1810. [SHS.1.14/15; SHS.6.224]

GORDON, ALEXANDER, tenant in Dalcharn, parish of Kildonan, Sutherland, in 1811. [SHS.8.102]

GORDON, ALEXANDER, son of John Gordon in Eldrable, Kildonan, Sutherland, was accused of rioting, resulting from the removal or eviction of tenants in Kildonan in 1813. [NRS.AD14.13.9; SC9.7.64]

GORDON, AUGUSTA, daughter of Alexander Gordon the Sheriff Substitute of Sutherland, married James H. Doyle of Toronto, at Christ Church Cathedral, Montreal, on 3 August 1862. [AJ.5982]

GORDON, CHRISTIAN, born 1765 in Culmaillie, Golspie, Sutherland, died 20 March 1832, wife of John McKay. [Millbrook gravestone, Pictou, NS]

GORDON, DONALD, emigrated from Cromarty or Thurso aboard the Lady Gray bound for Pictou, Nova Scotia, in 1841. [NRS.RH1.2.908]

GORDON, DONALD, minister of the Free Church in Edderton, Ross-shire, a petition, 1845. [NRS.GD112.51.84.13]

GORDON, GEORGE, born 1775, his wife and four children, in Balloan, Culmaily, Sutherland, in 1810. [SHS.8.14-15]

GORDON, GEORGE, born 1779, died 15 September 1849, husband of Catherine Grant, born 1793, died 28 May 1873, both born in Sutherland. [Gunn cemetery, Pictou, NS]

GORDON, GEORGE, born 1825, farmer at Whitebog, died 26 November 1883, husband of Catherine Bishop, born 1827, died 11 March 1888. [Rosemarkie gravestone, Ross and Cromarty]

GORDON, Reverend GEORGE, tenant in Lothmore, parish of Loth, Sutherland, in 1808, 1811. [SHS.8.99/230/231]

GORDON, Lieutenant GEORGE, tenant in Skelpick mill, Farr, Sutherland, in 1815. [SHS.8.224]

GORDON, GEORGE, with family, emigrated from Lochbeg, Loth, Sutherland, to Canada in 1829. [NLS.313.878]

GORDON, HUGH, a joint tenant in Rhiorn, Golspie, Sutherland, in 1808. [SHS.8.224]

GORDON, HUGH, a farm servant of Alexander Graham the tacksman of Ardillie, Dornoch, Sutherland, was accused of fraud in 1843. [NRS.AD14.43.76]

GORDON, Mrs ISABELLA, born 1787 in Clyne, Sutherland, wife of Donald Sutherland, emigrated in 1802, settled in New Lairg, Nova Scotia, died 19 November 1853. [New Lairg gravestone]

GORDON, JOHN, joint tenant in Breakacy, Kildonan, Sutherland, 1811. [SHS.8.108]

GORDON, JOHN, a tenant in Wester Killerman, Kildonan, Sutherland, was accused of rioting, resulting from the removal or eviction of tenants in Kildonan in 1813. [NRS.AD14.13.9; SC9.7.64]

GORDON, Lieutenant JOHN, joint tenant in Skelpick, Farr, Sutherland, in 1811. [SHS.8.112]

GORDON, JOHN, from Dalcharn, Kildonan, died at Scotch Hill, Pictou, Nova Scotia, on 30 May 1835. [AJ.4572]

GORDON, JOHN, son of John Gordon, [1780-1863], and his wife Jane Gordon, [1790-1879], settled in Melbourne, Australia. [Dornoch gravestone, Sutherland]

GORDON, JOSEPH, tenant in Carrol, Clyne, also in Achrindle and Prescan, Kildonan, Sutherland, in 1811. [SHS.8.91/107]

GORDON, KENNETH, a carter in Dingwall, Sutherland, was accused of rioting, mobbing, and assault at the Caledonian Hotel, Dingwall, in 1837. [NRS.AD14.37.36]

GORDON, Miss LUCY, joint tenant of Clyne Milnton, parish of Clyne, Sutherland, in 1811. [SHS.8.95]

GORDON, Mrs MARGARET, in Rhimoy and Auchumore, Farr, Sutherland, in 1811. [SHS.8.111]

GORDON, ROBERT, tenant in Langdale, Golspie, Sutherland, in 1808. [SHS.8.225]

GORDON, Captain ROBERT, joint tenant in Rhine and Mearlig, Rogart, Sutherland, in 1808, 1811. [SHS.8.72230]

GORDON, ROBERT, tenant in Blarich, Rogart, Sutherland, in 1811, 1815. [SHS.8.79/232]

GORDON, ROBERT, in Reisk, son of Alexander Gordon in Dalcharn, was accused of rioting in Kildonan, Sutherland, in 1813. [SHS.8.135]

GORDON, ROBERT, with family, emigrated from Golspie, Sutherland, to Canada in 1829. [NLS.313.878]

GORDON, THOMAS, joint tenant in Brachachy, Kildonan, Sutherland, in 1811, 1815. [SHS.8.108/227]; was granted a 15 year lease of Brachachy and of Garnsary on 29 December 1812. [SHS.9/2.175]

GORDON, WILLIAM, joint tenant in Kerrow of Kinbrace, Lairg, Sutherland, in 1808. [SHS.8.229]

GORDON, Captain WILLIAM, tenant in the parish of Farr, Sutherland in 1808, and 1811. [SHS.8.109/222]

GORDON, WILLIAM, tenant in Invernaver Inn, Golspie, Sutherland, in 1808. [SHS.8.225]

GORDON, WILLIAM, born 1795 in Sutherland, died 28 March 1892. [Landsdowne gravestone, Pictou, Nova Scotia]

GORDON, Mrs, born 1774, a widow, with four children, in Wester Culmaily, Sutherland, in 1810. [SHS.1.14/15]

GOUDIE, CATHERINE, born 1793, died 6 April 1871, wife of Robert Lourenson. [Lerwick gravestone, Shetland]

GOUDIE, JAMES, born 1811 in Stromness, Orkney, a blacksmith in Hudson Bay Company Service, settled in Victoria, British Columbia, around 1829, died there on 23 April 1887. [Ross Bay gravestone, B.C.]

GOUDIE, JANE, born 1814 in Stromness, Orkney, settled in Victoria, British Columbia, around 1858, died there on 17 July 1888. [Ross Bay gravestone, B.C.]

GOW, GEORGE, born 1807, a millwright, died in Bilbster, Caithness, on 14 September 1874, husband of Jean Macadam, born 16 July 1812, died 8 May 1896, parents of Peter Gow in Napier, New Zealand. [Watten gravestone, Caithness]

GOW, JAMES PETER, in Stromness, Orkney, versus Redpath Brown and Company, Candlemaker Row, Edinburgh, 1837. [NRS.CS46.1837.226]

GRAEME, ALEXANDER, of Graemeshall, an Admiral of the Blue, a sasine, 1805. [NRS.R.S.Orkney.633]

GRAEME, ALEXANDER SUTHERLAND, of the township of Paplay, parish of Holm, Orkney, 1828, [OA.SC11.58.19]; of Graemshall, versus Robert Stove in North Windbreck, Deerness, re illegal peat cutting, 1847. [NRS.SC11.5.1847.99]

GRAHAM, ALEXANDER, miller at Milnchlaren, Lairg, Sutherland, in 1811, 1815. [SHS.8.57/229]

GRAHAM, ALEXANDER, joint tenant of Doll, Clyne, Sutherland, in 1811. [SHS.8.90]

GRAHAM, ALEXANDER, born in Sutherland on 1787, died at Six Mile Brook on 23 September 1862, husband of Christy Munro, born 1793 in Ross-shire, died 18 November 1883. [Caledonia gravestone, Pictou, NS]

GRAHAME, CATHERINE, a widow with six children, emigrated from Kilfeddar, Strathbrora, Sutherland, to Nova Scotia in 1820.

GRAHAME, DONALD, son of Hugh Grahame, a tenant farmer in Lynnmeanoch, Assynt, Sutherland, was accused of the murder of Murdoch Grant an itinerant pedlar of Strathbeg, Loch Broom, in 1830. [NRS.AD14.30.384]

GRAHAM, JAMES, in Freester, Nesting, Shetland, versus James Law and Robert Law there, a petition, 1802. [SA.SC12.6.1802.26]

GRAHAM, WILLIAM, born 1803, died 16 May 1871, his wife Ann ....., born 1805, died 9 December 1877, both natives of Sutherland. [Caledonia gravestone, Pictou, NS]

GRANT, A., sr. and jr., joint tenants in Achnagarron, Rogart, Sutherland, in 1815. [SHS.8.231]

GRANT, ALEXANDER, born 1787, from Sutherland, emigrated via Cromarty aboard the Ossian of Leith bound for Pictou, Nova Scotia, on 25 June 1821. [Inverness Journal.29 June 1821]

GRANT, ALEXANDER, second son of William Grant in Strathpeffer, Ross and Cromarty, died in Valparaiso, Chile, on 16 October 1849. [AJ.5324]

GRANT, or MILLER, ANGUS, a soldier of the Ross and Caithness Militia, accused of assaulting a Revenue officer in 1812. [NRS.JC26.1812.1]

GRANT, ANNE, born 1770, with her sister, born 1775, and three girls, in Balloan, Culmaily, Sutherland, in 1810. [SHS.8.14-15]

GRANT, DANIEL, born 1752 in Sutherland, died in St Andrews parish, New Brunswick, on 28 December 1833. [New Brunswick Courier, 18.1.1834]

GRANT, DANIEL, in Roster, Latheron, a deed re the land of Ribigill, Sutherland, in 1829. [NRS.GD84.2.116]

GRANT, DONALD, born 1780, his wife and two children, in Balloan, Culmaily, Sutherland, in 1810. [SHS.8.14-15]

GRANT, DONALD, a shoemaker in Urrachal, Clyne, Sutherland, was accused of rioting, resulting from the removal or eviction of tenants in Kildonan in 1813. [NRS.AD14.13.9; SC9.7.64]

GRANT, DUNCAN, born 1802, a labourer in Achlorachen, Strathconan, Contin, Ross-shire, was accused of murder in 1835. [NRS.AD14.35.14]

GRANT, EBENEZER, born 1784, with wife and son in Balloan, Culmaily, Sutherland, in 1810. [SHS.8.14-15]

GRANT, D., in Halkirk, Caithness, a letter to Dr Carnaby in Thurso in 1817. [NRS.GD136.526]

GRANT, JAMES, born 1780, a tenant farmer, and his wife, in Rhiorn, Culmaily, Golspie, Sutherland, in 1808 and 1810. [SHS.1.14/15; SHS.8.224]

GRANT, JAMES, born 28 August 1804 in Cross and Burness parish, Orkney, son of Reverend William Grant and his wife Isabella Haggart, died in Jamaica. [F.7.259]

GRANT, JOHN, born 1745, his wife and three children, in Balloan, Culmaily, Sutherland, in 1810. [SHS.8.14-15]

GRANT, JOHN, born 1780, a farmer, with his second wife and six children, in Loanmore, Culmaily, Sutherland, in 1810. [SHS.1.14/15]

GRANT, JOHN, a joint tenant in Milnton of Evelix, Dornoch, in 1811. [SHS.8.67]

GRANT, MURDOCH, born 1809, in Little Reathes, Dornoch, Sutherland, was accused of theft in 1838. [NRS.AD14.38.233]

GRANT, ROBERT, born 1770, his wife and seven children, in Balloan, Culmaily, Sutherland, in 1810. [SHS.8.14-15]

GRANT, ROBERT LAING, born 29 April 1794 in Cross and Burness parish, Orkney, son of Reverend William Grant and his wife Isabella Haggart, died in St Ann's, Jamaica, on 17 July 1824. [F.7.259]

GRANT, WILLIAM, born 21 December 1797 in Cross and Burness parish, Orkney, son of Reverend William Grant and his wife Isabella Haggart, died 1819 in Jamaica. [F.7.259]

GRANT, Reverend WILLIAM, in parish of Cross and Burness, Sanday, Orkney, versus William Trail, and James Drever a shipowner in Kirkwall, in 1833. [OA.SC11.5.1833.38]

GRANT, Mrs, born 1750, with three children, in Rhiorn, Culmaily, Sutherland, in 1810. [SHS.1.14/15]

GRANT, Mrs, born 1750, a widow, in Balloan, Culmaily, Sutherland, in 1810. [SHS.8.14-15]

GRANT, Mrs, born 1749, a widow with two children, in Balloan, Culmaily, Sutherland, in 1810. [SHS.8.14-15]

GRAY, ALEXANDER, tenant in Crofteroonie, formerly in Hepernich of Kilcoy, Killearnan, Ross-shire, accused of assaulting a Revenue officer in 1816. [NRS.JC26.1816.37]

GRAY, GEORGE, a tenant in Raefirth, Mid Yell, Shetland, summons of removal, 1800. [SA.SC12.6.1800.17]

GRAY, JAMES, joint tenant in Culmaily, Lairg, Sutherland, in 1815. [SHS.8.229]

GRAY, LAURENCE, a skipper in Lerwick, a sasine, 1793. [NRS.R.S.Shetland.279]

GRAY, WILLIAM T., in Ulsta, Mid Yell, Shetland, accused of theft in 1849. [NRS.RH9.15.155]

GRAY, Mrs, widow of Lieutenant John McKay, tenant in Oldnay, Assynt, Sutherland, in 1811. [SHS.8.52]

GREENFIELD, WILLIAM, born 1765 in Caithness, died in Detroit, Michigan, on 16 January 1845. [AJ.5071]

GREENHILL, PETER, from Redcastle, Ross-shire, a passenger aboard the Edward Lambe was drowned in the shipwreck off New South Wales, Australia, on 17 August 1847. [AJ.4548]

GREIG, MARGARET HEDDELL, third daughter of James Greig of Sandsound, married John Cowie, a surgeon of the Hudson Bay Company, in Lerwick, Shetland, on 21 May 1839. [EEC.19904]

GREIG, WILLIAM, in Salachy, Lochalsh, Wester Ross, a victim of theft in Glasgow in 1837. [NRS.AD14.37.377]

GREY, BETTY, born 1796, emigrated via Stromness, Orkney, on the Prince of Wales to the Hudson Bay Company settlement at Fort Churchill on 29 June 1813. [PAC.M155.165-8]

GREY, CATHERINE, born 1790, emigrated via Stromness, Orkney, on the Prince of Wales to Fort Churchill on 29 June 1813. [PAC.M155.165-8]

GREY, JEAN, emigrated via Stromness, Orkney, on the Prince of Wales to Fort Churchill on 29 June 1813. [PAC.M155.165-8]

GRIERSON, ANDREW, of Quendale, Aithsling, Shetland, versus Robert Ross of Sound, re the division of the runrig lands of Trusta in 1806. [SA.SC12.6.1806.43]

GROAT, ALEXANDER GRAEME, versus the Earl of Zetland and the heritors of Durness, Sutherland, in 1839. [NRS.CS46.1839.7.216]

GROAT, Dr ROBERT, a physician in Kirkwall, Orkney, versus Thomas Gordon, Writer to the Signet, 1810, decreet. [NRS.CS38.1.96]

GROUNDWATER, EDWARD, a merchant in Stromness, Orkney, versus Alexander Sclatter in Funnigar in 1804. [OA.SC11.5.1804.78]

GRUBB, JAMES, a salmon fisher and trader in Ardock, Ross-shire, sederunt book 1817-1819. [NRS.CS96.843]

GUNN, ALEXANDER, a shoemaker in Halkirk, Caithness, accused of assaulting a Revenue officer in 1812. [NRS.JC26.1812.1]

GUNN, ALEXANDER, born 1761, his wife Christian born 1761 [she died on 20 September 1813], and son William, born 1795, from Strathullie, Kildonan, Sutherland, emigrated via Stromness on the Prince of Wales to the Hudson Bay Company settlement at Fort Churchill on 29 June 1813, settled on the Red River in 1814. [PAC.M155.165-8]

GUNN, ALEXANDER, born 1755, with his nieces Elizabeth McKay and Betty McKay, from Ascaig, Kildonan, Sutherland, emigrated via Stromness on the Prince of Wales to the Hudson Bay Company settlement at Fort Churchill on 29 June 1813. [PAC.M155.165-8]

GUNN, ALEXANDER, a tenant in Kildonan, Sutherland, was accused of rioting, resulting from the removal or eviction of tenants in Kildonan in 1813. [NRS.AD14.13.9; SC9.7.64][SHS.8.135]

GUNN, ALEXANDER, joint tenant in Culmaily, Lairg, Sutherland, in 1815. [SHS.8.229]

GUNN, ALEXANDER, tenant in Drumdivan, Dornoch, Sutherland, in 1815. [SHS.8.221]

GUNN, ALEXANDER, in Miniart, was accused of stealing two black stots from Auchintail, Kildonan, Sutherland, in 1818. [NRS.JC26.1818.106; JC26.1819.4]

GUNN, ALEXANDER, clerk of the Free Presbytery of Caithness, a petition, 1845. [NRS.GD112.51.192]

GUNN, ANGUS, joint tenant in Balquhairn, Lairg, Sutherland, in 1815. [SHS.8.229]

GUNN, ANGUS, born 1792, his wife Janet, from Borroba, Kildonan, Sutherland, emigrated via Stromness on the Prince of Wales to the Hudson Bay Company settlement at Fort Churchill on 29 June 1813, settled on the Red River in 1814, moved to the Holland River in 1815. [PAC.M155.165-8]

GUNN, ANNE, born 1750, with five children, in Sallichtown, Culmaily, Sutherland, in 1810. [SHS.1.14/15]

GUNN, BENJAMIN, with his wife Flora and son Donald, emigrated via Loch Laxford, Sutherland, on the Ellen of Liverpool bound for Pictou, Nova Scotia, on 22 May 1848. [PANS.257.110]

GUNN, CATHERINE, an innkeeper in Thurso, Caithness, a victim of theft in 1794. [NRS.JC26.1802.19]

GUNN, DANIEL, born 1841, second officer on the Cumberland died on 12 November 1870 in San Francisco. [Dunnet gravestone, Caithness]

GUNN, DAVID, a shoemaker, tenant in Golspie, Sutherland, in 1815. [SHS.8.225]

GUNN, DONALD, born 1748, his wife Janet born 1763, son George born 1797, daughter Esther born 1789, daughter Katherine born 1793 [died 29 August 1813], daughter Christian born 1803, from Borrobal, Kildonan, Sutherland, emigrated via Stromness on the Prince of Wales to the Hudson Bay Company settlement at Fort Churchill on 29 June 1813, settled at the Red River in 1814, and on the Holland River in 1815. [PAC.M155.165-8]

GUNN, DONALD, and his son Robert Gunn in Kildonan, Sutherland, were accused of rioting in 1813. [SHS.8.135]

GUNN, DONALD, born 1780, his wife and two daughters, in Sallichtown, Culmaily, Sutherland, in 1810. [SHS.1.14/15]

GUNN, DONALD, born 1797, eldest son of William Gunn in Braehouse, Halkirk, Caithness, to Canada as a Hudson Bay Company employee in 1813, settled at the Red River in 1821. [CG]

GUNN, GEORGE, in Rhives, a letter to James Loch re the herring fishing at Helmsdale, Sutherland, in 1827. [NRS.GD1.1169.4]

GUNN, HUGH, born 1760, with his wife and five children, in Sallichtown, Culmaily, Sutherland, in 1810. [SHS.1.14/15]

GUNN, ISOBEL, from Orkney, an employee of the Hudson Bay Company around 1806. [OL.ms21.1]

GUNN, JEAN, in Tuibeg of Sherray, Tongue, Sutherland, daughter of Alexander Gunn, accused of stealing sheep, failed to turn up for trial, and was subsequently outlawed in 1818. [NRS.JC26.1818.106]

GUNN, JESSE, infant son of Marcus Gunn, formerly a merchant in Thurso, Caithness, died in Newcastle, New Brunswick, on 14 June 1833. [Gleaner, 25.6.1833]

GUNN, JOHN, born 1761, emigrated from Caithness to Canada in 1802, died on 5 May 1835 at Black River, New Brunswick. [Gleaner:12.5.1835]

GUNN, JOHN, born 1794 in Caithness, died 29 January 1841. [Caledonia gravestone, Pictou, NS]

GUNN, JOHN, late tenant in Knockfin, Kildonan, Sutherland, accused of sheep stealing in 1802. [NRS.JC26.1802. 56]

GUNN, JOHN, a joint tenant of Glen, Golspie, Sutherland, in 1811. [SHS.8.87]

GUNN, JOHN, in Dunbeath, Latheron, Caithness, a victim of rioting in 1829. [NRS.AD14.29.350]

GUNN, JOHN, born 1794 in Caithness, died at West River, Pictou, Nova Scotia, on 28 January 1841. [Halifax Journal, 8.2.1841]

GUNN, JOHN, of Hastygrew, and James Steven tacksman of Stangerguie, a bond of caution, 1803. [NRS.CS27.1.624]

GUNN, JOHN, son of Alexander Gunn in Reisgill, Latheron, Caithness, accused of horse stealing in 1821. [NRS.AD14.21.207; JC26.1802.56]

GUNN, JOHN, born 1806 in Farr, Sutherland, was educated at King's College, Aberdeen, in 1830, a missionary on Cape Breton from 1838, died at Broad Cove there on 2 November 1870. [F.7.607]

GUNN, KENNETH, and DONALD GUNN, in Achalibister, Watten, Caithness, accused of murder in 1828. [NRS.AD14.28.235]

GUNN, MARGARET, from Thurso, Caithness, was found guilty of infanticide, petitioned for, and was granted, banishment from Scotland for life, at Inverness on 24 September 1799. [SM.61.721]

GUNN, MARGARET, third daughter of George Gunn in Rhives, Sutherland, married Malcolm Charles MacHardy, assistant manager of the London Chartered Bank, in St Kilda, Melbourne, Australia, on 31 December 1861. [AJ.5958]

GUNN, MARY, from Kildonan, Sutherland, to Hudson Bay, Canada, aboard the Prince of Wales in 1813, settled on the Red River in 1814. [PACAN]

GUNN, PETER, born 1816 in Caithness, son of John Gunn, was educated at Marischal College, Aberdeen, later a minister in Australia from 1842 until his death on 5 June 1864. [F.7.589]

GUNN, ROBERT, born 1784, emigrated via Thurso, Caithness, on the Elizabeth and Ann bound for Prince Edward Island on 8 November 1806. [PAPEI]

GUNN, ROBERT, born 1773 in Kildonan, Sutherland, died at West River on 8 June 1843, husband of Sarah Dunn, born 1782, died 1867. [Millbrook gravestone, Pictou, NS]

GUNN, ROBERT, a piper, from Kildonan, Sutherland, emigrated via Stromness on the Prince of Wales to the Hudson Bay Company settlement at Fort Churchill on 29 June 1813, moved to the Red River in 1814, and to the Holland River in September 1815. [PAC.M155.165]

GUNN, Reverend ROBERT, minister in Latheron, Caithness, letters, 1782-1816. [NRS.GD136.451]

GUNN, ROBERT, born 1830, son of Gilbert Gunn and his wife Helen Gray, died in Mudgie, New South Wales, on 20 October 1898. [Rogart gravestone, Sutherland]

GUNN, SINCLAIR MANNERS, youngest son of Reverend Alexander Gunn in Watten, Caithness, died aboard the George off the Banks of Newfoundland on 2 August 1843. [AJ.4998]

GUNN, WILLIAM, joint tenant in Fourpenny, Farr, Sutherland, in 1808. [SHS.8.223]

GUNN, WILLIAM, born 1765, twice married with five children, in Wester Culmaily, Sutherland, in 1810. [SHS.1.14/15]

GUNN, Lieutenant WILLIAM, tenant in Achnahow, Lairg, Sutherland, in 1808, and in the parish of Kildonan, Sutherland, in 1811. [SHS.8.103/229]

GUNN, WILLIAM, a tailor, emigrated from Cromarty or Thurso aboard the Lady Grey bound for Pictou, Nova Scotia, in June 1841. [NRS.RH1.2.908]

GUNN, WILLIAM, born 1784, a farmer in Houstry, Dunbeath, died 27 March 1858, husband of Elizabeth Sutherland, born 1794, died 28 January 1862. [Old Latheron gravestone, Caithness]

GUNN, Mrs, born 1774, a widow with five children, in Sallichtown, Culmaily, Sutherland, in 1810. [SHS.1.14/15]

GUNN, Mrs, a widow, joint tenant in Kinbrace and its mill, Lairg, Sutherland, in 1808. [SHS.8.229]

GUNN, Mrs, born 1775, a widow, with Alexander Gunn, born 1799, a labourer, Christian Gunn, born 1796, Adam Gunn, born 1802, and Robert Gunn, born 1803, emigrated on the Prince of Wales to York Fort on Hudson Bay in 1815. [PACAN]

GUTHRIE, JAMES BAILL only brother of Colonel Charles Seton Guthrie of Scotscalder, Caithness, died in Swellendam, Cape of Good Hope, South Africa, on 1 February1862. [AJ.5861]

HALCROW, ADAM, in Aith, Cunningsburgh, Shetland, a summons of removal in 1804. [SA.SC12.6.1804.22]

HALCROW, CHARLES, born 1790, died 16 August 1846, husband of Marrion Bain, born 1795, died 21 June 1856. [Cunningburgh gravestone, Shetland]

HALCROW, JAMES, in Aith, Bressay, Shetland, was accused of plundering the wrecked sloop Polly of Dover on Bressay in 1800. [SA.SC12.6.1800.27]

HALCRO, JOSHUA, baptised 8 August 1787 son of William Halcro and his wife Janet Flett in Orphir, Orkney, a clerk and trader in the service of the Hudson Bay Company from 1810. [OL.ms21.5]

HALCROW, LAURENCE, in Blosta, Cunningsburgh, Shetland, was accused of appropriating hay in 1807. [SA.SC12.6.1807.6]

HALCREW, MARGARET, in Aith, Cunningsburgh, Shetland, versus Laurence Davidson in Easter Quarff, Shetland, re aliment for a child in 1820. [SA.SC12.6.1820.56]

HALCROW, UMPHRA, from Burra, Shetland, an employee of the Hudson Bay Company from 1842 to 1850, then settled in Canada. [HBRS.16.360]

HAMILTON, JOHN MACAULAY, born 28 November 1799, son of Reverend Gavin Hamilton and his wife Penelope MacAulay, a physician who emigrated to Canada. [F.7.244]; a surgeon in Stromness, Orkney, a petition, 1849. [NRS.SC11.5.1849.28]

HAMILTON, JOHN, born 1823, born 1823, died in Brawl on 25 February 1908, husband of Janet Mackay, born 1829, died 4 December 1913, parents of John Hamilton, born 1849, died in Leadville, Colorado, on 21 March 1882, and James Hamilton, born 1853, died in Wellington, New Zealand, on 4 March 1895. [Halkirk gravestone, Caithness]

HAMILTON, JAMES, born 1786, died in Brabster, Bower, Caithness, on 2 June 1851, and his wife Ann Cameron, born 1789, died 22 June 1871, parents of Alexander Hamilton in Melbourne, Victoria, Australia, [Halkirk gravestone, Caithness]

HAMILTON, Reverend ZACHARY MACAULAY, in Bressay, Shetland, petition, 1849. [NRS.SC11.5.1849.28]

HARPER, NICHOL, born 1777, emigrated from Birsay, Orkney, via Stornaway on the Prince of Wales bound for the Hudson Bay Company settlement on the Red River in 1811. [PAC.M155.145]

HARRISON, CHARLES, from North Mavine, Shetland, a Hudson Bay Company employee from1852 to 1856. [HBRS.16.357]

HARRISON, JOHN, in North Setter, Aithsting, Shetland, was accused of pillaging a stranded ship, the Norges Constitution of Drontheim on Vementy, Shetland, in 1842, was outlawed. [NRS.AD2.13]

HARROLD, MARJORY, wife of Henry Craig in Wester Wick, Caithness, accused of resisting an officer of the law in 1821. [NRS.AD14.21.97]

HASSOCK, ALEXANDER, from Cromarty, emigrated to North Georgetown, Quebec, in 1801. [AC]

HAY, ANDREW, in Lerwick, letters from his nephew Andrew Hay in Singapore, 1839. [NRS.RH1.2.811]

HAY, JAMES, born 22 May 1791 in Lerwick, Shetland, son of James Hay of Laxfirth, [1750-1830], a merchant in New York by 1817, died in Pelhamville, N.Y., on 5 May 1854. [ANY.II.69]

HAY, WILLIAM, in Quoybank, St Ola, Orkney, versus Annabella Chisholm or Drever, re debt, 1822. [OA.SC11.5.1842.46]

HAY, WILLIAM, of Hayfield, born 8 October 1787, died 28 May 1858, husband of Margaret Ogilvy, born 8 July 1792, died 27 August 1838. [Lerwick gravestone, Shetland]

HEDDLE, ROBERT, in Melsetter, Eday, versus Andrew Swanney in Blow, Shapinsay, in 1822. [OA.C11.5.1822.45]; purchased Papa Stronsay in 1817. [NRS.GD263.39]; petitioned re land on Walls, Shetland, in 1824. [NRS.E341.38]

HENDERSON, ALEXANDER, in Thurso, Caithness, a victim of theft in 1830. [NRS.JC26.1830.90]

HENDERSON, BARTHOLEMEW, tenant in Norby, Foula, Shetland, a summons of removal in 1804. [SA.SC12.6.1804.6]

HENDERSON, GEORGE, born 1797 in Halkirk, Caithness, emigrated to Canada in 1817, moved to Boston in 1819, naturalised in Rockingham County, in October 1840. [NARA]

HENDERSON, GILBERT, jr., second son of William Henderson of Pettister, Shetland, died at Thebes, Upper Egypt, on 2 June 1839. [SG.816]

HENDERSON, JOHN, born 1760, died 4 April 1853, and his wife Isabella Campbell, born 1770, died in Upper Haster on 22 June 1823, parents of Ester McDougall in Berbice. [Halkirk gravestone, Caithness]

HENDERSON, ROBERT, formerly of the 78th Regiment, in Achow, Reisgill, Latheron, Caithness, accused of shopbreaking in 1823. [NRS.AD14.23.193]

HENDERSON, WILLIAM, the grieve at Sandside, Reay, Caithness, a prisoner in Inverness Tolbooth accused of theft and housebreaking, petitioned for banishment in 1802. [NRS.JC26.1802.54]

HENDERSON, WILLIAM, a writer in Thurso, Caithness, letters, 1815. [NRS.GD136.517]

HENRY, Captain ARCHIBALD, born 1793, son of Thomas Henry of Buraston, and his wife Lillias Henry, died on the Mississippi River in March 1837. [Walls gravestone, Shetland]

HENRY, GEORGE, in South Lodge, Aithsling, Shetland, summons of removal in 1807, [Shetland Archives.SC12.6.1807.6]

HENRY, JAMES, tenant in Colliesburgh, Bressay, Shetland, a summons of removal, 1800. [SA.SC12.6.1800.59]

HEPBURN, JOHN, son of John Hepburn a tinsmith in Kirkwall, Orkney, accused of robbery and theft in 1838. [NRS.AD14.38.552]

HEPBURN, WILLIAM, from Orphir, Orkney, an employee of the Hudson Bay Company from 1845 to 1851, died in London in 1851. [HBRS.16.359]

HERCULSON, JAMES, born 1839, in Flugarth, died 27 December 1909. [Lunnasting gravestone, Shetland]

HERCUS, ANN, in Park of Cora, South Ronaldsay, Orkney, versus William Sinclair in Ness, Burray, re aliment in 1828. [OA.SC11.5.1828.87]

HERD, JAMES, and his wife Marion Ross, were parents of William Herd, born 1860, died in Brisbane, Queensland, Australia, on 18 August 1910. [Dornoch gravestone, Sutherland]

HOGG, ALEXANDER, born 1823, a fisher in Cromarty, accused of robbery in 1841. [NRS.AD14.41.164]

HOGG, GILBERT, born 1824, a fisher in Cromarty, accused of robbery in 1841. [NRS.AD14.41.164]

HOGG, ROBERT, a fisher in Cromarty, accused of mobbing and prison breaking in 1844. [NRS.AD14.44.443]

HOGG, ROBERT, a seaman in Cromarty, dead by 1854. [NRS.S/H]; grandfather of Robert Hogg, a brass finisher in New York. [NRS.GD1.478.5-7]

HOGSTON, WILLIAM, a cooper in Wick, Caithness, had his hand shattered and dismembered at the grain riot of Wick in 1847. [NRS]

HOLLAND, JAMES, born 1823 in Orkney, 'former messenger to James Douglas', died in Victoria, British Columbia, on 10 October 1868. [Ross Bay gravestone, B.C.]

HOME, HECTOR, emigrated from Cromarty or Thurso, on the Lady Gray bound for Pictou, Nova Scotia, in June 1841. [NRS.RH1.2.908]

HONYMAN, WILLIAM, of Graemsay, and his factor John Gillies, versus Archibald Sinclair tenant in Pow, Rousay, Orkney, summons of removal, in 1800. [OA.SC11.5.1800.59]; versus Magnus Yorston, in Steinbrow, Evie, re disrepair of dykes in 1823. [OA.SC11.5.1823.23]

HOSEASON, HOSEA, of Aywick, Shetland, versus Charles Scott, Bonar More, and James Nisbet, all on Yell, Shetland, in 1804. [SA.SC12.6.1804.7]

HOSEASON, JAMES DAVID, in Greenbank, Yell, Shetland, versus James Fraser a tenant in Yell, in 1836. [NRS.CS46.1836.2.46]

HOSEASON, JOHN, of Udhouse, Delting, Shetland, versus Joseph Peterson of Midgarth in 1800. [SA.SC12.6.1800.42]

HOSEASON, WILLIAM, jr., of Uthouse, Delting, Shetland, was accused of plundering a Norwegian shipwreck in 1803. [SA.SC12.6.1803.47]

HOSSACK, JOHN D., from Kirkwall, Orkney, died in Tompkinsville, Staten Island, New York, on 6 March 1885. [S.13010]

HOURSTON, MAGNUS, in Benzieclat, Sandwick, versus William Hourston in Cott of Birsay, Orkney, in 1830. [OA.SC11.5.1830.63]

HOURSTON, SAMUEL, a mariner aboard HMS Ramillies, a sasine, 1790. [NRS.R.S. Orkney.439]

HOURSTON, THOMAS, a farmer in Firth, Orkney, 1829, brother of John Hourston in Halifax, Nova Scotia. [NRS.S/H]

HOUSTON, HUGH, tenant in Glaslochan, the parish of Clyne, also the schoolhouse at Brora, Sutherland, in 1811. [SHS.8.95/96]

HOUSTON, LEWIS, in Golspie and in Proney, Dornoch, Sutherland, 1848. [NRS.CS285.148]

HOUSTON, THOMAS, tenant in Lothbeg, and part of Slatel Forest, parish of Loth, also in Suisgall, Kildonan, Sutherland, in 1811, 1815. [SHS.8.99/106/227/228/230/231]

HOWSTON, L., from Orkney, then in Maryville, California, married Maggie Harcus, daughter of Reverend F. Harcus from Orkney, in Port Colborne, Canada, on 9 August 1870. [S.8455]

HUGHSON, JAMES, in Hascusay, Shetland, was accused of plundering a Norwegian shipwreck in 1803. [SA.SC12.6.1803.47]

HUNTER, ROBERT, of Lunna, and John Bruce and Company tacksmen, versus Robert Robertson, tenant in Lunna, and Lillias Anderson, also Erasmus Harry tenant in Firth, Delting, Shetland, 1800. [SA.SC12.6.1800.29]

HUTCHISON, EDWARD, from Papa Westray, Orkney, an employee of the Hudson Bay Company from 1843 to 1847. [HBRS.16.360]

INKSETTER, JOHN, a mariner in Stromness, Orkney, a sasine, 1798. [NRS.R.S.Orkney.427-428]

INNES, BARBARA ST CLAIR, third daughter of Major Innes in Thrumster, Caithness, married George MacLeay, in Sydney, Australia, on 27 April 1842. [AJ.4952]

INNES, GEORGE, tenant in the Mains of Strathy, Golspie, Sutherland, in 1808. [SHS.8.225]

INNES, HUGH, of Lochalsh, Wester Ross, versus Alexander Downie minister of Lochalsh in 1806. [NRS.CS271.58884]

INNES, KENNETH, born 1797 at Loch Broom, Wester Ross, emigrated to Nova Scotia in 1803, died 13 April 1864. [Caledonia gravestone, Pictou, N.S.]

INNES, THOMAS NEWMAN, born 1813 in Orkney, emigrated on the brig Vancouver, settled in Victoria, British Columbia, in 1853, died there on 26 March 1888. [Ross Bay gravestone, B.C.]

INNES, HUGH, born 1760, twice married with seven children, in Wester Culmaily, Sutherland, in 1810. [SHS.1.14/15]

INNES, JOHN, born 1780, his wife and three children, in Balloan, Culmaily, Sutherland, in 1810. [SHS.8.14-15]

INNES, MARTIN, born 1745, his wife and four children, in Balloan, Culmaily, Sutherland, in 1810. [SHS.8.14-15]

IRVINE, ANNE JANE, born 1843 in Stromness, Orkney, married ...McNiffe, settled in Victoria, British Columbia, in 1862, died there on 17 November 1896. [Ross Bay gravestone, B.C.]

IRVINE, ARTHUR A., born 1848 in Stromness, Orkney, died in Victoria, British Columbia, on 28 March 1885. [Ross Bay gravestone, B.C.]

IRVINE, GEORGE, a merchant in Quoylon, Orkney, 1801. [NRS.CS97.111,134/1]

IRVINE, ISABELLA, died 16 December 1798, wife of Robert Crookshank a skipper in Stromness, Orkney, deceased. [AJ.2661]

IRVINE, JOHN, born 1828 at Calf Sound, Eday, Orkney, a labourer in Hudson Bay Company Service, settled in Victoria, British Columbia, in 1851, died there on 18 February 1906. [Ross Bay gravestone, B.C.]

IRVINE, JOHN, born 1845 in Orkney, died in Victoria, British Columbia, on 8 March 1915. [Ross Bay gravestone, B.C.]

IRVINE, MARGARET, born 30 March 1846, daughter of William Irvine and his wife Ursula Tait, died in Compeigne, France, on 2 May 1867. [Lerwick gravestone, Shetland]

IRVINE, PETER, born 1818 in Stromness, Orkney, a labourer and shoemaker in Hudson Bay Company Service, settled in Victoria, British Columbia, in 1856, died 20 September 1880. [Ross Bay gravestone, B.C.]

IRVINE, WILLIAM, in South Lee, Tingwall, Shetland, versus Thomas and John Laurenceson, also James Nicolson in Dale, Tingwall, re swine rooting in 1807. [SA.SC12.6.1807.64]

IRVINE, WILLIAM, born 2 January 1841, son of William Irvine and his wife Ursula Tait, died in Akyab, British Burma, on 1 August 1885. [Lerwick gravestone, Shetland]

IRVINE, WILLIAM JOHN M., born in Orkney, died in Victoria, British Columbia, on 26 May 1876. [Ross Bay gravestone, B.C.]

IRVING, ANDREW, a skipper in Stromness, a sasine, 1802. [NRS.R.S.Orkney.6]

IRVING, THOMAS, born in Shetland, was naturalised in Craven County, North Carolina, on 17 February 1825. [Craven County Court Records]

ISBISTER, JAMES, a fisherman in Orkney, an employee of the Hudson Bay Company at Fort Wedderburn from 1803 to 1821. [OL.ms21.5] [HBRS.1.443]

ISBISTER, JAMES, born 1832 in Orkney, died in Victoria, British Columbia, on 14 March 1910. [Ross Bay gravestone, B.C.]

ISBISTER, MARGARET, on Flotta, Orkney, versus William Simpson in Bull of Flotta, re the ownership of a lamb in 1827. [OA.SC11.5.1827.73]

ISBISTER, THOMAS, a fisherman in Orkney, an employee of the Hudson Bay Company at Fort Wedderburn from 1803 to 1821. [OL.ms21.5] [HBRS.1.443]

JACK, PETER, a fisherman at St Margaret's Hope, South Ronaldsay, a sasine, 1803, [NRS.R.S.Orkney 554]; versus James Laird a farmer in Weddel, Burray, in 1805. [OA.SC11.5.1805.38]

JACK, WILLIAM, emigrated from Scrabster, Caithness, on the Superior of Peterhead bound for Pictou, Nova Scotia, landed there in June 1842. [PO.21.6.1842]

JAFFREY, GEORGE, tenant of Michaelwells, Torrinroy, Dornoch, Sutherland, in 1811. [SHS.8.60]

JAMESON, BARCLAY, in Brake, Aithsling, Shetland, summons of removal in 1807, [Shetland Archives.SC12.6.1807.6]

JAMESON, MAGNUS, in Grimister, Lerwick, Shetland, versus Lawrence Smith, Lawrence Johnson, and Arthur Lawrenson in Northmavine, in 1805. [SA.SC12.6.1805.6]

JAMESON, MAGNUS, a merchant in Lochend, Northmavine, Shetland, versus James Jameson a merchant in Lerwick in 1807. [SA.SC12.6.1807.22]

JAMESON, MATTTHEW, in Aairt, Aithsling, Shetland, summons of removal in 1807, [SA.SC12.6.1807.6]

JAMESON, PETER, tenant in Quoy in Vaila, Foula, Shetland, a summons of removal in 1804. [SA.SC12.6.1804.6]

JOHNSON, JOHN, born 1776, a tenant farmer in Aith, Aithsting, Shetland, was accused of theft from a stranded ship in 1816. [NRS.AD14.16.26]

JOHNSON, MAGNUS, of Snarraness, Sanness, Shetland, 1803. [NRS.SC12.6.1803.6]

JOHNSON, PETER, in Houll, Weisdale, Aithsting, Shetland, a victim of sheep-stealing in 1837. [NRS.AD14.37.471; JC26.1837.534]

JOHNSTON, ANN, aged 20-30, a servant, Castle Street, Dingwall, Ross and Cromarty, accused of theft, fraud, and embezzlement, in 1829. [NRS.AD14.29.344]

JOHNSTON, DANIEL, alias David Ross, a watchmaker, imprisoned in Dornoch Tolbooth, Sutherland, found guilty of fraud and embezzlement, was sentenced to transportation beyond the seas for seven years in 1827. [NRS.JC26.1827.81]

JOHNSTON, DAVID, born 1770, master of the sloop Betsy of Thurso, died on 24 September 1827. [Dunnet gravestone, Caithness]

JOHNSTON, HARRY, a planter in St Kitts, West Indies, a sasine in 1791. [NRS.R.S.Orkney, 250]

JOHNSTON, JAMES, born 1769 in Outbrecks, Stenness, a former carpenter in Hudson Bay Company service, died on 17 April 1842. [Stenness gravestone, Orkney]

JOHNSTON, JAMES, born 1782, from Birsay, Orkney, emigrated via Stornaway on the Prince of Wales to the Hudson Bay Company settlement on the Red River in 1811. [PAC.M155.145]

JOHNSTONE, JAMES, a merchant in Dornoch, Sutherland, a sequestration, 1807. [NRS.CS235.SEQN.IJ.1.19]

JOHNSTON, JAMES, born 1832 on Orkney, a Hudson Bay Company employee, settled in Victoria, British Columbia, in 1857, died there on 4 November 1895. [Ross Bay gravestone, B.C.]

JOHNSTON, JOHN, a famer in Houbensetter, Delting, Shetland, versus Elizabeth Goodlad, relict of .... Harryson a sailor in Delting, 1801. [SA.SC12.6.1801.23]

JOHNSTON, LAURENCE, a shoemaker in Hoore, Uphouse, Bressay, Shetland, accused of theft in 1822. [SA.NRS.AD14.22.]

JOHNSTONE, WILSON, born 1780, died 14 June 1850, father of Joseph G. Johnstone in St John's, New Brunswick. [Wick gravestone, Caithness]

JOYNER, JOHN, a grocer in Tain, Ross and Cromarty, died 28 March 1846. [NRS.S/H.1876]

KEITH, ALEXANDER, born 5 October 1795 in Halkirk, Caithness, settled in Halifax, Nova Scotia, in 1817, a brewer, banker, and politician, died on 14 December 1873. [BNA]

KEITH, CHARLES, born 1777, a mason, died 6 July 1858, husband of Ann..., born 1760, died 23 March 1840, parents of Donald Keith of the 75th Regiment, born 1810, who died in Quebec on 7 June 1837. [Halkirk gravestone, Caithness]

KEITH, DONALD, in Halkirk, Caithness, died 21 September 1847, father of Alexander Keith in Halifax, Nova Scotia. [NRS.S/H.1868]

KEITH, LEWIS, youngest son of Reverend William Keith in Golspie, Sutherland, died in Halifax, Nova Scotia, in June 1843. [AJ.4984]

KEITH, MARY, servant to the Duke of Sutherland at Dunrobin Castle, testament, 28 March 1843. [NRS.CS228.L9.53]

KEITH, PATRICK, eldest son of Reverend Keith in Golspie, Sutherland, died in Berbice on 10 August 1805. [SM.68.78]

KEITH, ROBERT, born 1800 in Auchengillie, Caithness, died in Fountain City, Wisconsin, on 23 October 1876. [EC.28788]

KEITH, WILLIAM, in Golspie, Sutherland, wrote to the Justice of the Peace of the parishes of Clyne and Golspie, on 26 April 1804. [NRS.JP32.7.5]

KEITH, Reverend, WILLIAM, tenant in Golspie Tower in 1808, a joint tenant of Glen, Golspie, Sutherland, in 1811. [SHS.8.87/227]

KELLY, ALEXANDER, factor in Dingwall, Ross and Cromarty, letters, 1830-1833. [NRS.GD46.1.366]

KEMP, HECTOR, a cattle and barley also a manufacturer of bark and salves at Cumrie, Contin, Ross-shire, in 1826. [NRS.CS233.SEQN.K1.14]

KENNEDY, Reverend ANGUS, joint tenant in Lower Lairg, Sutherland, in 1808, 1815. [SHS.8.228/229]

KENNEDY, ALEXANDER, born 1781 at St Margaret's Hope, South Ronaldsay, Orkney, an employee of the Hudson Bay Company at York Factory, from 1798 to 1830, sailed from Stromness to York Factory aboard the King George, died 1832 in London. [HBRS.2.225][HBCA.PAM.A36/8.fos.99-100D]

KENNEDY, ALEXANDER, son of Alexander Kennedy of Braehead Hope and his wife Agatha Isbister, was born on 2 February 1808 at Mouse Lake, North America was baptised in South Ronaldsay on 26 June 1822.

KENNEDY, Captain WILLIAM, born 1813, died 1890, in Hudson Bay Company Service in 1851, wrote from on board the Prince Albert off Cape Shackleton, Hudson Bay, to his cousin John Laughton jr., St Margaret's Hope, South Ronaldsay, Orkney. [NRS.GD1.460.43]

KIRKNESS, GEORGE, from Sandwick, Shetland, a boatbuilder in Hudson Bay Company service from 1845 to 1851. [HBRS.16.361]

KNARSTON, JAMES, a merchant in Kirkwall, Orkney, 1804. [NRS.CS230.SEQN.K1.11]

LAIDLAW, WILLIAM, factor at Brahan, Ross-shire, letters, 1832-1834. [NRS.GD46.1.378]

LAING, MALCOLM, of Strynzie, a heritor of St Ola, Orkney, a memorandum in 1815. [NRS.GD31.489]

LAING, ROBERT, in Strenzie, Stronsay, versus Hugh Bews in Saliskerry, Eday, Orkney, 1802. [NRS.SC11.5.1802.9]

LARNACH, WILLIAM, born 1831, son of William Larnach, [1799-1878], and his wife Barbara McDonald, [died 1879], died in Buenos Ayres, Argentina, on 2 January 1864, buried in the British Cemetery there. [Watten gravestone, Caithness]

LAUGHTON, ALEXANDER, a mariner in Kirkwall, Caithness, dead by 1807. [NRS.GD31.467]

LAUGHTON, JOHN, jr, at St Margaret's Hope, South Ronaldsay, Orkney, in 1851. [NRS.GD1.460.43]

LAUGHTON, PATRICK, a merchant in Kirkwall, versus David Traill, a farmer in Deerness, Orkney, 1800. [OA. SC11.5.1800.46]

LAUGHTON, WILLIAM, a mariner from Orkney, was naturalised in Charleston, South Carolina, on 18 January 1796. [NARA.M1183.1]

LAUGHTON, WILLIAM, born on South Ronaldsay, Orkney, died in Victoria, British Columbia, on 12 May 1869. [Ross Bay gravestone, B.C.]

LAURENSON, WILLIAM, tenant in Melbie, Foula, Shetland, a summons of removal in 1804. [SA.SC12.6.1804.6]

LAW, JOHN, a merchant in Golspie, Sutherland, versus Hugh Reid a writer in Cromarty, 1828-1830. [NRS.SC24.4A.50]

LAWRENCESON, THOMAS, in Park, Bressay, Shetland, a summons of removal, 1800. [SA.SC12.6.1800.59]

LEARMONTH, Reverend PETER, in Stromness, Orkney, letters, 1833-1844. [NRS.GD217.1131]

LEASK, ELIZABETH, daughter of Thomas Leask in Crown, Delting, Shetland, versus William Petrie in Uresland, Tingwall, re alimony for a child in 1842. [SA.SC12.6.1842.13]

LEASK, JAMES CHARLES, born 1834 on Orkney, settled in Victoria, British Columbia, in 1853, died there on 13 October 1901. [Ross Bay gravestone, BC]

LEASK, JANET, in Burra of Tingval, Shetland, versus Mathew Yorston in Southerhouse, Nossound, Bressay, a petition for aliment in 1801. [SA.SC12.6.1801]

LEASK, MARGARET, born 1819 in Orkney, married .... Merriman on 27 December 1849, settled in Victoria, British Columbia, in 1856, died there on 7 November 1879. [Ross Bay gravestone, BC]

LEASK, ROBERT, and Henry Leask in Rendall, versus Reverend James Bremner in Walls and Flotta, Orkney, 1800. [OA.SC11.5.1800.6]

LEASK, THOMAS, born 1768, a shipmaster, died 13 July 1833, husband of Elizabeth Johnston, born 1767, died 19 November 1850. [Lerwick gravestone, Shetland]

LEISK, ISABEL, in Trusta, Aithsling, Shetland, a victim of sheep-stealing in 1837. [NRS.AD14.37.471; JC26.1837.534]

LEISK, JEREMY, a cottar in Weisdale, Aithsting Shetland, a victim of sheep-stealing in 1837. [NRS.AD14.37.471; JC26.1837.534]

LEISK, WILLIAM, in Trusta, Aithsting, Shetland, a victim of sheep-stealing in 1837. [NRS.AD14.37.471; JC26.1837.534]

LEITH, Miss C., tenant in Culgower and Wester Garry, Clyne, Sutherland, in 1811. [SHS.8.100]

LEITH, WILLIAM, a boatman from Firth, Orkney, a Hudson Bay Company employee at Peace River around 1802. [OL.ms21.5]

LEITH, Mrs, tenant in Culgower, Loth, Sutherland, in 1815. [SHS.8.231]

LESLIE, HUGH, tenant in Proncynain, Farr, in 1808. [SHS.8.223]

LESLIE, HUGH, a writer in Dornoch, tenant of the Mill of Cyderhall, also Dalvevie, Teachlybe, and Loanmore, Dornoch, Sutherland, in 1811 and 1815. [SHS.8.61/221]

LESLIE, WILLIAM, born 1847, son of James Leslie and his wife Isabel Shearer, died in New South Wales, Australia, on 21 January 1881. [St Peter's gravestone, Stronsay, Orkney]

LESLIE, Captain J. M., married Barbara Heddle, both from Orkney, at 203 West Buren Street, Chicago, on 27 August 1873. [GH.10523]

LESLIE, WILLIAM, born 1849, son of James Leslie and his wife Isabel Shearer, died at Lake Michigan on 7 November 1872. [St Peter's gravestone, Stronsay, Orkney]

LEVACK, DAVID, born 1800, a fish curer and farmer, died in Willowbank, Wick, Caithness, on 10 May 1886, husband of Esther McBeath, born 1800, died 28 October 1862. [Wick gravestone]

LIDDLE, PETER, born 1824, died at the Gilbert River goldfield, Northern Queensland, Australia,on 23 September 1869. [Lady gravestone, Stronsay, Orkney][St Magnus Cathedral gravestone, Kirkwall]

LILLIE, ROBERT, emigrated from Cromarty or Thurso aboard the Lady Grey bound for Pictou, Nova Scotia, in June 1841. [NRS.RH1.2.908]

LILLINGTON, WILLIAM, at Lochalsh, Wester Ross, a letter in 1836. [NRS.GD46.4.82]

LINDSAY, ANDREW, an ironmonger in Golspie, Sutherland, 28 September 1844. [NRS.CS228.L9.53]

LINKLATER, ANDREW, from Orkney, a Hudson Bay Company employee around 1818. [OL.ms.21.5]

LINKLATER, ANN, born 1837 in Orkney, wife of .... Logan, settled in Victoria, British Columbia, in 1865, died there on 5 January 1916. [Ross Bay gravestone, BC]

LINKLETTER, WILLIAM, a Hudson Bay Company employee, a sasine 6 August 1798. [NRS.R.S.Orkney.426]

LINKLETTER, WILLIAM, born 1802, son of Magnus Linkletter, an apprentice mason in Louisburgh, Caithness, accused of mobbing and rioting in 1827. [NRS.AD14.27.218]

LINKLETTER, WILLIAM, born 8 October 1830, died 10 February 1869. [Lerwick gravestone, Shetland]

LOCH, THOMAS, a shepherd in Contin, Ross-shire, accused of sheep stealing in Aird, Duirinish, in 1837. [NRS.AD14.37.4]

LOCHORE, Reverend GAVIN, and his wife Sarah Wilkin, in St Andrews parish, Orkney, parents of Willian Brodie Lochore, born 2 April 1851, who settled in Melbourne, Australia. [F.7.212]

LOERBACH, PETRAS DOROTHEOS, born 1815, died in Lerwick, Shetland, on 30 September 1871, husband of Annie Loerbach. [Lerwick gravestone]

LOGAN, DONALD, emigrated from Sutherland to Nova Scotia in 1803, a timber merchant there in 1818.

LOGGAN, GEORGE, born 1748, wife Christian Gair born 1855, children Jean born 1782, George born 1786, Robert born 1782, Walter born 1792, Alexander born 1794, William born 1790, Peter born 1798, and Dougald born 1800, emigrated via Thurso, Caithness, on the Elizabeth and Ann bound for Prince Edward Island on 8 November 1806. [PAPEI]

LOGAN, JOHN, a skipper in Stromness, Orkney, a sasine, 1805. [NRS.R.S.Orkney.625]

LOGIE, MARGARET LENDRUM, born 1815 in Kirkwall, Orkney, daughter of Reverend William Logie, married Reverend George Smellie on 19 June 1843, settled in Fergus, Ontario, died 11 March 1904. [F.7.265]

LOGIN, JOHN, a merchant in Stromness, Orkney, versus James Ewan a tanner in Seater, Orkney, in 1803. [OA.SC11.5.1803.43]

LOGIN, JOHN SPENCE, MD, son of John Login and his wife Margaret Moar Spence in Stromness, Orkney, settled in Bengal before 1841. [NRS.S/H]

LORDAN, JAMES, residing in Berridale, Latheron, Caithness, a coach driver between Port Gower and Berridale, was accused of reckless driving causing the coach to overturn and James Sutherland, an outside passenger, being thrown over the bridge into the Water of Langwell on 12 March 1824, found not guilty. [NRS.JC26.1824]

LOUTIT, JAMES, in Thieveshall, Deerness, Orkney, and Isabel Smith of Loutit there, versus Ann Delday in Groutley, Deerness, and John Delday in Gairth, Deerness, 1800. [OA.SC11.5.1800.22]

LOUTIT, JAMES, a famer in Deerness, Orkney, versus John Harper in Harray, 1800. [OA.SC11.5.1800.36]

LOUTIT, JAMES, in Groathall, Eday, Orkney, versus William Scott in Stenaquoy, Eday, 1810. [OA.SC11.5.1810.97]

LOUTIT, JOHN, of the Hudson Bay Company, grandson of William Loutit in Lyking, Stromness, a sasine, 13 July 1808. [NRS.R.S.Orkney.755]

LOUTIT, Dr WILLIAM, a physician in Kirkwall, Orkney, versus Kenneth McKenzie an apothecary in Edinburgh, 1810. [NRS.CS36.1.69]

LOUTIT, WILLIAM, born 1804 in Orkney, emigrated in 1817, a declaration to naturalise dated 20 June 1831. [Norfolk County Circuit Records, Virginia]

LYON, STEWART, tailor in Contin, Ross-shire, accused of forging a bill of exchange in 1840. [NRS.AD14.40.12]

MACADAM, ALEXANDER, son of Peter MacAdam in Watten, Caithness, a merchant who died in Detroit, Michigan, on 13 April 1872. [S.676]

MCADIE, DAVID, a merchant in Watten, Caithness, later in Belleville, Ontario, died 9 March 1860, father of William McAdie in Belleville. [NRS.S/H.1877]

MCANDIE, JAMES, in British Guiana, 1855. [NRS.Tain.242.70.6.183]

MCANDREW, DAVID, former town clerk of Fortrose, died in Adelaide, South Australia, on 22 June 1839, 'one day after his arrival there'. [EEC.19989]

MCAULAY, ANGUS, born 1797, wife Ann born 1805, son Donald born 1832, daughter Ann born 1834, daughter Flora born 1830, daughter Kate born 1838, daughter Marion born 1834, and son Donald born 1851, from Kildonan, emigrated via Liverpool aboard the Priscilla bound for Victoria, Australia, on 15 October 1852. [NRS.HD4/5]

MCBARNET, A., of Attadale and Torridon, Ross-shire, late of H.M. Council of St Vincent, died in Inverness on 25 November 1838. [AJ.4744]

MCBEATH, ANDREW, born 1794, his wife Janet, from Borrobal, Sutherland, emigrated via Stromness on the Prince of Wales to the Hudson Bay Company settlement at Fort Churchill on 29 June 1813. [PAC.M155.165-8]

MCBEATH, ANDREW, joint tenant in Fenofal, Dallagan, Kildonan, Sutherland, 1815. [SHS.8.227]

MCBEATH, ANDREW, born 1745 in Sutherland, died in Lanark, Ontario, on 3 August 1847. [QCG]

MCBEATH, ANDREW, with wife Janet, from Kildonan, Sutherland, emigrated on the Prince of Wales to Hudson Bay in 1813, landed at Churchill in August 1813, settled on the Red River in 1814, moved to the Holland River in September 1815. [PAC]

MCBEATH, ANGUS, a joint tenant in Reisk, Lairg, Sutherland, in 1808. [SHS.8.229]

MCBEATH, BARBARA, born 1768, a widow, son Charles born 1797, daughter Hanny born 1790, from Borrobal, Sutherland, emigrated via Stromness on the Prince of Wales to the Hudson Bay Company settlement at Fort Churchill on 29 June 1813. [PAC.M155.165-8]

MCBEATH, GEORGE, in Old Wick, Caithness, a victim of theft in Edinburgh in 1843. [NRS.AD14.43.321]

MCBEATH, JOHN, born 1785, a labourer in Kinloch, Latheron, formerly a tailor in Langdale, Strathnaver, in Badlean, Watten, Caithness, accused of housebreaking at Carnachy, Farr, Sutherland, in 1824. [NRS.AD14.24.118; JC26.1824.26]

MCBEATH, JOHN, born 1792 in Sutherland, died 2 November 1878 at the Red River settlement, Manitoba. [Kildonan gravestone, Winnipeg] [PAM.HBCA.D5.11]

MCBEATH, WILLIAM, born 1767 in Sutherland, emigrated to August 1840. [Gleaner, 25.8.1840]

MCBETH, ALEXANDER, born 1760, a labourer, wife Christian Gunn born 1765, son George born 1799, son Roderick born 1803, son Robert born 1805, son Adam born 1809, son Morrison born 1811, daughter Margaret born 1797, daughter Molly born 1797, daughter Christian born 1801, from Sutherland, emigrated via Stromness on the Prince of Wales to the Hudson Bay Company settlement at York Fort on 23 June 1815, landed there on 26 August 1815. [PAC.M1659/61] [MG19.E4.1.165/8]

MACCULLOCH, DUNCAN, in Alnasou, Lochalsh and Plockton district, to emigrate to America around 1850. [NRS.HD21.53]

MCCULLOCH, HUGH, son of Kenneth McCulloch and his wife Barbara Ross, settled in Calloa, South America, before 1857. [Balnakeil gravestone, Durness, Sutherland]

MCCULLOCH, WILLIAM, a Captain of the Sutherland Volunteers, the muster roll of 1807. [NRS.SC9.87.56]; tenant of Cyderhall, Sandcroft, Achinchainnter and Castle Yards, Dornoch, in 1811. [SHS.8.57/221]

MCCULLOCH, Mrs, tenant in Kilmote, Loth, Sutherland, in 1808. [SHS.8.230]

MCDIALIG, or MACHOMAISH, JANET, daughter of Murdo McDialig or McHomaish, wife of Alexander Cumming a labourer in Dingwall, accused of sheep stealing in 1820. [NRS.AD14.20.128]

MCDONALD, ANGUS, in Ascoilemore, Strathbrora, Sutherland, father of Alexander McDonald who had a land grant on the Tatamagouche River, Nova Scotia, in 1822.

MCDONALD, ALEXANDER, born 1775 in Ross-shire, emigrated to Cape Breton in 1803, later settled at Little Brook, Black River, Northumberland County, New Brunswick, died in St John, N.B., on 31 October 1843. [Weekly Chronicle, 17.11.1843]

MCDONALD, ALEXANDER, a merchant in Dornoch, Sutherland, financial records, 1807 – 1811. [NRS.RH9.1.249]

MCDONALD, ALEXANDER, born 1792, a merchant, with his mother, sister and brother, in Webster Culmaily, Sutherland, in 1810. [SHS.1.14/15]

MCDONALD, ALEXANDER, joint tenant in Fenofal, Dallagan, Kildonan, Sutherland, 1815. [SHS.8.227]

MCDONALD, ALEXANDER, joint tenant in Bank, Rogart, Sutherland, in 1815. [SHS.8.231]

MCDONALD, Reverend ALEXANDER, in Plockton Manse, Lochalsh, Wester Ross, a letter, 1836. [NRS.GD46.12.81]

MCDONALD, ALEXANDER, emigrated from Cromarty or Thurso aboard the Lady Grey bound for Pictou, Nova Scotia, in June 1841. [NRS.RH1.2.908]

MCDONALD, ANN, widow of Donald Sutherland, and their son William Sutherland, in Achness, Sutherland, accused of resisting officers of the law, failed to appear at their trial, and was therefore outlawed in 1821. [NRS.JC26.1821.9]

MCDONALD, ANN, eldest daughter of John McDonald of the Customs House in Ullapool, Wester Ross, married Murdoch McKenzie from St Vincent, in Ullapool on 17 March 1825. [S.547.224]

MCDONALD, ANN, daughter of Colin McDonald in Aultgowrie, died 1861, and his wife Helen Gollan, died 1864, wife of ... Brown, settled in Nearee, New Zealand. [St Clement's gravestone, Dingwall]

MCDONALD, CHRISTY, born 1770 in Sutherland, wife of Robert Sutherland, settled in New Lairg, Nova Scotia, died on 27 June 1842. [New Lairg gravestone]

MCDONALD, COLIN, emigrated from Cromarty or Thurso aboard the Lady Grey bound for Pictou, Nova Scotia, in June 1841. [NRS.RH1.2.908]

MCDONALD, COLIN, a carpenter from Armadale, Sutherland, married Mary Duffy in Toronto on 15 February 1872. [S.8927]

MCDONALD, DONALD, a labourer from Alness, Ross-shire, emigrated via Fort William aboard the Sarah bound for Pictou, Nova Scotia, in June 1801. [NRS.RH2.4.87.66-71]

MCDONALD, DONALD, born 1765 in Sutherland, his wife Isabella born 1763 in Sutherland, they married there around 1788, emigrated to Nova Scotia in 1807, both died in Carleton Village near Shelburne, N.S., in November 1843. [Times, 12.12.1843]

MCDONALD, DONALD, of Tanera, a tenant in Assynt, Sutherland, in 1811. [SHS.8.52]

MCDONALD, DONALD, in Inverinate, Kintail, Ross-shire, accused of assault in 1828. [NRS.AD14.28.276]

MCDONALD, DONALD, born 1805, with family, from Sutherland, emigrated via Cromarty aboard the Ossian bound for Pictou, Nova Scotia, on 25 June 1821. [Inverness Journal.29 June 1821]

MCDONALD, DUNCAN, emigrated from Cromarty or Thurso aboard the Lady Grey bound for Pictou, Nova Scotia, in June 1841. [NRS.RH1.2.908]

MCDONALD, DUNCAN, a merchant in Charlestown, Gairloch, Wester Ross, letters, 1850-1854. [NRS.GD1.1196.2]

MCDONALD, ELIZABETH, born 1789 in Sutherland, wife of Angus Murray, died at Mount Thom, Nova Scotia, on 25 November 1840. [Nova Scotian, 24.12.1840]

MCDONALD, FRANCIS, born in December 1714, in Halkirk, Caithness, died on 23 November 1824 in St Mary's, Nashwaak, New Brunswick. [Acadian Recorder, 18 December 1824]

MCDONALD, FRANCIS, born in Caithness, formerly in Halifax, Nova Scotia, died in Berbice in March 1830. [Nova Scotian, 3.6.1830]

MCDONALD, GEORGE, born 1765 [he died 1 September 1813], wife Janet born 1783, emigrated via Stromness on the Prince of Wales to the Hudson Bay Company settlement at Fort Churchill on 29 June 1813. [PAC.M155.165-8]

MCDONALD, GEORGE, a tenant in Dalvait, Kildonan, Sutherland, was accused of rioting, resulting from the removal or eviction of tenants in Kildonan in 1813. [NRS.AD14.13.9; SC9.7.64] [SHS.8.136]

MCDONALD, GEORGE, born 1828, son of William McDonald and his wife Christy Campbell, died in Victoria on 13 June 1910. [Dornoch gravestone, Sutherland]

MCDONALD, HECTOR, with his wife Jessie Kennedy, son of Murdo McDonald a tenant farmer at Auchtercairn, emigrated from Gairloch, Wester Ross, to Australia in 1849, a farmer at Goulburn, New South Wales, later a publican, letters from 1849 to 1869. [NRS.GD1.1196.1-4]

MCDONALD, HUGH, tenant in Portskerra, Golspie, Sutherland, in 1808. [SHS.8.225]

MACDONALD, JAMES, son of Angus MacDonald a tenant in Achlorachban, Contin, Ross-shire, was murdered in 1835. [NRS.AD14.35.14]

MCDONALD, JANET, born 1735, wife of Murdo McDonald in Leadchouick, Dingwall, Sutherland, accused of sheep stealing in 1820. [NRS.AD14.20.128]

MCDONALD, JOHN, born 1781, a cooper in Leackachan, Glenshiel, Ross-shire, accused of forgery in 1835. [NRS.AD14.35.12; JC26.1835.10]

MACDONALD, JOHN, tenant in Polly, Clyne, also in Dallagan, parish of Kildonan, Sutherland, in 1811. [SHS.8.93/104]; was granted a lease of the Pollyour Lot, Sutherland, for 5 years on 29 December 1812. [SHS.9/2/175]

MCDONALD, JOHN, born 1793, a saddler, from Sutherland, emigrated via Stromness, Orkney, on the Prince of Wales to York Fort on 23 June 1815, landed on 26 August 1815. [PAC.M1659/61] [MG19.E4.1.165/8]

MCDONALD, JOHN, joint tenant in Fourpenny, Dornoch, Sutherland, in 1815. [SHS.8.222]

MCDONALD, JOHN, miller at Powsin, Contin, Ross-shire, was accused of assault of a Revenue officer in 1820. [NRS.JC26.1820.2]

MCDONALD or AIRD, JOHN, a postboy in Dingwall, Ross and Cromarty, was accused of rioting, mobbing, and assault at the Caledonian Hotel, Dingwall, in 1837. [NRS.AD14.37.36]

MCDONALD, JOHN, labourer, in Kirktomy, Farr, Sutherland, accused of theft in 1839. [NRS.AD14.39.7]

MCDONALD, JOHN, jr, tenant and fisher in Armadale, Farr, Sutherland, accused of theft in 1839. [NRS.AD14.39.7]

MCDONALD, JOHN, born 1848, son of Thomas McDonald and his wife Margaret Cameron, died in Melbourne, Australia, on 9 March 1908. [Golspie gravestone, Sutherland]

MCDONALD, MARGARET, born 1761, a widow with family, from Sutherland, emigrated via Cromarty aboard the Ossian bound for Pictou, Nova Scotia, on 25 June 1821. [Inverness Journal.29 June 1821]

MCDONALD, MURDO, born 1746, in Leadchouick, Dingwall, Ross and Cromarty, accused of sheep stealing in 1820. [NRS.AD14.20.128]

MCDONALD, MURDO, clerk of works to the Lewis Estate in Stornaway, father of Neil McDonald a clerk of the London and San Francisco Bank died at sea on 18 October 1883 when bound from New York to Liverpool. [S.12580]

MCDONALD, NEIL, [1824-1874], and his wife Margaret Ross, [1838-1899], parents of Alexander McDonald, born 1857, died in USA in 1883. [Farr gravestone, Sutherland]

MCDONALD, NEIL, a fisher in Armadale, Farr, Sutherland, accused of theft in 1839. [NRS.AD14.39.7]

MCDONALD, WILLIAM, joint tenant in Achtomliny, Rogart, Sutherland, in 1815. [SHS.8.231]

MCDONALD, WILLIAM, born 1766, with family, from Sutherland, emigrated via Cromarty aboard the Ossian bound for Pictou, Nova Scotia, on 25 June 1821. [Inverness Journal.29 June 1821]

MCDONALD, WILLIAM, with his wife Margaret Johnstone, and family, from Sutherland, emigrated to Canada in 1836, settled in Megantic County, Quebec. [AMC.48]

MCDONALD, WILLIAM, emigrated from Cromarty or Thurso aboard the Lady Grey bound for Pictou, Nova Scotia, in June 1841. [NRS.RH1.2.908]

MCDONALD, WILLIAM, born 1830, son of Murdo McDonald and his wife Catherine McDonald, settled in Westland, Otago, New Zealand, died on 24 December 1916. [Annot, Loch Torridon, gravestone]

MCDOUGAL, WILLIAM, in Lochinver, Sutherland, 1849. [NRS.CS279.1875]

MACEANVOIR, or MCKENZIE, MURDOCH, in Achmore of Rhoagie, Ross-shire, accused of theft in 1801. [NRS.JC11.45]

MACEUSIE, Mrs JOHN BAIN, a widow in Aronisk, Lochalsh and Plockton district, to emigrate to America around 1850. [NRS.HD21.53]

MCFARLANE, RODERICK, born1810, late in St Kitts and in New York, died in Tain, Ross and Cromarty, on 10 September 1835. [AJ.4577]

MCGILLIVRAY, CHARLES C., born 26 May 1818, son of Reverend Donald McGillivray and his wife Ann Allan in Berriedale, Caithness, settled in Grenada, died there on 6 April 1845. [F.4.135][Kilmallie gravestone]

MCGLASHAN, WILLIAM, a merchant in Cromarty in 1832, nephew of A. McGlashan a merchant in Newfoundland. [NRS.S/H]

MCGREGOR, DUNCAN, and his wife Margaret Dingwall who died on 21 December 1871, parents of Duncan McGregor who died in Australia. [St Clement's gravestone, Dingwall, Ross and Cromarty]

MCGREGOR, MURDOCH, innkeeper at Gairloch, Wester Ross, 1844. [NRS.CS280.30.75]

MACGREGOR, ROBERT, born 1777, with his wife and three children, children in Corgrain, Culmaily, Sutherland, in 1810. [SHS.1.14/15]

MCGREGOR, RODERICK, born 1783, a fisher in Ullapool, Wester Ross, was accused of rioting in 1833. [NRS.AD14.33.117]

MACGREGOR, THOMAS D., born 1818 in Dingwall, son of Alexander MacGregor, died on Plantation Endeavour, Leguan, Demerara, on 28 May 1846. [AJ.5142]

MCGRIGOR, DAVID, born 1799, son of Alexander McGrigor and his wife Ann Mackay, a house carpenter in La Belle Alliance, Demerara, died on 15 September 1839. [Croick gravestone, Ross-shire]

MCINNES, JOHN, born 1846, son of Malcolm McInnes and his wife Margaret Matheson, died in Australia in June 1924. [Lairg gravestone, Sutherland]

MCINNES, PAUL, born 1848, son of Malcolm McInnes and his wife Margaret Matheson, died in Australia in February 1917. [Lairg gravestone, Sutherland]

MACINTOSH, CHARLES C., minister of Tain Free Church, a petition, 1845. [NRS.GD1.2.51.178]

MCINTOSH, DONALD, from Sutherland, settled in Earlstown, Nova Scotia in 1813. [History of Tatamagouche, Halifax, 1917]

MCINTOSH, GEORGE, born 1797 in Sutherland, died at Canso, Nova Scotia, aboard the schooner Margaret when bound for Buren, Newfoundland, on 17 July 1830. [New Brunswick Courier, 7.8.1830]

MCINTOSH, GEORGE, with Barbara his wife and daughter Elizabeth, emigrated from Loch Laxford, Sutherland, on the Ellen of Liverpool bound for Pictou, Nova Scotia, on 22 May 1848. [PANS.257.110]

MCINTOSH, HUGH, emigrated from Loch Laxford, Sutherland, on the Ellen of Liverpool bound for Pictou, Nova Scotia, on 22 May 1848. [PANS.257.110]

MCINTOSH, HUGH, in Dornoch, Sutherland, was a victim of theft in 1850. [NRS.AD14.50.552]

MCINTOSH, JAMES, from Ross-shire, educated at King's College, Aberdeen, in 1818, a minister in Charlottetown, Prince Edward Island, from 1830 to 1836. [F.7.621]

MCINTOSH, JANET, emigrated from Loch Laxford, Sutherland, on the Ellen of Liverpool bound for Pictou, Nova Scotia, on 22 May 1848. [PANS.257.110]

MCINTOSH, KENNETH, and Roderick McIntosh in Knockbain, Ross and Cromarty, accused of assaulting a Revenue officer in 1811. [NRS.JC26.1811.4]

MCINTOSH, WILLIAM, a joint tenant in Auchluie, Dornoch, Sutherland, in 1811. [SHS.8.58]

MCINTOSH, WILLIAM, with family, from Sutherland, emigrated via Cromarty or Thurso aboard the Prince William bound for Pictou, Nova Scotia, in 1815. [NSARM.mg100, vol.226.30]

MCINTOSH, WILLIAM, emigrated from Cromarty or Thurso aboard the Lady Grey bound for Pictou, Nova Scotia, in June 1841. [NRS.RH1.2.908]

MCINTOSH, W. and G., joint tenants in Dalvevy, Teachlybe, Dornoch, Sutherland, in 1815. [SHS.8.221]

MACINTYRE, Reverend ALEXANDER CAMPBELL, and his wife Mary Ralston in Shieldaig, Ross and Cromarty, were parents of Alexander Campbell MacIntyre, born 17 December 1864, who died in Toowoomba, Australia. [F.4.90]

MCIVER, DONALD, born 1 November 1778, son of Reverend Murdoch McIver and his wife Mary McKenzie, a merchant in New York, died in Bermuda. [F.7.155]

MCIVER, ELIZABETH, servant of William Waters tenant of Barnyards of Garth, Olrick, Caithness, was found guilty of child murder and banished from Scotland for life in 1807. [NRS.JC11.48]

MCIVOR, MARCUS, born 1807, a coal merchant, died 14 June 1858, husband of Margaret Harrold, born 1809, died 21 March 1881. [Wick gravestone, Caithness]

MCIVER, MURDO, born 1852, son of Evander McIver and his wife Mary MacDonald, died 1891 in South Africa. [Scourie gravestone]

MCIVER, WILLIAM WALKER, born 1825, son of Lewis McIver in Gress, Isle of Lewis, died in Hong Kong on 25 February 1849. [EEC.21811]

MCKAY, ADAM, a piper, a joint tenant of Glen, Golspie, Sutherland, in 1811. [SHS.8.87]

MACKAY, ADAM, accused of murder at Helmsdale Bridge, Kildonan, Sutherland, in 1817. [NRS.AD14.17.2]

MACKAY, AENEAS, son of James Mackay in Ross-shire, died in Havanna, Cuba, in May 1817. [GM.87.629]

MCKAY, Lieutenant ALEXANDER, tenant in Ironhill and Baddin, parish of Golspie, in 1808, 1811 and 1815, tenant in Brachie, Rogart, Sutherland, in 1811. [SHS.8.77/82/224/225]; was granted a 6 year lease of Knockinachalich on 29 December 1812. [SHS.9/2.175]

MCKAY, ALEXANDER, tenant in Altindown, parish of Kildonan, Sutherland in 1811. [SHS.8.104]

MCKAY, ALEXANDER, a tailor, from Sutherland, settled in Earlstown, Nova Scotia in 1815. [History of Tatamagouche, Halifax, 1917]

MCKAY, ALEXANDER, with family, from Brora, East Muir, Clyne, Sutherland, emigrated to Canada, in 1829. [NRS.313.878]

MCKAY, ALEXANDER, with family, from Torbreck, Rogart, Sutherland, emigrated to Canada, in 1829. [NRS.313.878]

MCKAY, ALEXANDER, with family, from Auchlomliny, Rogart, Sutherland, emigrated to Canada, in 1829. [NRS.313.878]

MCKAY, or MORE, ALEXANDER, a fisher in Armadale, Farr, Sutherland, accused of theft in 1839. [NRS.AD14.39.7]

MACKAY, ALEXANDER, born in Sutherland, died on Williamsfield Estate, St Thomas in the East, Jamaica, on 15 September 1841. [AJ.4910]

MCKAY, ALEXANDER, born 1837, son of Donald McKay and his wife Ann Gordon, died in Australia on 12 April 1873. [Creich gravestone, Sutherland]

MCKAY, ANDREW, joint tenant in Fourpenny, Farr, Sutherland, in 1808. [SHS.8.223]

MCKAY, ANDREW, a joint tenant in Auchluie, Dornoch, Sutherland, in 1811. [SHS.8.58]

MCKAY, Captain ANGUS, tenant of the Mains of Rogart, Sutherland, in 1808, 1811. [SHS.8.72/230]

MCKAY, ANGUS, born 1789, his wife Jean, from Kildonan, Sutherland, bound for the Hudson Bay Company settlement at Fort Churchill on 29 June 1813, settled on the Red River in 1814, moved to the Holland River in September 1815. [PAC.M155.165-8]

MACKAY, ANGUS, and his wife Marion, in Rhiniskain, Clyne, Sutherland, accused of resisting officers of the law, failed to appear at their trial, and were therefore outlawed in 1821. [NRS.JC26.1821.9]

MCKAY, ANGUS, tenant in Golspie Mill, Sutherland, in 1811, 1815. [SHS.8.87/226]

MACKAY, ANGUS, born 1781, a miller, from Sutherland, emigrated via Cromarty aboard the Ossian of Leith bound for Pictou, Nova Scotia, on 25 June 1821. [Inverness Journal.29 June 1821]

MACKAY, ANGUS, and family, from Banscol, Rogart, Sutherland, emigrated to Canada in 1829. [NLS.313-878]

MACKAY, ANGUS, and family, from Inchcap, Rogart, Sutherland, emigrated to Canada in 1829. [NLS.313-878]

MCKAY, ANGUS, with wife Elizabeth and four children, emigrated from Loch Laxford, Sutherland, on the Ellen of Liverpool bound for Pictou, Nova Scotia, on 22 May 1848. [PANS.257.110]

MCKAY, ANNE, born 1782, in Corgrain, Culmaily, Sutherland, in 1810. [SHS.1.14/15]

MCKAY, ANN, born 1792, from Cain, emigrated on the Prince of Wales bound for Hudson Bay 1813, landed at Churchill in August 1813, settled on the Red River in 1814. [PAC]

MCKAY, ANN, with Elizabeth and Margaret, emigrated from Loch Laxford, Sutherland, on the Ellen of Liverpool bound for Pictou, Nova Scotia, on 22 May 1848. [PANS.257.110]

MCKAY, ANN, born 1830, emigrated from Loch Laxford, Sutherland, on the Ellen of Liverpool bound for Pictou, Nova Scotia, on 22 May 1848. [PANS.257.110]

MACKAY, BESSY, daughter of Donald Mackay a tenant farmer in Inveran, Creich, Sutherland, accused of infanticide in 1814. [NRS.AD14.14.13]

MCKAY, BETSY, born 1776, emigrated via Thurso, Caithness, on the Elizabeth and Ann bound for Prince Edward Island on 8 November 1806. [PAPEI]

MCKAY, BETTY, born 1792, from Kildonan, Sutherland, emigrated on the Prince of Wales bound for Hudson Bay 1813, landed at Churchill in August 1813, settled on the Red River in 1814, moved to the Holland River in September 1815. [PAC]

MACKAY, CATHERINE, servant to Benjamin Calder tacksman in Thurso, Caithness, found guilty of child murder and banished from Scotland for life in 1807. [NRS.JC11.48]

MCKAY, COLIN, tenant in Cerkall of Strathalladale, Reay, Caithness, trial papers, 1819. [NRS.JC26.1819.3]

MACKAY, DAVID, in Tannach, Wick, Caithness, accused of mobbing and rioting in 1827. [NRS.AD14.27.218]

MCKAY, DAVID, emigrated from Loch Laxford, Sutherland, on the Ellen of Liverpool bound for Pictou, Nova Scotia, on 22 May 1848. [PANS.257.110]

MACKAY, DAVID SCOTT, born 1847, son of Hugh Mackay, died in Auckland, New Zealand, on 27 December 1874. [Lochinver gravestone, Sutherland,]

MCKAY, Mrs DIANA, tenant in Carnachy, Farr, Sutherland, in 1811. [SHS.8.113]

MACKAY, Mrs DIANA, born 1765, from Carnachy, Sutherland, died 14 August 1847 in Pickering, Canada. [SG.1760]

MCKAY, DIANNA, emigrated from Loch Laxford, Sutherland, on the Ellen of Liverpool bound for Pictou, Nova Scotia, on 22 May 1848. [PANS.257.110]

MCKAY, DONALD, born 1782, wife Ann born 1782, and Hugh born 1805, emigrated via Thurso, Caithness, on the Elizabeth and Ann bound for Prince Edward Island on 8 November 1806. [PAPEI]

MCKAY, DONALD, joint tenant in Kinbrace and its mill, Lairg, Sutherland, in 1808. [SHS.8.229]

MCKAY, DONALD, born 1794, from Uig, Ross-shire, emigrated via Stornaway on the Prince of Wales to the Hudson Bay Company settlement on the Red River in 1811. [PAC.M155.145]

MCKAY, DONALD, born 1784, a labourer, wife Catherine Bruce born 1785, son John born 1814, from Sutherland, emigrated via Stromness on the Prince of Wales to the Hudson Bay Company settlement at York Fort on 23 June 1815, landed there on 26 August 1815. [PAC.M1659/61] [MG19.E4.1.165/8]

MACKAY, DONALD, sr., with family, from Sutherland, emigrated via Cromarty or Thurso aboard the Prince William bound for Pictou, Nova Scotia, in 1815. [NSARM.mg100, vol.226.30]

MACKAY, DONALD, jr., with family, from Sutherland, emigrated via Cromarty or Thurso aboard the Prince William bound for Pictou, Nova Scotia, in 1815. [NSARM.mg100, vol.226.30]

MCKAY or BAIN, DONALD, a fisherman, in Armadale, Farr, Sutherland, accused of theft in 1839. [NRS.AD14.39.7]

MACKAY, DONALD, born 1808, died 19 July 1848, and his wife Christian Bain, born 1805, died 25 January 1875, parents of Elizabeth Mackay in Australia. [Halkirk gravestone, Caithness]

MCKAY, DONALD, with wife Jean and daughter Maria, emigrated from Loch Laxford, Sutherland, on the Ellen of Liverpool bound for Pictou, Nova Scotia, on 22 May 1848. [PANS.257.110]

MACKAY, DONALD, in Thurso, Caithness, father of Mary Mackay who married Robert M. Easdale of Morrion, Whiteside County, Illinois, in Brooklyn on 17 October 1874. [EC.28117]

MCKAY, DONALD, born 1845, son of Donald McKay and his wife Mary Ross, died in Wyalong, Australia, on 5 September 1899. [Durness gravestone, Sutherland]

MACKAY, DUNCAN, a ship carpenter, son of Rupert MacKay in Caithness, died of Asiatic cholera in Portland parish, New Brunswick, on 26 October 1834. [New Brunswick Courier, 1.11.1834]

MACKAY, DUNCAN, born 1815, son of James Mackay, [1774-1847], and his wife Mary McPherson, [1778-1847], died in Detroit, Michigan, in June 1868. [St Clement's gravestone, Dingwall, Ross and Cromarty]

MCKAY, ELIZABETH, from Kildonan, Sutherland, emigrated via Thurso, Caithness, on the Prince of Wales bound for Hudson Bay in 1813, landed at Churchill in August 1813, settled on the Red River in 1814. [PAC]

MACKAY, ELIZABETH, daughter of John Mackay a crofter in Newlands, Lybster, Caithness, accused of housebreaking and theft in 1828. [NRS.AD14.28.279]

MACKAY, ELIZABETH, eldest daughter of Findlay Mackay in Caithness, married Andrew Taylor from Caithness, in Rampart Street, New Orleans, Louisiana, on 11 March 1874. [S.9581]

MCKAY, ELSPET, emigrated from Loch Laxford, Sutherland, on the Ellen of Liverpool bound for Pictou, Nova Scotia, on 22 May 1848. [PANS.257.110]

MACKAY, ERIC, in Scourie, Edrachillis, Sutherland, accused of horse theft, was outlawed in 1829. [NRS.AD14.29.134; JC26.1829.80]

MCKAY, FAIRLY, born 1824, with Jean McKay born 1822, emigrated from Loch Laxford, Sutherland, on the Ellen of Liverpool bound for Pictou, Nova Scotia, on 22 May 1848. [PANS.257.110]

MCKAY, GEORGE, born 1769 in Sutherland, died in South Carolina on 18 December 1819. [Old Scots gravestone, Charleston]

MACKAY, GEORGE, a tenant in Craigtown, Golspie, Sutherland, in 1808. [SHS.8.224]

MACKAY, GEORGE, a catechist in Lirrapul, was accused of rioting in Kildonan, Sutherland, in 1813. [SHS.8.136]

MCKAY, GEORGE, born 1769 in Sutherland, died in South Carolina on 18 December 1819. [Old Scots gravestone, Charleston, S.C.]

MCKAY, GEORGE, born 1765, a weaver, wife Isabella Mathewson born 1765, son Roderick born 1796 a labourer, son Robert born 1804, daughter Roberta born 1799, from Sutherland, emigrated via Stromness on the Prince of Wales to the Hudson Bay Company settlement at York Fort on 23 June 1815, landed there on 26 August 1815. [PAC.M1659/61] [MG19.E4.1.165/8]

MCKAY, GEORGE, tenant in Craigtown, Golspie, Sutherland, in 1811. [SHS.8.82]

MACKAY, GEORGE, born 1800, son of Kenneth Mackay of Torboll, the Convenor of Sutherland, died in Montreal in 1820. [SM.89]

MCKAY, GEORGE, tenant in Rhilochan, Rogart, Sutherland, in 1811. [SHS.8.76]

MCKAY, GEORGE, joint tenant in Achunoluechrach, Rogart, Sutherland, in 1815. [SHS.8.232]

MCKAY, GEORGE, sr., with family, from Rhilechan, Rogart, Sutherland, emigrated to Canada, in 1829. [NRS.313.878]

MCKAY, GEORGE, jr., with family, from Rhilechan, Rogart, Sutherland, emigrated to Canada, in 1829. [NRS.313.878]

MCKAY, or BAIN, GEORGE, a fisherman, in Armadale, Farr, Sutherland, accused of theft in 1839. [NRS.AD14.39.7]

MCKAY, GEORGE, emigrated from Cromarty or Thurso aboard the Lady Gray bound for Pictou, Nova Scotia, in June 1841. [NRS.RH1.2.908]

MACKAY, GEORGINA AENEAS, youngest daughter of Kenneth Mackay of Ledbeg, married James Sutherland from St Vincent, in Felim, Sutherland, on 11 February 1829. [S.955.144]

MCKAY, GEORGINA, emigrated from Loch Laxford, Sutherland, on the Ellen of Liverpool bound for Pictou, Nova Scotia, on 22 May 1848. [PANS.257.110]

MACKAY, HECTOR, born 1831, son of Charles Mackay and his wife Hectorina Morrison, died in Sydney, Australia, on 13 April 1895. [Durness gravestone, Sutherland]

MACKAY, HUGH, son of George Mackay of Bighouse, Sutherland, and his wife Louisa Campbell, died 1818 in Antigua. [BM.332]

MCKAY, HUGH, with family, from Lednobirichen, Dornoch, Sutherland, emigrated to Canada, in 1829. [NRS.313.878]

MACKAY, Colonel HUGH, born 1751 in Sutherland, a Lieutenant of the Queen's American Rangers during the American War of Independence, died at Suther Hall, St George, Lairg, New Brunswick, on 29 January 1848. [SG.1697]

MCKAY, Captain HUGH, tenant in Rhiphail, parish of Farr, Sutherland, in 1808, and 1811, in Mudle Tubeg, Farr, in 1815. [SHS.8.110/222/224]

MACKAY, HUGH, [1], with family, from Sutherland, emigrated via Cromarty or Thurso aboard the Prince William bound for Pictou, Nova Scotia, in 1815. [NSARM.mg100, vol.226.30]

MCKAY, HUGH, [2], with family, from Sutherland, emigrated via Cromarty or Thurso aboard the Prince William bound for Pictou, Nova Scotia, in 1815. [NSARM.mg100, vol.226.30]

MCKAY, HUGH, son of Mary McLeod or McKay, widow, a fisherman, residing with mother in Armadale, Farr, Sutherland, accused of theft in 1839. [NRS.AD14.39.7]

MCKAY or BAIN, HUGH, jr, tenant in Armadale, Farr, Sutherland, accused of theft in 1839. [NRS.AD14.39.7]

MACKAY, HUGH, emigrated from Cromarty or Thurso aboard the Lady Grey bound for Pictou, Nova Scotia, in June 1841. [NRS.RH1.2.908]

MACKAY, or MCLEOD, INNES, in Auldnabrekach, was accused of rioting in Kildonan, Sutherland, in 1813. [SHS.8.136]

MCKAY, ISABEL, born 1788, emigrated via Thurso, Caithness, on the Elizabeth and Ann bound for Prince Edward Island on 8 November 1806. [PAPEI]

MACKAY, JAMES, born 1759 in Kildonan, Sutherland, son of George Mackay and his wife Elizabeth McDonald, emigrated to Canada in 1776, an explorer for the Spanish in Louisiana, after1800 an explorer, militia officer and politician in Missouri, died on 16 March 1822.

MCKAY, JAMES, born 1784, a miller, with wife and two children, at the Mill House, Wester Culmaily, Sutherland, in 1810. [SHS.1.14/15]

MCKAY, JAMES, and John Ross, were granted a joint lease of Muiemore, Sutherland, on 29 December 1812. [SHS.9/2.175]

MCKAY, JAMES, born 1794, with sister Ann born 1792, from Cain, emigrated via Stromness on the Prince of Wales to Fort Churchill on 29 June 1813. [PAC.M155.165-8]

MCKAY, JAMES, with family, from Sutherland, emigrated via Cromarty or Thurso aboard the Prince William bound for Pictou, Nova Scotia, in 1815. [NSARM.mg100, vol.226.30]

MACKAY, JAMES, from Durness, Sutherland, a member of the Scots Charitable Society of Boston in 1817. [SCS/NEHGS]

MCKAY, or COOPER, JAMES, son of Angus McKay or Cooper, tenant in Cerkall of Strathalladale, Reay, Caithness, trial papers, 1819. [NRS.JC26.1819.3]

MACKAY, JAMES, born 1774, a tenant farmer in Druimlinach, Doulay, Lairg, Sutherland, was accused of rioting in 1821. [NRS.AD14.21.93]

MACKAY, JAMES, born 1812, son of James Mackay, [1774-1847], and his wife Mary McPherson, [1778-1847], died in Brooklyn, New York, on 15 November 1861. [St Clement's gravestone, Dingwall]

MACKAY, JAMES, born in Durness, a cattle drover in Sutherland, was accused of cattle theft in 1833. [NRS.AD14.33.15]

MCKAY, JAMES, with wife Bessy, emigrated from Loch Laxford, Sutherland, on the Ellen of Liverpool bound for Pictou, Nova Scotia, on 22 May 1848. [PANS.257.110]

MACKAY, JAMES, and his wife Jessie Sutherland, parents of George Sinclair Mackay born 1868, died in Oklahoma City on 2 September 1889. [Halkirk gravestone, Caithness]

MACKAY, or MCKEACHEN, JANET, daughter of William Mackay or McKeachen, in Tongue, Sutherland, accused of stealing sheep, failed to appear at her trial, and consequently was declared an outlaw, in 1818. [NRS.JC26.1818.106]

MCKAY, JANET, a widow, tenant in Clachan Mill, Farr, Sutherland, in 1808. [SHS.8.222]

MCKAY, JANET, in Dornoch Tolbooth, accused of child murder at Drumswordland, Assynt, Sutherland, in 1801, banished from Scotland for life [NRS.JC11.45]

MACKAY, JESSIE, eldest daughter of Captain Mackay of Skail, Farr, Sutherland, married Roderick Young from Cuminsburgh, Demerara, in Inverness on 20 June 1810. [SM.73.553]; marriage contract, dated 19 June1811. [NRS.RD3.345.165]

MACKAY, JESSIE, youngest daughter of Donald Mackay in Borgie, Sutherland, married Robert Mackay a merchant in Toronto, in Niagara, Upper Canada, on 5 October 1840. [W.96]

MCKAY, JOHN, born 1750, a farmer, with his wife and five children, in Wester Culmaily, Sutherland, in 1810. [SHS.1.14/15]

MACKAY, JOHN, a piper, with his family, emigrated from Gairloch, Ross and Cromarty, on the Sir Sidney Smith bound for Nova Scotia in 1805, settled at East River, N.S. [SG]

MCKAY, JOHN, joint tenant of Shiness Sheep Farm, Lairg, Sutherland, in 1815. [SHS.8.229]

MACKAY, JOHN, tenant in Kintraid, Rogart, Sutherland, in 1815. [SHS.8.231]

MACKAY, JOHN, in Muir of Lairg, son of Donald Mackay a tenant in Lower Lairg, Sutherland, Sutherland, was accused of rioting in 1821. [NRS.AD14.21.93]

MACKAY, JOHN, born 1773, a wright in Pitarxie, Gruids, Lairg, Sutherland, and his wife Margaret McDonald, were accused of rioting in 1821. [NRS.AD14.21.93]

MACKAY, JOHN, with family, from Sutherland, emigrated via Cromarty or Thurso aboard the Prince William bound for Pictou, Nova Scotia, in 1815. [NSARM.mg100, vol.226.30]

MCKAY, JOHN., with family, from Backies, Golspie, Sutherland, emigrated to Canada, in 1829. [NRS.313.878]

MACKAY, JOHN, born 1791 in Rogart, Sutherland, died at West River, Pictou, Nova Scotia, on 24 June 1847. [AJ.5194]

MACKAY, JOHN, born 1803, son of Donald Mackay on halfpay of the 42nd Highlanders, late in Quebec, died in New Ireland, Megantic County, Quebec, on 30 September 1848. [AJ.5262] [SG.1765]

MCKAY, JOHN, with wife Jess and daughter Georgina, emigrated from Loch Laxford, Sutherland, on the Ellen of Liverpool bound for Pictou, Nova Scotia, on 22 May 1848. [PANS.257.110]

MCKAY, JOHN, from Androcullis, Sutherland, emigrated via Stornaway on the Prince of Wales to the Hudson Bay Company settlement on the Red River in 1811. [PAC.M155.145]

MACKAY, JOHN, son of Donald Mackay deceased a tenant in Kildonan, Sutherland, was accused of rioting, resulting from the removal or eviction of tenants in Kildonan in 1813. [NRS.AD14.13.9; SC9.7.64]

MCKAY, JOHN, with family, from Sutherland, emigrated via Cromarty or Thurso aboard the Prince William bound for Pictou, Nova Scotia, in 1815. [NSARM.mg100, vol.226.30]

MACKAY, JOHN, with family, from Sutherland, emigrated via Cromarty or Thurso aboard the Prince William bound for Pictou, Nova Scotia, in 1815. [NSARM.mg100, vol.226.30]

MCKAY, JOHN, tenant in Corrigall, Reay, Caithness, later in Millhill, Olrig, Caithness, trial papers, 1819. [NRS.JC26.1819.3]

MACKAY, JOHN, from Bettyhill, Sutherland, a Captain of the 27th Regiment, married Amelia Isabella de Wolff, third daughter of Benjamin de Wolff of Windsor, Nova Scotia, there in 1821. [BM.10.489]

MACKAY, JOHN, born around 1800, second son of Kenneth Mackay of Torboll, the Convenor of Sutherland, died in Nassau, New Providence, on 20 October 1823. [SM.91.519]

MCKAY, Lieutenant JOHN, joint tenant in Moriness, Rogart, Sutherland, in 1808, and in Grubbeg, Farr, Sutherland, in 1815. [SHS.8.224/230]

MCKAY, JOHN, with family, from Sutherland, emigrated via Cromarty or Thurso aboard the Prince William bound for Pictou, Nova Scotia, in 1815. [NSARM.mg100, vol.226.30]

MACKAY, JOHN, born 1823, son of John Mackay and his wife Elizabeth Sutherland, died in Melbourne, Australia, on 18 January 1853. [Rogart gravestone, Sutherland]

MACKAY, JOHN, was accused of murder at Duncansby, Caithness, in 1829. [NRS.JC26.1829.85]

MACKAY, JOHN, a tailor in Wick, Caithness, a victim of housebreaking and theft in 1836. [NRS.AD14.36.4]

MACKAY, JOHN, born 1826 in Ross-shire, a tea merchant in New York, died in Hudson County on 3 April 1885. [ANY.II.260]

MCKAY, JOHN, emigrated from Cromarty or Thurso aboard the Lady Grey bound for Pictou, Nova Scotia, in June 1841. [NRS.RH1.2.908]

MACKAY, JOHN, son of John Mackay in Lower Brora, Sutherland, settled in the East Indies before 1852. [Clyne Kirkton gravestone]

MACKAY, JOHN, son of John Mackay in Oldtown, [1774-1856], and his wife Christy McLeod, [1784-1851], settled in Horseshoebush, New Zealand, by 1865. [Clyne, Kirkton, gravestone, Sutherland]

MCKAY, Captain KENNETH, a tenant in Mudle Tubeg, Golspie, Sutherland, in 1808, and in the parish of Dornoch, Sutherland, in 1811, also in 1815. [SHS.8.63/221/222/225]

MCKAY, LILLY, born 1790, in Corgrain, Culmaily, Sutherland, in 1810. [SHS.1.14/15]

MCKAY, MARGARET, born 1780, a soldier's wife with one boy, a tenant in Corgrain, Culmaily, Sutherland, in 1810. [SHS.1.14/15]

MCKAY, MARGARET, daughter of Captain McKay from Arichteing, Sutherland, wife of William Ross, died at Margaree, Cape Breton, on 11 March 1836. [Gleaner, 3.5.1836]

MACKAY, MARY, servant to Dr Ross in Golspie, Sutherland, was accused of theft in 1813. [NRS.AD14.13.56]

MACKAY, NEIL, born 1842, son of Neil Mackay, [1807-1882], died in Texas on 17 June 1879. [Kildonan gravestone, Sutherland]

MCKAY, NORMAN, born 1770, with Jean born 1802, Ann born 1804, and Isobell born 1805, emigrated via Thurso, Caithness, on the Elizabeth and Ann bound for Prince Edward Island on 8 November 1806. [PAPEI]

MCKAY, PHILIP, a wright in Dornoch, tenant of Croftkaill, Dornoch, Sutherland, in 1811. [SHS.8.60]

MACKAY, ROBERT, with family, from Sutherland, emigrated via Cromarty or Thurso aboard the Prince William bound for Pictou, Nova Scotia, in 1815. [NSARM.mg100, vol.226.30]

MCKAY, ROBERT, born 1751, with family, from Sutherland, emigrated via Cromarty aboard the Ossian bound for Pictou, Nova Scotia, on 25 June 1821. [Inverness Journal.29 June 1821]

MACKAY, ROBERT, second son of George Mackay of Bighouse, Sutherland, died in Antigua in 1793. [SM.56.62]

MACKAY, ROBERT, son of Donald Mackay, [1803-1883], and his wife Henrietta Matheson, [1812-1886], died in South Australia aged 30. [Rogart gravestone, Sutherland]

MACKAY, ROBERT, youngest son of George Mackay of Bighouse, Sutherland, died in Antigua on 29 September 1816 [DPCA.752][BM.332] [GM.86.566]

MCKAY, ROBERT, born 1801 in Cromarty, died in Milledgeville, Georgia, on 10 August 1833. [Southern Recorder, 14.8.1833]

MACKAY, ROBERT, born 1818, son of John Mackay and his wife Ann Alexander, died in Whampoa, China, on 6 July 1843. [Auchness gravestone]

MACKAY, RODERICK, born 1794 at Loch Broom, Ross-shire, died in Montreal on 16 January 1841. [AJ.4861][W.II.117]

MCKAY, RODERICK, with Barbara McKay, emigrated from Loch Laxford, Sutherland, on the Ellen of Liverpool bound for Pictou, Nova Scotia, on 22 May 1848. [PANS.257.110]

MACKAY, RUPERT, fourth son of George Mackay of Bighouse, Sutherland, died in Jamaica in 1802. [SM.64.183]

MCKAY, WILLIAM, born 1748, with wife Jean Scobie born 1756, Kenneth born 1791, George born 1792, Duncan born 1793, Jean born 1794, Hugh born 1799, John born 1801, and William born 1804, emigrated via Thurso, Caithness, on the Elizabeth and Ann bound for Prince Edward Island on 8 November 1806. [PAPEI]

MCKAY, WILLIAM, born 1766, with wife Christian McKay born 1767, and John born 1790, Neil born 1793, William born 1794, and Janet born 1806, emigrated via Thurso, Caithness, on the Elizabeth and Ann bound for Prince Edward Island on 8 November 1806. [PAPEI]

MCKAY, WILLIAM, tenant in Achlean of Pitfure, Rogart, Sutherland, in 1811. [SHS.8.70]

MCKAY, Captain WILLIAM, tenant in Skaill, Farr, Sutherland, in 1811. [SHS.8.114]

MCKAY, WILLIAM, born 1771, a shoemaker, wife Barbara Sutherland born 1780, daughter Betty born 1805, daughter Dorothy born 1811, and daughter Ann born 1813, from Sutherland, emigrated via Stromness on the Prince of Wales to the Hudson Bay Company settlement at York Fort on 23 June 1815, landed there on 26 August 1815. [PAC.M1659/61] [MG19.E4.1.165/8]

MACKAY, WILLIAM, [1], with family, from Sutherland, emigrated via Cromarty or Thurso aboard the Prince William bound for Pictou, Nova Scotia, in 1815. [NSARM.mg100, vol.226.30]

MCKAY, WILLIAM, [2], with family, from Sutherland, emigrated via Cromarty or Thurso aboard the Prince William bound for Pictou, Nova Scotia, in 1815. [NSARM.mg100, vol.226.30]

MCKAY, WILLIAM, joint tenant in Grubbeg, Farr, Sutherland, in 1815. [SHS.8.224]

MCKAY, WILLIAM, emigrated from Sutherland to Nova Scotia, settled in Earltown, Nova Scotia, in 1815. [History of Tatamagouche, Halifax, 1917]

MCKAY, WILLIAM, accused of assault, found guilty, sentenced to four months in Dornoch Tolbooth, Sutherland, in 1826. [NRS.JC26.1826.50]

MACKAY, or BAIN, WILLIAM, tenant in Armadale, Farr, Sutherland, accused of theft in 1839. [NRS.AD14.39.7]

MCKAY, WILLIAM, son of Barbara McDonald or McLeod, widow, a fisherman, residing with mother, Armadale, Farr, Sutherland, accused of theft in 1839. [NRS.AD14.39.7]

MACKAY, or ABRACH, WILLIAM, a cottar in Durness, Sutherland, accused of assault in 1848. [NRS.AD14.48.184]

MCKAY, WILLIAM, and wife Janet with four children, emigrated from Loch Laxford, Sutherland, on the Ellen of Liverpool bound for Pictou, Nova Scotia, on 22 May 1848. [PANS.257.110]

MCKAY, Mrs, tenant in Carnachy, Golspie, Sutherland, in 1808. [SHS.8.225]

MCKAY, Mrs, a tenant in Proncynaird, Dornoch, Sutherland, in 1808, 1811, also in 1815. [SHS.8.66/222/223]

MCKAY, a widow, with family, from Sutherland, emigrated via Cromarty or Thurso aboard the Prince William bound for Pictou, Nova Scotia, in 1815. [NSARM.mg100, vol.226.30]

MCKAY, Captain, in Torbell, tenant in Eiden, parish of Rogart, Sutherland, in 1811. [SHS.8.69]

MCKAY, Lieutenant, tenant in the parish of Clyne, Sutherland, in 1811. [SHS.8.101]

MCKENLEY, WILLIAM, a labourer in Upper Quendale, Rousay, Orkney, versus David Murray a contractor in Frotoft, Rousay, re wage arrears in 1848. [OA.SC11.5.1848.135]

MCKENZIE, ALEXANDER, tenant in Edracalda, Assynt, Sutherland, in 1811. [SHS.8.51]

MCKENZIE, Ensign ALEXANDER's heirs, tenants of Elphine, Assynt, Sutherland, in 1811. [SHS.8.49]

MCKENZIE, ALEXANDER, born 1800 in Dornoch, Ross and Cromarty, died at Mount Dalhousie, Nova Scotia, on 6 January 1839. [Nova Scotia Royal Gazette, 23.1.1839]

MCKENZIE, ALEXANDER, born 1818 in Strathpeffer, emigrated to New York in 1840, died in Vermont on 25 August 1874. [ANY.II.260]

MCKENZIE, Captain ALEXANDER, in Applecross, Wester Ross, was a victim of in Dingwall, in 1837. [NRS.AD14.37.36]

MCKENZIE, ANDREW, born 1823 in Ross-shire, late of St John, New Brunswick, died in New York on 25 August 1840. [New Brunswick Courier, 19.9.1840]

MCKENZIE, ANGUS, born in Kylestrome, Sutherland, a banker in St John, New Brunswick in 1820s, settled in New York in 1836. [ANY.II.253]

MCKENZIE, ANGUS, a fisher in Armadale, Farr, Sutherland, accused of theft in 1839. [NRS.AD14.39.7]

MCKENZIE, ANGUS, emigrated from Loch Laxford, Sutherland, on the Ellen of Liverpool bound for Pictou, Nova Scotia, on 22 May 1848. [PANS.257.110]

MCKENZIE, ANN, in Drynie, Knockbain, Ross and Cromarty, a letter to James Grant of Bught, re death of Captain McQueen in Madras, India, 1827. [NRS.GD23.6.619]

MCKENZIE, CATHERINE, wife of Angus Gunn a tenant in Tongue, Sutherland, accused of stealing sheep, failed to appear for trial and consequently was declared an outlaw in 1818. [NRS.JC26.1818.106]

MCKENZIE, COLIN, born 1803, of Mount Gerard, Ross-shire, and Spanish Town, Jamaica, died on 1 December 1847. [AJ.4700][Spanish Town Cathedral gravestone]

MCKENZIE, D., tenant in Pitfure and Carranlorkan, Rogart, Sutherland, in 1811. [SHS.8.71]

MCKENZIE, Reverend DAVID, in Farr, Sutherland, a victim of theft in 1830. [NRS.JC26.1830.90]

MCKENZIE, DONALD, [1758-1846], a farmer in Balnagra, and his wife Ann McKenzie, [1773-1854], parents of John McKenzie who settled in California. [Lochcarron gravestone, Ross and Cromarty]

MCKENZIE, DONALD, born 1769, a soldier of the Ross and Cromarty Rangers, Fencibles, accused of discharging a pistol in Inverness in 1801. [NRS.JC11.45; AD14.33.117]

MCKENZIE, DONALD, born 1797 in Ross-shire, died at Plaster Mines, Cape Breton, on 12 June 1856, husband of Margaret McKenzie, born 1805 in Ross-shire, died 24 February 1868. [Plaster Mines gravestone]

MCKENZIE, DONALD, joint tenant of Rovykirkton, Rogart, Sutherland, in 1808. [SHS.8.230]

MCKENZIE, DONALD, emigrated from Cromarty or Thurso aboard the Lady Grey bound for Pictou, Nova Scotia, in June 1841. [NRS.RH1.2.908]

MCKENZIE, DONALD, emigrated from Loch Laxford, Sutherland, on the Ellen of Liverpool bound for Pictou, Nova Scotia, on 22 May 1848. [PANS.257.110]

MCKENZIE, DONALD, born 1758, a farmer in Balnagra, died 1846, husband of Ann, born 1773, died 1854, parents od John MacKenzie in California. [Lochcarron gravestone, Ross and Cromarty]

MCKENZIE, DONALD, with wife Mary, and seven children, emigrated from Loch Laxford, Sutherland, on the Ellen of Liverpool bound for Pictou, Nova Scotia, on 22 May 1848. [PANS.257.110]

MCKENZIE, DONALD, with Ann, Robina, Donaldina, Cina, Roderick, and Hughina, all Mcintoshes, emigrated from Loch Laxford, Sutherland, on the Ellen of Liverpool bound for Pictou, Nova Scotia, on 22 May 1848. [PANS.257.110]

MACKENZIE, DUNCAN, in Ardelvie, Lochalsh and Plockton district, Wester Ross, to emigrate to America around 1850. [NRS.HD21.53]

MCKENZIE, GEORGE, eldest son of Colin McKenzie a writer in Dingwall Ross and Cromarty, a planter in Jamaica, by 1803 in America. [NRS.RS38.195; CS17.1.22.370]

MCKENZIE, GEORGE, tenant in Inchnadamff, Assynt, 1811. [SHS.8.50]

MCKENZIE, GEORGE, with family, from Achrinsdale, Clyne, Sutherland, emigrated to Canada in 1829. [NLS.Dep.313.878]

MACKENZIE, GEORGE, third son of Sir George Stewart Mackenzie of Coul, Ross-shire, died in Madeira on 2 June 1839. [EEC.19920]

MCKENZIE, GEORGE, late from Demerara, died at Leamington Park, Ross-shire, on 14 May 1840. [A.4820]

MACKENZIE, GEORGE, in Invergordon, Ross and Cromarty, dead by 1860. [NRS.S/H.1860]

MACKENZIE, GEORGE, son of .... Mackenzie and his wife Isabella Cameron, [1789-1871], settled in Canada West. [Dornoch gravestone]

MCKENZIE, GEORGE, father of George McKenzie born 1862, died in Chifwoo, China, on 11 October 1903. [Lochinver gravestone, Sutherland]

MCKENZIE, HECTOR, in New York State, son of Kenneth McKenzie of Redcastle, married Diana Davidson, second daughter of Dr Davidson, in Edinburgh on 29 March 1800. [GM.70.588]

MCKENZIE, HECTOR, born 1750, a weaver, with his wife and three children, in Balloan, Culmaily, Sutherland, in 1810. [SHS.8.14-15]

MCKENZIE, HECTOR, emigrated from Loch Laxford, Sutherland, on the Ellen of Liverpool bound for Pictou, Nova Scotia, on 22 May 1848. [PANS.257.110]

MACKENZIE, HELEN, in Blackmuir, Invergordon, Ross and Cromarty, was murdered in 1830. [NRS.AD14.30.101A; JC26.549]

MACKENZIE, HENRIETTA, of Suddie, Ross-shire, married James Wemyss Mackenzie, from Jamaica, on 26 March 1810. [SM.72.399]

MCKENZIE, HUGH, born 1821, son of Reverend David McKenzie, died in Demerara in 1844. [Farr gravestone, Sutherland]

MCKENZIE, HUGH, with wife Betty, and Christy Gunn, William Gunn, and Donald Gunn, emigrated from Loch Laxford, Sutherland, on the Ellen of Liverpool bound for Pictou, Nova Scotia, on 22 May 1848. [PANS.257.110]

MCKENZIE, ISABEL, wife of Neil McKenzie a tenant in Tongue, Sutherland, accused of stealing sheep, failed to appear for trial and consequently was declared an outlaw in 1818. [NRS.JC26.1818.106]

MCKENZIE, JAMES, born 1784, emigrated via Thurso, Caithness, on the Elizabeth and Ann bound for Prince Edward Island on 8 November 1806. [PAPEI]

MACKENZIE, JAMES, youngest son of John MacKenzie a mason in Fortrose, Ross and Cromarty, married Margaret Lyon from Edinburgh, at 21 Wall Street, Boston, Massachusetts, on 15 October 1868. [S.7882]

MACKENZIE, JANE, born 1802, daughter of Kenneth MacKenzie of Ledbeg, Sutherland, wife of James Clarke of Glen Dhu, died on 8 March 1847. [St Andrew's gravestone, Hobart, Tasmania, Australia]

MCKENZIE, JOHN, youngest son of Reverend William McKenzie minister of Tongue, Sutherland, a surgeon, died in Jamaica in March 1809. [SM.71.398] [EA.91.4734]

MCKENZIE, JOHN, born 1772 in Ross-shire, emigrated to America in 1774, died 12 September 1847. [Cross Creek gravestone, North Carolina]

MCKENZIE, JOHN, born 1750, late farmer in Balnacra, died 2 May 1812, husband Mary McCauley, born 1777, died 12 February 1817. [Lochcarron gravestone, Ross and Cromarty]

MCKENZIE, JOHN, son of Hugh McKenzie deceased, in Achrieskill, Sutherland, guilty of horse theft, was outlawed in 1829. [NRS.AD14.29.134; JC26.1829.80]

MCKENZIE, JOHN, son of Kenneth McKenzie, tenant in Muncastle, Loch Broom, Wester Ross, was accused of wilful fire-raising in 1828. [NRS.AD14.28.392]

MCKENZIE, JOHN, of Castle Street, Dingwall, Ross and Cromarty, a victim of theft, fraud, and embezzlement, in 1829. [NRS.AD14.29.344]

MCKENZIE, JOHN, son of Simon McKenzie or Buie a boatman or boat carpenter in Badlucherach, Ullapool, Wester Ross, was accused of wilful fireraising in 1828. [NRS.AD14.28.392]

MCKENZIE, JOHN, a cattle dealer and general merchant in Ledbeg, Assynt, Sutherland, a sederunt book 1824-1832. [NRS.CS96.4262]

MCKENZIE, JOHN, born 1804, a mason, son of Alexander McKenzie in Kinrive, Kilmuir Easter, Ross-shire, accused of culpable homicide in 1827. [NRS.AD14.7.203]

MCKENZIE, JOHN, a rabbit killer at Meikle Ferry, Dornoch, Sutherland, was accused of sheep stealing and breaking prison in 1843. [NRS.AD14.43.12]

MACKENZIE, JOHN, born 1778, a tenant in Balnacra, died 4 January 1825, father of Roderick MacKenzie, a merchant on Cape Breton. [Lochcarron gravestone, Ross and Cromarty]

MCKENZIE, JOHN, born 1783 in Caithness, died 29 October 1827 in Charleston, South Carolina. [Old Scots gravestone, Charleston]

MCKENZIE, JOHN, born 1804, a carter in Wellhouse, Kilcoy, Killearnan, Ross-shire, accused of forging a bill of exchange in 1844. [NRS.AD.44.470]

MCKENZIE, JOHN, son of Donald McKenzie, [1758-1846], a farmer in Balnagra, and his wife Ann McKenzie, [1773-1854], settled in California. [Lochcarron gravestone, Ross and Cromarty]

MACKENZIE, JOHN BAIN, in Aronisk, Lochalsh and Plockton district, Wester Ross, to emigrate to America around 1850. [NRS.HD21.53]

MACKENZIE, JOHN BEG, in Aronisk, Lochalsh and Plockton district, Wester Ross, to emigrate to America around 1850. [NRS.HD21.53]

MCKENZIE, KATHERINE, born 1804, at Bridge of Edderton, Ross-shire, daughter of Robert McKenzie a soldier, was accused of concealing a pregnancy, sentenced to six months in prison in 1824. [NRS.AD14.1824.86; JC26.1824.117]

MCKENZIE, KENNETH, tenant in Leadbeg, Assynt, in 1811. [SHS.8.50]

MCKENZIE, KENNETH, born in Ross-shire, a painter and glazier in New York in 1797, died in Bloomingdale, N.Y., in October 1803. [ANY.I.363]

MCKENZIE, KENNETH, tenant of Invershin, Creich, 1811. [SHS.8.55]

MCKENZIE, KENNETH, born 15 April 1797 in Ross and Cromarty, son of Alexander and Isabella McKenzie, emigrated to Canada in 1816, a fur trader and merchant in Missouri after 1822, died on 26 April 1861.

MCKENZIE, KENNETH, of the Caledonian Hotel, Dingwall, Ross and Cromarty, was a victim of rioting, mobbing, and assault at the Caledonian Hotel, Dingwall, in 1837. [NRS.AD14.37.36]

MACKENZIE, KENNETH, in Kirkwall, Orkney, a victim of robbery in 1847. [NRS.AD14.47.486]

MACKENZIE, KENNETH, in Ardelvie, Lochalsh and Plockton district, Wester Ross, to emigrate to America around 1850. [NRS.HD21.53]

MACKENZIE, KENNETH, in Invergordon, Ross and Cromarty, died 14 May 1868, father of George Mackenzie in Cumberland Hill, Dundas, Prince Edward Island, Canada. [NRS.S/H]

MCKENZIE, MALCOLM, merchant in Jeantown, Loch Carron, Ross and Cromarty, a ledger 1819-1823. [NRS.GD1.1202]

MCKENZIE, MALCOLM, born 1835, died in New Zealand on 16 June 1909. [Olrig gravestone, Caithness]

MCKENZIE, MARGARET, second daughter of Alexander McKenzie of Ord, married John McLean from Richmond, Grenada, in Peterhead, Aberdeenshire, on 6 October 1820. [EA.5934.231]

MCKENZIE, MARGARET, emigrated from Loch Laxford, Sutherland, on the Ellen of Liverpool bound for Pictou, Nova Scotia, on 22 May 1848. [PANS.257.110]

MACKENZIE, MARGARET, in Invergordon, Ross and Cromarty, dead by 1856. [NRS.S/H.1856]

MCKENZIE, MARY, emigrated from Loch Laxford, Sutherland, on the Ellen of Liverpool bound for Pictou, Nova Scotia, on 22 May 1848. [PANS.257.110]

MCKENZIE, MURDOCH, born 1742 at Loch Broom, Sutherland, died at Springs on the West River, Pictou, Nova Scotia, on 16 July 1831. [New Brunswick Royal Gazette, 20.7.1831]

MCKENZIE, MURDOCH, tenant in Stonechrubie, Assynt, Sutherland, in 1811. [SHS.8.50]

MCKENZIE, MURDOCH, of Ardross, tenant of Water of Shin, Lairg, Sutherland, in 1811. [SHS.8.57]

MCKENZIE, MURDOCH, born 1804, from Gairloch, Wester Ross, settled at Plaster Mines, Cape Breton, around 1845, died 1868, husband of Barbara born 1812 died 2 January 1890. [Plaster Mines gravestone]

MACKENZIE, MURDOCH, born 1816 in Assynt, Sutherland, died in Port Elizabeth, Cape Province, South Africa, on 26 October 1859. [St George gravestone, Port Elizabeth]

MCKENZIE, M., MD, son of Alexander McKenzie of Letterewe, Ross and Cromarty, died in Canton, China, on 5 November 1831. [AJ.4394][EEC.18780]

MCKENZIE, NORMAN, born 1848, son of Alexander McKenzie and his wife Jane MacRae, died in Kenona, Canada, in December 1910. [Stoer gravestone, Sutherland]

MCKENZIE, ROBERT, son of Reverend David McKenzie, [1783-1868], and his wife Barbara Grace Gordon, [1797-1868], settled in Otago, New Zealand. [Farr gravestone, Sutherland]

MACKENZIE, ROBERT, with family, from Sutherland, emigrated via Cromarty or Thurso aboard the Prince William bound for Pictou, Nova Scotia, in 1815. [NSARM.mg100, vol.226.30]

MCKENZIE, Lieutenant ROBERT, in Borgie, Tongue, Sutherland, a victim of theft in 1830. [NRS.JC26.1830.90]

MCKENZIE, RODERICK, born 1772 in Inver Assynt, Sutherland, emigrated to Canada in 1800, an employee of the North West Company from 1800 until 1821, then with the Hudson Bay Company, until 1852, later settled on the Red River, died on 2 January 1859. [HBRS]

MACKENZIE, RODERICK, son of Captain MacKenzie of Redcastle, Ross-shire, died in Jamaica in 1801. [GC.1522] [GM.71.483]

MCKENZIE, RODERICK, son of Alexander McKenzie, [died 1802], chief factor of the Hudson Bay Company. [Lochinver gravestone, Sutherland]

MCKENZIE, RODERICK, born 1791 at Gairloch, Wester Ross, an employee of the Hudson Bay Company in Canada from 1811 until his death on 10 January 1830 at Port Neuf, Mille Vache district. [HBRS]

MCKENZIE, RODERICK, in Knockbain, Ross and Cromarty, a letter, 1806. [NRS.GD403.64.14]

MCKENZIE, RODERICK, joint tenant of Leadmore, Badgrinan, Assynt, Sutherland, in 1811. [SHS.8.49]

MACKENZIE, Captain RODERICK, youngest son of Sir Hector Mackenzie of Gairloch, Ross and Cromarty, died in Port Philip, Australia, on 30 June 1849. [AJ.5328]

MCKENZIE, RODERICK, the Sheriff Substitute in Stornaway, died on 1 April 1853, father of Duncan Roderick McKenzie in Brooklyn, New York. [NRS.S/H]

MCKENZIE, RODERICK, son of John McKenzie, [1778-1825], a farmer in Balnacra, a merchant on Cape Breton. [Lochcarron gravestone, Ross and Cromarty]

MACKENZIE, Dr SIMON, son of Dr John Mackenzie in Fortrose, Ross and Cromarty, died at Fortrose on the Bay of Honduras on 2 August 1787. [SM]

MCKENZIE, THOMAS, of Applecross, Wester Ross, a letter to J. A. Stewart McKenzie of Seaforth in 1831. [NRS.GD46.1.370]

MCKENZIE, THOMAS, in Mealmill of Ord, Urray, Ross-shire, victim of housebreaking and theft in 1835. [NRS.AD14.35.3]

MCKENZIE, THOMAS WILMOR, born in Ross-shire, landed in New Zealand in 1840. [St Clement's gravestone, Dingwall]

MCKENZIE, Reverend WILLIAM, tenant on Coulin, Assynt, Sutherland, in 1811. [SHS.8.51]

MCKENZIE, WILLIAM, with family, from Doll, Clyne, Sutherland, emigrated to Canada in 1829. [NLS.Dep.313.878]

MCKENZIE, WILLIAM, born 1772 in Sutherland, to Nova Scotia by 1810, died in Kenzieville on the Barney's River, Nova Scotia, on 19 May 1834. [Halifax Journal, 26.5.1834]

MCKENZIE, WILLIAM JOHN, son of Reverend David McKenzie, [1783-1868], and his wife Barbara Grace Gordon, [1797-1868], died in Otago, New Zealand, aged 44. [Farr gravestone, Sutherland]

MCKENZIE, WILLIAM, born 1835 in Torridon, '33 years in New Zealand', died in Achnasheen in 1908. [Annat gravestone, Ross and Cromarty]

MACKENZIE, Miss, eldest daughter of Lord Seaforth, married Sir Samuel Hood, in Barbados on 6 November 1804. [SM.67.71]

MCKENZIE, Mrs, tenant of Kintraid, Rogart, in 1808. [SHS.8.230]

MACKENZIE, Mr, a merchant in Wester Garty, Loth, Sutherland, in 1815. [SHS.8.231]

MCKIDD, ALEXANDER, from Thurso, Caithness, graduated MA from King's College, Aberdeen, in 1842, a missionary in Canada. [KCA.295]

MCKID, ROBERT, tenant in Kirkton and part of Balblair, Golspie, Sutherland, in 1811 and 1815. [SHS.8.83/225]

MCKID, ROBERT, a writer in Thurso, versus Adam McRae a merchant in Cromarty, 1820. [NRS.CS34.25.39]

MACKID, Mrs, widow of John MacKid in Watten, Caithness, died in Goderich, Upper Canada, on 18 August 1850. [AJ.5359]

MACKIMEON, JOHN, in Crimminuie, Lochalsh and Plockton district, Wester Ross, to emigrate to America around 1850. [NRS.HD21.53]

MCKINLAY, ROBERT, a skipper in London, a sasine, 1807. [NRS.R.S.Orkney.723]

MCLAREN, ROBERT GREENLAW, born 3 August 1833, son of James McLaren and his wife Mary Greenlaw in Wick, Caithness, educated at St Andrews University from 1847 to 1853, a minister at Three Rivers, Canada, from 1862 to 1882. [SAU]

MCLEA, DONALD, born in September 1816 in Urray, Ross-shire, died in San Francisco, California, in November 1885.

MCLEAN, ANGUS, emigrated from Cromarty or Thurso aboard the Lady Gray bound for Pictou, Nova Scotia, in June 1841. [NRS.RH1.2.908]

MCLEAN, DONALD, emigrated from Cromarty or Thurso aboard the Lady Gray bound for Pictou, Nova Scotia, in June 1841. [NRS.RH1.2.908]

MCLEAN, HUGH, born 1791, a wright in Clunel of Gruids, Lairg, Sutherland, was accused of rioting in 1821. [NRS.AD14.21.93]

MCLEAN, JOHN, son of Roderick McLean a tailor at Shallagar, Auchtascaill, Loch Broom, was accused of fireraising in 1828. [NRS.AD14.28.392]

MCLEAN, JOHN, born 1815, in Rattar, died 24 March 1864, husband of Marion Stewart, born 1820, died 11 February 1900, parents of M. McLean in New South Wales, Australia. [Dunnet gravestone, Caithness]

MCLEAN, WILLIAM, born 1836, died in New Zealand on 24 September 1866. [Dunnet gravestone, Caithness]

MCLEAY, WILLIAM, born 1811, son of Alexander McLeay in Invershin, Sutherland, and his wife Esther Grant, died in Geelong, New South Wales, Australia, on 17 July 1852. [Ardgay gravestone]

MCLENNAN, ALEXANDER STEWART, second son of R. McLennan in Polewe, Wester Ross, died in Demerara on 5 May 1838. [AJ.4724] [SG.7.683]

MCLENNAN, ALEXANDER, in Dunbeath, Caithness, father of Hugh McLennan born 1860, who died at Dutoit's Pan Diamond Fields, South Africa, on 20 August 1884. [S.12855]

MCLELLAN, JOHN, born 1788, from Uig, Ross-shire, emigrated via Stornaway on the Prince of Wales to the Hudson Bay Company settlement on the Red River in 1811. [PAC.M155.145]

MCLELLAN, JOHN, emigrated from Cromarty or Thurso aboard the Lady Grey bound for Pictou, Nova Scotia, in June 1841. [NRS.RH1.2.908]

MCLENNAN, ALEXANDER, born 1825, his wife Isabella born 1824, and an infant, from Lallochy, Kintail, Ross and Cromarty, emigrated via Liverpool on the Arabian bound for Victoria, Australia, on 27 October 1852. [NRS.HD4/5]

MCLENNAN, ALEXANDER STEWART, second son of Alexander McLennan in Poolewe, Wester Ross, died in Demerara on 5 May 1838. [AJ.4724][SG.683]

MCLENNAN, DONALD, a tenant in Balblair, Contin, Ross-shire, accused of assaulting Revenue officers in 1818, was outlawed. [NRS.JC11.59]

MCLENNAN, DONALD, born 1816, his wife Christianna born 1824, daughter Mary born 1846, and daughter Margaret born 1848, from Bundalloch, Ross and Cromarty, emigrated via Liverpool aboard the Priscilla bound for Victoria, Australia, on 15 October 1852. [NRS.HD4/5]

MCLENNAN, EWEN, born 1792, his wife Mary born 1796, son Rory born 1827, son John born 1829, daughter Christy born 1825, and daughter Janet born 1833, from Lallochy in Kintail, Wester Ross, emigrated via Liverpool aboard the Arabian bound for Victoria, Australia, on 27 October 1852. [NRS.HD.J4/5]

MCLENNAN, JOHN, born 1800 in Ross-shire, was educated at King's College, Aberdeen, later a minister on Prince Edward Island, Canada, from 1823 until 1849. [F.7.622]

MCLENNAN, JOHN, in Braes of Gargarton, Killearnan, Ross-shire, accused of assaulting a Revenue officer in 1816. [NRS.JC26.1816.39]

MCLENNAN, JOHN, born 1811, Matthew born 1815, Duncan born 1841, Murdoch born 1845, Janet born 1839, Isabella born 1848, and Christy born 1852, from Portnacloich in Kintail, Wester Ross, emigrated via Liverpool aboard the Arabian bound for Victoria, Australia, on 27 October 1852. [NRS.HD4/5]

MACLENNAN, JOHN BAIN, in Aronisk, Lochalsh and Plockton district, Wester Ross, to emigrate to America around 1850. [NRS.HD.21.53]

MCLENNAN, KENNETH, born 1792, his wife Christy born 1797, son Norman born 1822, daughter Christy born 1826, daughter Mary born 1831, daughter Catherine born 1833, son Samuel born1842, Duncan born 1824, Flora born 1824, and John born 1850, from Kilmaloag, emigrated via Liverpool aboard the Arabian bound for Victoria, Australia, on 27 October 1852. [NRS.HD4/5]

MCLENNAN, KENNETH, a fisher in Poolewe, Wester Ross, accused of forgery in 1840. [NRS.AD14.40.14]

MCLENNAN, MARY, born 1798, son John born 1825, son Roderic born 1830, daughter Mary born 1834, and daughter Jane born 1840, from Inverinate, Kintail, Wester Ross, emigrated via Liverpool aboard the Arabian bound for Victoria, Australia, on 27 October 1852. [NRS.HD4/5]

MCLENNAN, ROBERT PRINGLE, eldest son of Kenneth McLennan in Caithness, died in Pittsburgh, USA, on 14 May 1872. [S.9022],

MCLEOD, A., born 1775, a labourer, with his wife and daughter, in Sallichtown, Culmaily, Sutherland, in 1810. [SHS.1.14/15]

MCLEOD, ALEXANDER, tenant in Wattin, Caithness, guilty of theft, sentenced to 12 months imprisonment in Dornoch Tolbooth in 1819. [NRS.JC26.1819.89]

MCLEOD, ALEXANDER, born 1789, with family, from Sutherland, emigrated via Cromarty aboard the Ossian bound for Pictou, Nova Scotia, on 25 June 1821. [Inverness Journal.29 June 1821]

MCLEOD, ANGUS, born 1770, a Lieutenant of the 78th Regiment of Foot, later Captain of the Ross-shire Militia, died 7 October 1833, father of Justina McLeod in Upper Canada. [St Clement's gravestone, Dingwall, Ross and Cromarty]

MCLEOD, ANGUS, emigrated from Cromarty or Thurso aboard the Lady Gray bound for Pictou, Nova Scotia, in June 1841. [NRS.RH1.2.908]

MCLEOD, Mrs CHRISTIAN, widow of Kenneth McKenzie, and Lieutenant John McKenzie of the Sutherland Fencibles Regiment, tenants of Inverkirkaig, Assynt, Sutherland, in 1811. [SHS.8.54]

MCLEOD, COLIN, born 1806, a fisher in Ullapool, Wester Ross, was accused of rioting in 1833. [NRS.AD14.33.117]

MCLEOD, DONALD, in Gledfield, Kincardine, Ross-shire, was a victim of rioting, mobbing, and assault at the Caledonian Hotel, Dingwall, in 1837. [NRS.AD14.37.36]

MCLEOD, DONALD, with Johan, Hugh, Lucy, Robertina, David, and Betty, emigrated from Loch Laxford, Sutherland, on the Ellen of Liverpool bound for Pictou, Nova Scotia, on 22 May 1848. [PANS.257.110]

MCLEOD, DONALD, with wife Mary, and two children, emigrated from Loch Laxford, Sutherland, on the Ellen of Liverpool bound for Pictou, Nova Scotia, on 22 May 1848. [PANS.257.110]

MCLEOD, DONALD, with wife Margaret, and four children, emigrated from Loch Laxford, Sutherland, on the Ellen of Liverpool bound for Pictou, Nova Scotia, on 22 May 1848. [PANS.257.110]

MCLEOD, DONALD, with wife Betty, and three children, emigrated from Loch Laxford, Sutherland, on the Ellen of Liverpool bound for Pictou, Nova Scotia, on 22 May 1848. [PANS.257.110]

MCLEOD, DONALD, and his wife Jane McDonald, parents of John McLeod, who died in Sydney, Australia, on 15 February 1865. [Golspie gravestone, Sutherland]

MCLEOD, GEORGE's heirs, tenant in Morness, Rogart, Sutherland, in 1811. [SHS.8.76]

MCLEOD, GEORGE, a tenant in Wester Killerman, Kildonan, Sutherland, was accused of rioting, resulting from the removal or eviction of tenants in Kildonan in 1813. [NRS.AD14.13.9; SC9.7.64][SHS.8.135]

MCLEOD, GEORGE, born 1796 in Sutherland, a tailor in Columbia, South Carolina, was naturalised in South Carolina on 13 April 1830. [NARA.M1183.1]

MCLEOD, GEORGE, with family, from Achrinsdale, Clyne, Sutherland, emigrated to Canada in 1829. [NLS.Dep.313.878]

MCLEOD, GEORGE, with wife Nancy, and daughter Margaret, emigrated from Loch Laxford, Sutherland, on the Ellen of Liverpool bound for Pictou, Nova Scotia, on 22 May 1848. [PANS.257.110]

MCLEOD, GEORGE ROSS, born 1829 in Golspie, Sutherland, a merchant formerly of Hollin, Maryboro, later of Stratford, Ontario, died at 146 Ross Street, Winnipeg, on 20 June 1884. [DA.7268]

MCLEOD, GEORGE, born 1796 in Sutherland, a clerk in Charleston, South Carolina, was naturalised there on 19 October 1813. [NARA.M1183.1]

MCLEOD, HECTOR CHISHOLM, born 1790 in Sutherland, a tailor in Columbia, South Carolina, was naturalised in South Carolina on 13 April 1830. [NARA.M1183.1]

MCLEOD, HECTOR, born 1794, from Ascaig, emigrated to Canada on the Prince of Wales in 1813, landed at Churchill on Hudson Bay in August 1813, settled on the Red River in 1814, moved to the Holland River in September 1815. [PAC]

MCLEOD, HUGH, born 1771, with family, from Sutherland, emigrated via Cromarty aboard the Ossian of Leith bound for Pictou, Nova Scotia, on 25 June 1821. [Inverness Journal.29 June 1821]

MCLEOD, HUGH, in Redhouse, Nigg, Ross and Cromarty, versus Alexander McIver a fish curer in Cromarty in 1827. [NRS.SC24.10.18]

MCLEOD, HUGH, son of Roderick McLeod a tenant farmer in Lynnmeanoch, Assynt, Sutherland, was accused of the murder of Murdoch Grant an itinerant pedlar of Strathbeg, Loch Broom, in 1830. [NRS.AD14.30.384]

MCLEOD, J., joint tenant of Leadmore, Badgrinan, Assynt, Sutherland, in 1811. [SHS.8.49]

MCLEOD, JAMES, with family, from Doll, Clyne, Sutherland, emigrated to Canada in 1829. [NLS.Dep.313.878]

MCLEOD, JOHN, born 1747, wife Ann McKenzie, Donald born 1781, Barbara born 1788, Hugh born 1791, Neill born 1792, Wilhelmina born 1797, and Angus born 1801, emigrated via Thurso, Caithness, on the Elizabeth and Ann bound for Prince Edward Island on 8 November 1806. [PAPEI]

MCKENZIE, JOHN, born 1771, wife Mary McPherson born 1774, Isabel born 1794, Hugh born 1796, Christian born 1798, Donald born 1802, and Andrew born 1804, emigrated via Thurso, Caithness, on the Elizabeth and Ann bound for Prince Edward Island on 8 November 1806. [PAPEI]

MCLEOD, JOHN, born 1 January 1773 in Sutherland, died 10 March 1862 in North Carolina. [Union Baptist gravestone, Lenoir, Caldwell County, N.C.]

MCLEOD, JOHN, born 1775, his wife and three children, in Balloan, Culmaily, Sutherland, in 1810. [SHS.8.14-15]

MCLEOD, JOHN, born 1805, son of James McLeod and his wife Anne MacDonald, died in America in December 1861. [Creich gravestone, Sutherland]

MCLEOD, JOHN, with family, from Knockarthur, Clyne, Sutherland, emigrated to Canada in 1829. [NLS.Dep.313.878]

MCLEOD, JOHN, born 1809, a house carpenter in Ballintraid Pier, Kilmuir Easter, Ross-shire, accused of murder in Invergordon in 1830. [NRS.AD14.30.101A; JC26.549]

MCLEOD, JOHN, born 1785 in Ross-shire, died in Wallace, Nova Scotia, on 7 March 1832. [Halifax Journal, 26.3.1832]

MCLEOD, JOHN, a tenant in Costally, Kildonan, Sutherland, was accused of rioting, resulting from the removal or eviction of tenants in Kildonan in 1813. [NRS.AD14.13.9; SC9.7.64]

MCLEOD, JOHN, with wife Ann, and three children, emigrated from Loch Laxford, Sutherland, on the Ellen of Liverpool bound for Pictou, Nova Scotia, on 22 May 1848. [PANS.257.110]

MCLEOD, JOHN, son of Donald McLeod and his wife Jane McDonald, died in Sydney, Australia, on 15 February 1865. [Golspie gravestone, Sutherland]

MCLEOD, JOHN, born 1858 in Golspie, Sutherland, died in Sydney, New South Wales, Australia, on 15 February 1885. [S.13030]

MCLEOD, KENNETH, born 1769, wife Nancy Morrison born 1776, John born 1794, Marion born 1796, George born 1801, Kenneth born 1803, Nancy born 1805, and James born 1805, emigrated via Thurso, Caithness, on the Elizabeth and Ann bound for Prince Edward Island on 8 November 1806. [PAPEI]

MCLEOD, KENNETH, was granted a tack of Lemirvay, Lochs, Lewis, for nineteen years at £96 per annum, in 1812. [NRS.GD46.1.286]

MCLEOD, MARGARET, a widow, joint tenant of Clyne Milnton, parish of Clyne, Sutherland, in 1811. [SHS.8.95]

MCLEOD, or BELCHES, MARGARET, sister of Donald McLeod of St Kilda, died in Cincinatti, Ohio, on 13 August 1835. [AJ.4602]

MCLEOD, NEIL, with wife Catherine, emigrated from Loch Laxford, Sutherland, on the Ellen of Liverpool bound for Pictou, Nova Scotia, on 22 May 1848. [PANS.257.110]

MCLEOD, NORMAN, born 1801, a fisher in Gidcascraig, Loch Broom, Wester Ross, was accused of rioting in 1833. [NRS.AD14.33.117]

MCLEOD, R., joint tenant of Leadmore, Badgrinan, Assynt, Sutherland, in 1811. [SHS.8.49]

MCLEOD, ROBERT BRUCE AENEAS, son of Lieutenant Alexander McLeod in Tain, Ross and Cromarty, died in Turama, St Vincent, on 25 November 1831. [AJ.4387]

MCLEOD, ROBERT, a saddler from Ross-shire, married Grace Polson second daughter of Hugh Polson a merchant in Aberdeen, in Montreal on 19 May 1834. [AJ.4507]

MCLEOD, RODERICK, a tenant farmer in Elphin, Assynt, Sutherland, tried for murder on 2 May 1800, case dismissed. [NRS.JC26.1800.59]

MCLEOD, RODERICK, son of Alexander McLeod in Tain, Ross and Cromarty, was drowned off St Vincent on 30 July 1830. [BM.28.861]

MCLEOD, WILLIAM, from Achaveregie, Toftingall, Watten, Caithness, a prisoner in Inverness Tolbooth, guilty of theft, sentenced to 12 months imprisonment in Dornoch Tolbooth in 1819. [NRS.JC26.1819.89; JC26.1820.107]

MCLEOD, WILLIAM, with family, from Doll, Clyne, Sutherland, emigrated to Canada in 1829. [NLS.Dep.313.878]

MCLEOD, WILLIAM J., born 1803 in Caithness, died in Halifax, Nova Scotia, on 3 April 1841. [Acadian Recorder, 10.4.1841]

MCLEOD, W. MERAN, emigrated from Loch Laxford, Sutherland, on the Ellen of Liverpool bound for Pictou, Nova Scotia, on 22 May 1848. [PANS.257.110]

MCLEOD, Mrs, a tenant in Morvich, Golspie, Sutherland, in 1811, 1815. [SHS.8.90/226]

MCLEOD, Mrs, a widow, joint tenant in Balblair, Golspie, Sutherland, in 1815. [SHS.8.226]

MCMILLAN, ANGUS, in Inverinate, Kintail, Wester Ross, accused of assault in 1828. [NRS.AD14.28.276]

MCMILLAN, DUNCAN, in Inverinate, Kintail, Wester Ross, accused of assault in 1828. [NRS.AD14.28.276]

MCMILLAN, JOHN, in Dornie, Lochcarron, Kintail, Wester Ross, applied to settle in Canada on 25 January 1819. [TNA.C0384.5.15]

MCNAB, ALEXANDER, PETER, and JOHN, were granted a tack of Lochs, Lewis, for fifteen years in 1812. [NRS.GD112.10.2/11]

MCPHAIL, JOHN, a drover in Farr, Strathnavin, Sutherland, 1800. [NRS.CS223.SEQN.M1.33]

MCPHEARSON, ALEXANDER, master of the Adventure of Wick, Caithness, in 1794. [DCA.CE70.1.8/96]

MCPHERSON, ALEXANDER, born 1770, with his wife and four children, in Sallichtown, Culmaily, Sutherland, in 1810. [SHS.1.14/15]

MCPHERSON, ALEXANDER, imprisoned in Dornoch Tolbooth, Sutherland, accused of child murder, trial papers, 1826. [NRS.JC26.1826.49]

MCPHERSON, ARCHIBALD, in Achine, Assynt, Sutherland, shepherd of Reverend George Tulloch in Edrachillis, was accused of sheep stealing in 1841. [NRS.AD14.41.287]

MCPHERSON, CATHERINE, born 1788, from Gailable, emigrated on the Prince of Wales bound for Hudson Bay, landed at Churchill in August 1813, settled at the Red River in 1814. [PAC]

MCPHERSON, DONALD, was granted a 15 year lease of Achnamoin, Sutherland, on 29 December 1812. [SHS.9/2/175]

MCPHERSON, DONALD, [1827-1800], father of William McPherson born 1878, died in Caldwell, Idaho, on 6 February 1910. [Croick gravestone, Ross-shire]

MCPHERSON, GEORGE, born 1787, a farmer with his wife and five children, in Sillichtown, Culmaily, Sutherland, in 1810. [SHS.1.14/15]

MCPHERSON, HECTOR, and his wife Christine McKenzie, parents of Donald born 1858, died in Sydney, Australia, on 26 February 1902. [Gairloch gravestone, Ross and Cromarty]

MCPHERSON, HUGH, from Sutherland, with three dependents, petitioned for a land grant in Nova Scotia on 6 October 1814, and was granted 250 acres. [NSARM.RG20.series A]

MCPHERSON, JAMES, born 1750, with his wife and one boy, in Sallichtown, Culmaily, Sutherland, in 1810. [SHS.1.14/15]

MCPHERSON, JAMES, emigrated from Cromarty or Thurso aboard the Lady Grey bound for Pictou, Nova Scotia, in June 1841. [NRS.RH1.2.908]

MCPHERSON, JOHN, tenant in Balblair, Golspie, Sutherland, in 1815. [SHS.8.226]

MCPHERSON, JOHN, born 1795, sister Catherine born 1787, from Gaible, Sutherland, emigrated via Stromness on the Prince of Wales to the Hudson Bay Company settlement at Fort Churchill on 29 June 1813. [PAC.M155.165-8]

MCPHERSON, JOHN, born 1796, from Gailable, emigrated on the Prince of Wales bound for Hudson Bay, landed at Churchill in August 1813, settled at the Red River in 1814. [PAC]

MCPHERSON, ROBERT, second son of Alexander McPherson of Elzy, Caithness, died in Nashville, Tennessee, on 11 August 1838. [AJ.4745]

MCPHERSON, THOMAS, from Ross-shire, was educated at King's College in Aberdeen, graduated MA in 1827, a minister in Lancaster, Canada. [KCA.283]

MCPHERSON, Mrs, born 1776, a widow with eight children, in Sallichtown, Culmaily, Sutherland, in 1810. [SHS.1.14/15]

MCQUARLISH, DONALD SUTHERLAND, born 1771, with his family of eight, from Sutherland, emigrated via Cromarty on the Ossian of Leith to Pictou, Nova Scotia, on 25 June 1821. [Inverness Journal, 29.6.1821]

MCQUEEN, ARCHIBALD, born 1786 in Applecross, Wester Ross, emigrated to Halifax, Nova Scotia, from there to Worcester, Massachusetts, by 1813.

MCQUILKIN, ARCHIBALD, a fisher in Lerwick, Shetland, accused of theft in 1837. [SA.AD14.37.342]

MCQUINAN, DUNCAN MCDONALD, tenant in Inverchoran, Urray, Ross-shire, accused of assaulting Revenue officers in 1818, was outlawed. [NRS.JC11.59]

MACRA, ALEXANDER, tacksman of Inchroe, a tenant in Kintail, Wester Ross, 1833. [NRS.GD46.1.246]

MACRA, ANGUS and Duncan Macra, in Dalcataig, Wester Ross, cattle dealers, 1831-1834, sederunt book, [NRS.CS96.4647]

MCRA, ARCHIBALD, tacksman of Ardintoul, Kintail, Wester Ross, a letter, 1793. [NLS.Acc.6945]

MACRA, JOHN, a surgeon from Plockton, emigrated via Obermory on the Glen Tannar to Cape Breton or Quebec in 1820. [NRS.E504.35.2]

MACRA, MURDOCH, in Ruroch, Kintail, Wester Ross, a cattle dealer, 1831-1834, sederunt book, [NRS.CS96.4647]

MCRAE, ADAM, a merchant in Cromarty, versus Robert McKid a writer in Thurso in 1820. [NRS.CS34.25.39]

MACRAE, ALEXANDER, Chief of his name in the Highlands, a member of the Court of Policy of Demerara, died there on 9 June 1812. [SM.74.727]

MCRAE, ALEXANDER, born 4 December 1803 in Applecross, Wester Ross, died at Middle River, Cape Breton, husband of Mary McLennan, born 12 March 1812 in Applecross, died at Middle River on 13 December 1875. [Middle River gravestone, C.B.]

MCRAE, ALEXANDER, born 1807, son of Alexander McRae alias Fear-a-mhonaidh, in Meikle or Wester Inverinate, Kintail, Wester Ross, accused of assault in 1828. [NRS.AD14.28.276]

MCRAE, ALEXANDER, alias Not Oig; Fear-a-mhonaidh, in Meikle, Kintail, Wester Ross, accused of assault in 1828. [NRS.AD14.28.276]

MCRAE, ALEXANDER, alias Fear-a-mhonaidh, in Wester or Meikle Innerinate, Kintail, Wester Ross, accused of assault in 1828. [NRS.AD1.28.276]

MCRAE, ALEXANDER, was found guilty in Dornoch, Ross and Cromarty, of assault and rape, then sentenced to death in 1841. [NRS.B15.5.13]

MCRAE, ALEXANDER, in Aronisk, Lochalsh and Plockton district, Wester Ross, to emigrate to America around 1850. [NRS.HD21.53]

MCRAE, ALEXANDER, in Alnasou, Lochalsh and Plockton district,Wester Ross, to emigrate to America around 1850. [NRS.HD21.53]

MCRAE, ALEXANDER, a carrier in Ardelvie, Lochalsh and Plockton district, Wester Ross, to emigrate to America around 1850. [NRS.HD21.53]

MCRAE, ANDREW, and Son, lint manufacturers in Cromarty, spinning book, 1794-1804. [NRS.CS96.1860]

MCRAE, ANDREW, a merchant in Cromarty, versus Alexander Liston Ramage, in 1813. [NRS.CS38.8.71]

MCRAE, ARCHIBALD, in Bendoloch, Lochalsh and Plockton district, Wester Ross, to emigrate to America around 1850. [NRS.HD21.53]

MCRAE, CATHERINE, born 1802, son Alexander born 1824, son John born 1830, and daughter Mary born 1834, from Inveraite, Wester Ross, emigrated via Liverpool aboard the Priscilla bound for Victoria, Australia, on 15 October 1852. [NRS.HD4/5]

MCRAE, CATHERINE, daughter of Alexander Macrae, Wester Inverinate, Kintail, Wester Ross, accused of assault in 1828. [NRS.AD14.28.276]

MCRAE, CHRISTOPHER, in Aronisk, Lochalsh and Plockton district, Wester Ross, to emigrate to America around 1850. [NRS.HD21.53]

MCRAE, DONALD, born 1801 in Kintail, Wester Ross, died 20 October 1881 at Middle River, Cape Breton, husband of Ann McDougall, born 1806 on Mull, died 23 December 1888 at Middle River. [Middle River gravestone, C.B.]

MACRAE, DONALD, born 3 October 1839 in Poolewe, Wester Ross, son of Reverend Donald MacRae and his wife Jessie Russell, a physician in Iowa. [F.7.163]

MCRAE, DOUGALD, in Aronisk, Lochalsh and Plockton district, Wester Ross, to emigrate to America around 1850. [NRS.HD21.53]

MACRAE, DUNCAN, born 16 April 1796, son of Reverend John MacRae and his wife Madeline, in Glen Shiel, Ross-shire, died in Florida. [F.7.151]

MCRAE, DUNCAN, from Glenshiel, Kintail, Wester Ross, emigrated to Montreal, Quebec, in June 1802, settled in Finch, Stormont County, Upper Canada, in 1804. [LAC.mg24.i.183][CMM]

MACRAE, DUNCAN, a weaver, in Dunmore, Kintail, Ross-shire, accused of assault in 1828. [NRS.AD14.28.276]

MCRAE, DUNCAN, in Ardelvie, Lochalsh and Plockton district, Wester Ross, to emigrate to America around 1850. [NRS.HD21.53]

MCRAE, DUNCAN, in Gallahy, Lochalsh and Plockton district, Wester Ross, to emigrate to America around 1850. [NRS.HD21.53]

MCRAE, DUNCAN, in Aronisk, Lochalsh and Plockton district, Wester Ross, to emigrate to America around 1850. [NRS.HD21.53]

MCRAE, DUNCAN, in Doune, Bendoloch, Lochalsh and Plockton district, Wester Ross, to emigrate to America around 1850. [NRS.HD21.53]

MCRAE, DUNCAN BAIN, in Killilan, Lochalsh and Plockton district, Wester Ross, to emigrate to America around 1850. [NRS.HD21.53]

MCRAE, FARQUHAR, born 1798, wife Peggy born 1804, son John born 1829, son Duncan born 1834, and daughter Mary born 1832, from Inveraite, Wester Ross, emigrated via Liverpool aboard the Priscilla bound for Victoria, Australia, on 15 October 1852. [NRS.HD4/5]

MCRAE, FARQUHAR, son of Alexander MacRae alias Fear-a-mhonaidh, in Meikle, Kintail, Ross-shire, accused of assault in 1828. [NRS.AD14.28.276]

MCRAE, GILCHRIST, from Lianish, Kintail, Wester Ross, emigrated to Montreal, Quebec, in June 1802, settled in Finch, Stormont County, Upper Canada, in 1804. [LAC.mg24.i.183][CMM] [CAN.MG24.1.183]

MACRAE, JAMES RUSSELL, born 1840s in Poolewe, Wester Ross, son of Reverend Donald MacRae and his wife Jessie Russell, a farmer at Council Bluffs, USA. [F.7.163]

MACRAE, JOHN son of Christopher MacRae, tailor, in Rhuneile, Kintail, Ross-shire, accused of assault in 1828. [NRS.AD14.28.276]

MACRAE, JOHN, in Meikle, Wester Inverinate, Kintail, Wester Ross, accused of assault in 1828. [NRS.AD14.28.276]

MCRAE, JOHN, a shopkeeper and carpenter in Auchterneed, Fodderty, Cromarty, accused of forgery in 1838. [NRS.AD14.38.26]

MCRAE, Reverend JOHN, in Killearnan, Ross-shire, a letter to William McKenzie of Muirton, 1846. [NRS.GD274.25]

MCRAE, JOHN, a tailor in Aronisk, Lochalsh and Plockton district, Wester Ross, to emigrate to America around 1850. [NRS.HD21.53]

MCRAE, JOHN, in Kirkton of Lochalsh, Lochalsh and Plockton district, Wester Ross, to emigrate to America around 1850. [NRS.HD21.53]

MCRAE, JOHN, in Auchtertyre, Lochalsh and Plockton district, Wester Ross, to emigrate to America around 1850. [NRS.HD21.53]

MCRAE, JOHN, in Reraig, Lochalsh and Plockton district, Wester Ross, to emigrate to America around 1850. [NRS.HD21.53]

MCRAE, JOHN BAIN, in Aronisk, Lochalsh and Plockton district, Wester Ross, to emigrate to America around 1850. [NRS.HD21.53]

MCRAE, JOHN, born 1788, wife Isabella born 1792, son Finlay born 1824, son Farquhar born 1827, son Duncan born 1831, and daughter Margaret born 1835, from Portnacloich, Kintail, Wester Ross, emigrated via Liverpool aboard the Arabian bound for Victoria, Australia, on 27 October 1852. [NRS.HD4/5]

MACRAE, JOHN FARQUHAR, born 1852 in Poolewe, Wester Ross, son of Reverend Donald MacRae and his wife Jessie Russell, settled in Toorak, Melbourne, Australia. [F.7.163]

MCRAE, MALCOLM, in Aronisk, Lochalsh and Plockton district, Wester Ross, to emigrate to America around 1850. [NRS.HD21.53]

MCRAE, MARY, daughter of Kenneth McRae late grasskeeper in Inverate, Ross-shire, accused of wilful fire-raising in 1821. [NRS.AD14.21.83]

MACRAE, MURDO, in Little Inverinate, Kintail, Ross-shire, was accused of assault in 1828. [NRS.AD14.28.276]

MCTAVISH, JOHN, and his wife Helen McGillivray, parents of Duncan McTavish, born 1864, died October 1904, buried in Gallag, Peru. [Golspie gravestone, Sutherland]

MCVINISH, JOHN, born 1831, late a pilot, died in Maryborough, Queensland, Australia, on 3 November 1886. [Kinnettas, Strathpeffer, Ross and Cromarty, gravestone]

MCWILLIE, ANN, born 1814, wife of James Peterkin a farmer in Rumster, died 7 June 1866, daughter Helen Peterkin, born 1844, died in Cullen on 24 January 1861. [Old Latheron gravestone, Caithness]

MAIR, THOMAS, a merchant from the Shetland Isles, was naturalised in South Carolina on 27 May 1798. [NARA.M1183.1]

MANSON, ALEXANDER S., born 1805, only son of Dr Manson in Thurso, died in Morpeth, New South Wales, Australia, on 10 September 1847. [AJ.5228]

MANSON, ANDREW, born 1786 in Ross-shire a merchant in Charleston, South Carolina, was naturalised there on 28 February 1820. [NARA.M1183.1]

MANSON, ANDREW, son of Thomas Manson a carrier in Kirkwall, Orkney, accused of robbery and theft in 1838. [NRS.AD14.38.552]

MANSON, DONALD, born 1785, emigrated via Thurso, Caithness, on the Elizabeth and Anne bound for Prince Edward Island on 8 November 1806. [PAPEI], possibly an employee of the Hudson Bay Company from 1817 to 1858. [HBRS]

MANSON, GILBERT, born 1800, died 24 November 1831, husband of Philadelphia Bain, born 1800, died 23 May 1893. [Cunningsburgh gravestone, Shetland]

MANSON, HENRY, born 1788, emigrated via Thurso, Caithness, on the Elizabeth and Ann bound for Prince Edward Island on 8 November 1806. [PAPEI]

MANSON, JAMES, born 1798, died 21 May 1889, husband of Wilhelmina Campbell, born 1816, died 28 June 1910. [Canisbay gravestone, Caithness]

MANSON, JAMES, born 1781, farmer in Easter Mey, Caithness, died 15 October 1830, husband of Mary Swanson, born 1784, died 28 June 1868. [Canisbay gravestone]

MANSON, JOHN, tenant in Toftkemp, Caithness, versus William Sinclair of Freswick, 1803. [NRS.CS271.624]

MANSON, MARGARET, born 7 September 1802, resided in Australia from 1839 to 1857, died in West Canisbay on 17 June 1857, wife of William Geddes. [Canisbay gravestone, Caithness]

MANSON, MURRAY, a messenger in Thurso, Caithness, accused of forgery in Kirkwall in 1818. [NRS.AD14.18.104]

MARSHALL, ROBERT, was accused of bigamy at Skibo, Sutherland, was outlawed in 1825. [NRS.AD14.25.29; JC26.1825.287]

MARWICK, DAVID, born 1827 in Orkney, died in Victoria, British Columbia, on 12 August 1888. [Ross Bay gravestone, B.C.]

MARWICK, JAMES H., born 1852 in Kirkwall, Orkney, died in Victoria, British Columbia, on 13 March 1882. [Ross Bay gravestone, B.C.]

MARWICK, JOHN HUME, born 1850 in Kirkwall, Orkney, died in Carbonada, Washington, USA, on 13 May 1882. [Ross Bay gravestone]

MARWICK, MARY HOLLAND, born 1828 in Orkney, settled in Victoria, British Columbia, in 1852, died there on 2 October 1892. [Ross Bay gravestone, B.C.]

MATHER, MICHAEL, in Sangomore, Durness, Sutherland, a victim of horse theft in 1829. [NRS.AD14.29.134]

MATHIESON, ALEXANDER, born 17 March 1773 in Achanarish, Lochalsh, Wester Ross, died 1 May 1826. [Old Scots gravestone, Charleston, S.C.]

MATHIESON, ALEXANDER, joint tenant in Fourpenny, Farr, Sutherland, in 1808. [SHS.8.223]

MATHESON, ALEXANDER, from Keanved, Kildonan, Sutherland, emigrated via Stromness on the Prince of Wales to the Hudson Bay Company settlement at Fort Churchill on 29 June 1813, settled on the Red River in 1814, moved to the Holland River in September 1815. [PAC.M155.165-8]

MATHESON, ALEXANDER GORDON, youngest son of Colin Matheson of Bennetsfield, Ross-shire, died in Berbice on 1 October 1820. [S.5.203]

MATHIESON, ALEXANDER, born 1806, a fisher in Ullapool, Wester Ross, was accused of rioting in 1833. [NRS.AD14.33.117]

MATHIESON, ALEXANDER, joint tenant in Fourpenny, Dornoch, Sutherland, in 1815. [SHS.8.222]

MATHIESON, ALEXANDER, son of Murdoch Mathieson and his wife Florence MacRae in Kintail, Wester Ross, settled in Charleston, South Carolina, in 1830. [CMR]

MATHESON, CHRISTOPHER, in Drumbuy, Lochalsh and Plockton district, Wester Ross, to emigrate to America around 1850. [NRS.HD21.53]

MATHESON, DANIEL, born 1764 in Invershin, Sutherland, a tailor who died, in Ashville, Buncombe County, North Carolina, on 8 January 1812. [Mirror of the Times, 24.2.1812]

MATHIESON, DONALD, born 1744, the miller at Fernaig, Ross and Cromarty, father of Duncan Mathieson who settled in Charleston, South Carolina. [HOM]

MATHIESON, DONALD, joint tenant in Kerrow of Kinbrace, Lairg, Sutherland, in 1808. [SHS.8.229]

MATHESON, DONALD, tenant in Wester Badnadielson, Lairg, Sutherland, in 1815. [SHS.8.229]

MATHESON, DONALD, born 1811 in Ross-shire, emigrated to Charleston, South Carolina, in November 1825, was naturalised in Marlborough, S.C., on 17 April 1837, died in 1890. [SCA][HOM]

MATHESON, DONALD, died 1875, and his wife Isabella, died 1885, parents of Duncan and Kenneth who settled in Colorado. [Gairloch gravestone, Wester Ross]

MATHIESON, DUGALD, in Aronisk, Lochalsh and Plockton district, Wester Ross, to emigrate to America around 1850. [NRS.HD21.53]

MATHIESON, DOUGALD, in Kirkton of Plockton, Lochalsh and Plockton district, Wester Ross, to emigrate to America around 1850. [NRS.HD21.53]

MATHESON, DUNCAN, born 1784 in Ross-shire, emigrated to USA in 1806, a merchant in Augusta, Georgia, died there on 30 September 1812, buried at St Paul's, Augusta. [Augusta gravestone, Ga.]

MATHIESON, DUNCAN, tenant in Shiness, Lairg, Sutherland, in 1811, 1815. [SHS.8.56/229]

MATHIESON, DUNCAN, tenant in Ardaavine of Mudle, Farr, Sutherland, in 1811. [SHS.8.113]

MATHESON, DUNCAN, in Clyne Manse, Sutherland, a letter, 1830. [NRS.GD46.12.38]

MATHESON, ELSPET, emigrated via Loch Laxford, Sutherland, on the Ellen of Liverpool bound for Pictou, Nova Scotia, on 22 May 1848. [PANS.257.110]

MATHIESON, FARQUHAR, in Aronisk, Lochalsh and Plockton district, Wester Ross, to emigrate to America around 1850. [NRS.HD21.53]

MATHIESON, GILBERT, joint tenant in Balblair, Golspie, Sutherland, in 1815. [SHS.8.226]

MATHIESON, JAMES, joint tenant in Bank, Rogart, in 1815. [SHS.8.231]

MATHESON, JOHN, from Kinved, Kildonan, Sutherland, emigrated via Stromness, Orkney, on the Prince of Wales to the Hudson Bay Company settlement at Fort Churchill on 29 June 1813, settled at the Red River in 1814, moved to the Holland River in September 1815. [PAC.M155.165-8]

MATHESON, JOHN, born 1791, from Aultbreakachy, Sutherland, emigrated via Stromness, Orkney, on the Prince of Wales to the Hudson Bay Company settlement at Fort Churchill on 29 June 1813, settled at the Red River in 1814, moved to the Holland River in September 1815. [PAC.M155.165-8]

MATHESON, JOHN, in Rhiniskain, Clyne, Sutherland, was accused of resisting officers of the law, pleaded guilty, and was imprisoned for six months in Dornoch Tolbooth in 1821. [NRS.JC26.1821.9]

MATHESON, JOHN, emigrated via Scrabster, Caithness, on the Superior of Peterhead bound for Pictou, Nova Scotia, landed there in June 1842. [Pictou Observer, 21.6.1842]

MATHESON, JOHN, born 1829 in Orkney, settled in British Columbia in 1858, died in Victoria, British Columbia, on 2 January 1889. [Ross Bay gravestone, Vancouver, B.C.]

MATHESON, JOHN, son of George Matheson, tenant in Height of Achterneed, Cromarty, was accused of forgery in 1838. [NRS.AD14.38.26]

MATHESON, JOHN, with his wife Johan and children, emigrated via Loch Laxford, Sutherland, on the Ellen of Liverpool bound for Pictou, Nova Scotia, on 22 May 1848. [PANS.257.110]

MATHESON, JOHN, born 1798 in Sutherland, died 20 March 1878 at the Red River settlement, Manitoba. [PAM.HBCA.D5.11]

MATHIESON, JOHN, in Aronisk, Lochalsh and Plockton district, Wester Ross, to emigrate to America around 1850. [NRS.HD21.53]

MATHESON, JOHN, son of James Matheson [died 1876] and his wife Isabel Mackay, [1802-1846], died in Melbourne, Australia. [Dornoch gravestone, Sutherland]

MATHESON, JOHN, born 1829 in Orkney, settled in British Columbia, in 1858, died in Victoria, B.C., on 2 January 1889. [Ross Bay gravestone]

MATHESON, Lieutenant PATRICK, tenant in Achnahuah, Kildonan, Sutherland, in 1808. [SHS.8.226]

MATHESON, RODERICK, son of Murdoch Matheson in Lochalsh, Ross and Cromarty, settled in the Carolinas, died in 1811. [HOM]

MATHESON, RODERICK, born 1795, a labourer in Fairburn, Ross-shire, accused of housebreaking and theft in 1835. [NRS.AD14.35.3]

MATHESON, RODERICK, in Kyleakin, Lochalsh, Wester Ross, a victim of forgery in 1835. [NRS.AD14.35.12; JC26.1835.10]

MATHESON, WILLIAM POPE, youngest son of James Matheson a cabinet-maker in Tain, Ross and Cromarty, died in Tobago on 30 June 1830. [S.1111]

MATHESON, WILLIAM, sr., tenant in Wester Canisbay, Caithness, versus James Geddes there, in 1801. [NRS.GD136.182]

MATHESON, WILLIAM, was proposed as fox-hunter for the parishes of Clyne and Golspie, Sutherland, in 1804. [NRS.JP32.7.5]

MATHESON, Captain, tenant in the parish of Lairg, in 1808. [SHS.8.228]

MATHEWSON, ALEXANDER, born 1781, a shoemaker, wife Ann born 1781, son Hugh born 1805, son Angus born 1809, son John born 1814, daughter Catherine born 1813, from Sutherland, emigrated via Stromness on the Prince of Wales to York Fort on 23 June 1815, landed there on 26 August 1815. [PAC.M1659/61] [MG19.E4.1.165/8]

MATHEWSON, ANGUS, born 1785, a tailor, with Christian Mathewson born 1797, from Sutherland, emigrated via Stromness on the Prince of Wales to York Fort on 23 June 1815, landed there on 26 August 1815. [PAC.M1659/61] [MG19.E4.1.165/8]

MATHEWSON, JANE, born 1793, from Sutherland, emigrated via Stromness on the Prince of Wales to York Fort on 23 June 1815, landed there on 26 August 1815. [PAC.M1659/61] [MG19.E4.1.165/8]

MATTHEWSON, RODERICK, born 1831, only son of Alexander Matthewson, a native of Lochalsh, died in the Scotch Settlement, Reechbridge, Williamston, Beauharnois, in 1856. [EEC.21007]

MATTHEWSON, Mrs, born 1755, a widow, with son John born 1797, a labourer, daughter Helen born 1794, from Sutherland, emigrated via Stromness on the Prince of Wales to York Fort on 23 June 1815, landed there on 26 August 1815. [PAC.M1659/61] [MG19.E4.1.165/8]

MEIKLEJOHN, ALEXANDER, born 1832, son of John Meiklejohn and his wife Agnes Trotter in Latheron, Caithness, died in Queenstown, Australia, on 28 July 1868. [Latheron Old gravestone]

MEIL, HENRY, born 1820, a farmer in Orkney, settled in Saltcoats, Assiniboia, North West Territories, Canada, in 1889. [BPP.9.484]

MEIL, HENRY, jr., born 1851, a farmer in Orkney, settled in Saltcoats, Assiniboia, North West Territories, Canada, in 1889. [BPP.9.484]

MEIL, JOHN, born 1854, a farmer in Orkney, settled in Saltcoats, Assiniboia, North-West Territories, Canada, in 1889. [BPP.9.484]

MELVILLE, JEAN, wife of Donald Murray a dram seller in Suisgill, who had been ejected from her home, was accused of rioting in Kildonan, Sutherland, in 1813. [SHS.8.136/139]

MERRYLEES, WILLIAM, born 1795, died 6 June 1859, husband of Mary Mouat, born 1801, died 18 April 1885. [Lerwick gravestone, Shetland]

MERRIMAN, GEORGE, born 1789, from Hara, Orkney, emigrated via Stornaway on the Prince of Wales to the Hudson Bay Company settlement on the Red River in 1811. [PAC.M155.145]

MERRYMAN, JOHN, a farmer in Hourston, Sandwick, Shetland, versus Elspeth Johnston there, summons of removal in 1803. [SA.SC11.5.1803.68]

MERRIMAN, PETER, born 1804 in Orkney, settled in Victoria, British Columbia, in 1851, manager of Fairfield Farm, died in Victoria on 29 December 1869. [Ross Bay gravestone, Vancouver, B.C.]

MESSER, ALEXANDER, son of Alexander Messer, an architect, and his wife Jane, died in 1861 in Andover, Massachusetts. [St Clement's gravestone, Dingwall, Ross and Cromarty]

MESSER, JANE, wife of Alexander Messer, [1810-1857], an architect, died in Andover, Massachusetts, aged 76. [St Clement's gravestone, Dingwall, Ross and Cromarty]

MILIKEN, JAMES, a fisher in Pultneytown, Caithness, accused of mobbing and rioting in 1827. [NRS.AD14.27.218]

MILLER, ALEXANDER, a farm servant of Robert Innes, in Crakaig, Loth, Sutherland, was accused of the culpable homicide of Elizabeth Gunn daughter of Donald Gunn, a carpenter in East Brora, Clyne, on the road from Golspie to Brora and Crakaig in 1847. [NRS.AD14.47.525]

MILLAR, Dr DANIEL, born 1779, died 12 April 1823, husband of Jean Rugg, born 1786, died 14 May 1819, parents of Mrs Ann Falconer in Dartmouth, Nova Scotia. [Wick gravestone, Caithness]

MILLER, DONALD, tenant in Greenequoy, Caithness, versus William Sinclair of Freswick, 1803. [NRS.CS271.624]

MILLER, GEORGE, born 1795, a fish-curer in Forse, died 17 January 1872, husband of Esther Levack, born 1782, died 6 December 1864. [Old Latheron gravestone, Caithness]

MILLER, JAMES, tenant in Greenequoy, Caithness, versus William Sinclair of Freswick, 1803. [NRS.CS271.624]

MILLER, PETER, in Papa Stronsay, Orkney, versus Robert Laing in Strenzie, Stronsay, Orkney, in 1801. [OA.SC11.5.1801.6]

MILLAR, ROBERT, born 1768 in Thurso, Caithness, a merchant, died in Georgia on 26 March 1808. [Savana Death Register] [Colonial Museum and Savanna Advertiser, 29.3.1808]

MILLAR, SAMUEL, son of Christian McKay in Thurso, Caithness, a doctor in St Philip's parish, Charleston, South Carolina, probate 9 June 1795, S.C.

MILLER, WILLIAM, born 1785, with family, from Sutherland, emigrated via Cromarty aboard the Ossian bound for Pictou, Nova Scotia, on 25 June 1821. [Inverness Journal.29 June 1821]

MILLER, ..., master of the Jean of Wick was shipwrecked near Thurso, Caithness, in March 1790. [AJ.2199]

MILNE, ROBERT, fish curer in Cromarty, versus Walter Ross of Nigg in 1829. [NRS.SC24.4A.57]

MITCHELL, GEORGE, Aithsling, Shetland, summons of removal in 1807, [Shetland Archives.SC12.6.1807.6]

MITCHELL, JOHN, a writer in Kirkwall, factor for the deceased William Lindsay of Caldale, Orkney, versus Mrs Catherine Lindsay and John Foreman, jr, a decreet, 1815. [NRS.CS32.12.46]

MOAR, JOHN, born 1851 in Stromness, Orkney, died in Victoria, British Columbia, on 1 December 1896. [Ross Bay gravestone, Vancouver]

MOAR, PETER CLOUSTON, died 1838, son of Jonathan Moar blacksmith in Stromness, Orkney, and brother of Jonathan Moar on Souvies Island, Oregon. [NRS.S/H.1862]

MONRO, WILLIAM, tenant in Achany, Lairg, Sutherland, in 1811. [SHS.8.57]

MONRO, Mrs, of Novar, Ross and Cromarty, died in St Thomas in the East, Jamaica, on 30 August 1823. [EA]

MONTGOMERY, DUNCAN, a distiller and grain dealer in Poyntzfield, Cromarty, sederunt book, 1823-1824. [NRS.CS96.4117]

MOODIE, JOHN, born 1754, a farmer in Setter, died 9 December 1814. [Canisbay gravestone, Caithness]

MOODIE, J. W., from Orkney, and his wife Susanna Strickland, emigrated via Leith to Montreal in 1832. [*Forest Life in Canada*, London, 1852]

MOODIE, THOMAS, born 1 June 1790 in the parish of Walls and Flotta, Orkney, son of James Moodie of Melsetter and his wife Elizabeth Dunbar, a Lieutenant of the 34th Bengal Native Infantry, died in Kali, India, on 27 April 1824, buried at Kalpi, probate 16 June 1824. [BA.3.317]

MORE, DAVID, a blacksmith in North Yell, Shetland, was accused of plundering a Norwegian shipwreck in 1803. [SA.SC12.6.1803.47]

MORE, GEORGE MONRO, son of George Monro, a farmer and corn merchant in Ross-shire, was educated at Marishal College, Aberdeen, around 1856, later an employee of the Standard Bank of South Africa. [MCA.II]

MORGAN, Reverend JOHN, AM, born 1804, minister of Lerwick for 14 years, then minister of St George's, Georgetown, Demerara, for 7 years, died in Lerwick on 28 March 1865. [Lerwick gravestone]

MORRISON, ALEXANDER, from Sutherland, a member of the Scots Charitable Society of Boston, Massachusetts, in 1805. [NEHGS/SCS]

MORRISON, ALEXANDER, born in Eddrachillis, Sutherland, a fisher in Pultneytown, Wick, accused of housebreaking and reset in 1832 in Port Dunbar, Bay of Wick. [NRS.JC26.1832.132]

MORRISON, DONALD, with his wife Catherine McKay, and Peter Morrison, emigrated from Loch Laxford, Sutherland, on the Ellen of Liverpool bound for Pictou, Nova Scotia, on 22 May 1848. [PANS.257.110]

MORRISON, ELIZABETH, with Ann, Alexander, John, and Donald, emigrated from Loch Laxford, Sutherland, on the Ellen of Liverpool bound for Pictou, Nova Scotia, on 22 May 1848. [PANS.257.110]

MORRISON, FINGAL, emigrated from Loch Laxford, Sutherland, on the Ellen of Liverpool bound for Pictou, Nova Scotia, on 22 May 1848. [PANS.257.110]

MORRISON, HECTOR, from Sutherland, a member of the Scots Charitable Society of Boston, Massachusetts, in 1805. [SCS/NEHGS]

MORRISON, HUGH, in Kirkiboll of Tongue, Sutherland, a victim of theft in 1830. [NRS.JC26.1830.90]

MORRISON, Reverend JOHN, in Delting, Shetland, versus Malcolm Stout in Scaista, a petition, 1802. [SA.SC12.6.1802.19]HS.8.227]

MORRISON, JOHN, tenant in Goldpie Mills, Kildonan, Sutherland, in 1808. [SHS.8.227]

MORRISON, JOHN, born 1786 in Eddrachillis, Sutherland, a fisher in Old Shorebeg, Eddrachillis, accused of housebreaking and reset in 1832 in Port Dunbar, Bay of Wick, Caithness. [NRS.JC26.1832.132]

MORISON, JOHN, a shipmaster in Stornaway, died 4 October 1859, father of John Morison in Chicago. [NRS.S/H.1874]

MORRISON, MURDO, emigrated from Loch Laxford, Sutherland, on the Ellen of Liverpool bound for Pictou, Nova Scotia, on 22 May 1848. [PANS.257.110]

MORRISON, RODERICK, from Sutherland, a member of the Scots Charitable Society of Boston, Massachusetts, in 1805. [SCS/NEHGS]

MORRISON, WILLIAM, born 1792, son of Reverend Roderick Morrison and his wife Jane Fraser in Kintail, Wester Ross, died in Demerara on 5 May 1814. [Kiel Duich gravestone]

MORRISON, WILLIAM, in Glenshiel, Ross and Cromarty, a victim of forgery in 1835. [NRS.AD14.35.12; JC26.1835.10]

MORTON and CULLEY, tenants in Invershin, Creich, Sutherland, in 1815. [SHS.221]

MOWAT, ALEXANDER, in Louisburgh, Port Dunbar, Bay of Wick, Caithness, a victim of housebreaking in 1832. [NRS.JC26.1832.132]

MOWAT, ALEXANDER, born 1845, son of Alexander Mowat of the Aberdeen Town and Country Bank in Lybster, Caithness, of the Union Bank of Australia, died at Staffa House, Brisbane, Queensland, Australia, on 19 February 1867. [AJ.6229]

MOWAT, EDWARD, born 1786 in Orphir, Orkney, a Hudson Bay Company employee from 1806 to 1833, later settled on the Red River. [HBRS]

MOWAT, GEORGE, born 1741, a farmer at Papigoe, died June 1803, husband of Christian Plowman, born 1763, died in December 1807. Wick gravestone, Caithness]

MOWAT, JOHN, son of Reverend Hugh Mowat and his wife Elizabeth Baikie, a planter at Orkney Hall, Jamaica, died 1800. [F.7.216]

MOWAT, JOHN, born 1752, tenant farmer in Easter Mey, died 1837. [Canisbay gravestone, Caithness]

MOWAT, JOHN, in the Customs House of Lerwick, Shetland, a letter to a Mr Waddell in 1807. [NRS.GD51.16.36]

MOWAT, WILLIAM, of Gowdie House, Uyeasound, Shetland, letters, 1821. [SA.RH4.35.1.46]

MOWAT, WILLIAM, a farm servant of Robert Innes in Crakaig, Loth, Sutherland, was accused of the culpable homicide of Elizabeth Gunn daughter of Donald Gunn, a carpenter in East Brora, Clyne, on the road from Golspie to Brora and Crakaig in 1847. [NRS.AD14.47.525]

MOUAT, PETER, of Wadbister, Shetland, died in March 1855, brother of Alexander Henderson Mouat in Guelph, Ontario. [NRS.S/H.1877]

MUIR, DAVID, son of David Muir a labourer in Kirkwall, Orkney, accused of robbery and theft in 1838. [NRS.AD14.38.552]

MUIR, STEPHEN, in Howbel, Burness, Orkney, a petition, 1801. [OA.SC11.5.1801.86]

MUNRO, ALEXANDER, with family, from Sutherland, emigrated via Cromarty or Thurso aboard the Prince William bound for Pictou, Nova Scotia, in 1815. [NSARM.mg100, vol.226.30]

MUNRO, ALEXANDER, a wright in Edderton, Ross-shire, accused of cutting and stealing timber in 1817. [NRS.JC26.1817.60]

MUNRO, ALEXANDER ROSE, born 20 May 1835 in Invernald, died in Montreal on 9 August 1869. [Creich gravestone, Sutherland]

MUNRO, ANDREW, born 1823, son of Andrew Munro and his wife Isabella Urquhart, died in San Francisco, California, on 29 June 1852. [Avoch gravestone, Ross and Cromarty]

MUNRO, ANGUS, born 1815, son of George Munro a crofter, a labourer and road-maker in Breekval, Migdale, Creich, Sutherland, was accused of assault in 1829. [NRS.AD14.29.347]

MUNRO, BARBARA, a cattle drover in Pitressie, Dornoch, Sutherland, was accused of fraud in 1843. [NRS.AD14.43.76]

MUNRO, BETTY, born 1829, daughter of Hector Munro and his wife Sarah Mann, died in Northcote, Melbourne, Australia, on 5 September 1906. [Dornoch gravestone, Sutherland]

MUNRO, DAVID, born 1835, son of William and Margaret Munro in Bettyhill, Sutherland, died in Kimberley, South Africa, on 29 June 1901. [Farr gravestone, Sutherland]

MUNRO, DAVID, and his wife Margaret McDonald, parents of Donald Munro who died in Helena, Montana, on 12 November 1886. [Kincardine, Ardgay gravestone, Ross and Cromarty]

MUNRO, DONALD, in Dornoch Tolbooth, accused of stealing sheep in Invershin, Creich, Sutherland, in 1801, banished from Scotland for ten years. [NRS.JC11.45]

MUNRO, DONALD, joint tenant in Skelpick, Farr, in 1811. [SHS.8.112]

MUNRO, DONALD, son of Hector Munro a tenant in Halsary, Watten, Caithness, accused of rioting in 1821. [NRS.AD14.21.82]

MUNRO, GEORGE, second son of Sir Harry Munro of Foulis, Ross and Cromarty, a Customs officer who died in Kingston, Jamaica, on 22 April 1802. [GM.72.686]

MUNRO, GEORGE, tenant in Whitehill, parish of Loth, 1811, also in Knockfin, parish of Kildonan, Sutherland, in 1808, 1811, 1815. [SHS.8.99/226/227/230/231]

MUNROE, Major GEORGE GUNN, of Poyntzfield, Ross-shire, married Jemima Charlotte Graham, widow of Francis Graham of Tulloch Castle, Jamaica, in Richmond on 26 April 1822. [DPCA.1032]; George Gunn Munro versus James Munro in Balichary in 1822. [NRS.SC24.4A.31]

MUNRO, GEORGE, in Tain, Ross-shire, dead by 1832, father of Hugh Munro on Green Island, Jamaica. [NRS.S/H]

MUNRO, HECTOR, born 1801, a tailor in Barbaraville, Kilmuir, Ross-shire, accused of murder in Invergordon in 1830. [NRS.AD14.30.101A]

MUNRO, HECTOR, born 1819, a teacher who died in Australia on 7 October 1890. [Dornoch gravestone, Sutherland]

MUNRO, HECTOR, born 1810, son of George Munro a crofter, a labourer and roadmaker in Breekval, Migdale, Creich, Sutherland, was accused of assault in 1829. [NRS.AD14.29.347]

MUNRO, HUGH, joint tenant in Blarich mill, Rogart, Sutherland, in 1815. [SHS.8.232]

MUNROE, JAMES, born 1769, son of the late Reverend James Munroe of Cromarty, died in Pictou, Nova Scotia, on 1 August 1843. [St Andrews Standard, 17.8.1843]

MUNRO, JAMES, born 1805, a shoemaker in Barbaraville, Kilmuir, Ross-shire, accused of murder in Invergordon in 1830. [NRS.AD14.30.101A; JC26.549]

MUNRO, JOHN, and later William Munro, tenant farmers in Balvellie of Rarichy, Nigg, Ross and Cromarty, a farm rent book 1783-1836. [NRS.GD1.519.1/2]

MUNRO, Captain JOHN, tenant in Kirkton of Golspie, Sutherland, in 1808, and tenant in the parish of Dornoch, Sutherland, in 1815. [SHS.221/224]

MUNRO, Dr JOHN POYNTZ, born 1801 in Sutherland, later in Grenada, died at the house of his brother Captain Hector Munro in Hamilton, Canada West, on 1 September 1851. [AJ.5418]

MUNRO, JOHN, from Kincardine, Easter Ross, settled in Renfrew, Ontario, by 1853. [NLS.Acc.7023]

MUNRO, JOHN, from Creich, Sutherland, married Mary Robinson from Yorkshire, in Windsor, Nova Scotia, in 1867. [S.7583]

MUNRO, Major General JOHN, in Teaninich, Ross-shire, was a victim of rioting, mobbing, and assault at the Caledonian Hotel, Dingwall, in 1837. [NRS.AD14.37.36]

MUNRO, JOHN, born 1831, son of William and Margaret Munro in Bettyhill, Sutherland, died in Kimberley, South Africa, on 8 April 1913. [Farr gravestone]

MUNRO, KENNETH, with family, from Sutherland, emigrated via Cromarty or Thurso aboard the Prince William bound for Pictou, Nova Scotia, in 1815. [NSARM.mg100, vol.226.30]

MUNRO, KENNETH, in Kirkibull, Tongue, Caithness, a victim of theft in 1830. [NRS.JC26.1830.90]

MUNRO, MARY, [1771-1830], daughter of William Munro and his wife Ann Fraser, her birth and baptismal certificates from the United Presbyterian Congregation in Nigg, Ross and Cromarty. [NRS.GD1.958.3]

MUNRO, R. F., born 1800, youngest son of D. Munro at the Bridge of Alness, Ross-shire, died on the Foulis Plantation, Berbice, on 15 July 1830. [S.1120]

MUNRO, ROBERT, born 1793 in Ross-shire, was naturalised in Laurens County, South Carolina, on 19 November 1823. [Citizenship Book, 100]

MUNRO, ROBERT, a cartwright in Jemimaville, Cromarty, accused of mobbing and prison breaking in 1844. [NRS.AD14.44.443]

MUNRO, SUTHERLAND, a joiner in Pultneytown, Wick, Caithness, died 24 August 1855. [NRS.S/H.1879]

MUNRO, THOMAS, a shopkeeper in Dornoch, Sutherland, was accused of fraudulent bankruptcy in 1845. [NRS.AD14.45.124]

MUNRO, WILLIAM, the post carrier between Denbeath and Thurso, Caithness, was accused of the theft of letters on 21 September 1799. [NRS.JC11.44]

MUNRO, WILLIAM, a schoolmaster in Thurso, a letter describing mermaids seen on the coast of Caithness in 1809. [NRS.GD87.2.28]

MUNRO, WILLIAM, in Dornoch, tenant of Davochfin, parish of Dornoch, Sutherland, in 1811. [SHS.8.62]

MUNRO, WILLIAM, sr., tenant in Acheroch and Michaelwells, parish of Dornoch, Sutherland, in 1815. [SHS.8.221]

MUNRO, WILLIAM, tenant in Snottersgill, Watten, Caithness, was accused of rioting in 1821. [NRS.AD14.21.82]

MUNRO, WILLIAM, born 1808, son of George Munro a crofter, a labourer and roadmaker in Breekval, Migdale, Creich, Sutherland, was accused of assault in 1829. [NRS.AD14.29.347]

MUNRO, WILLIAM, of Uppat, tenant of Muiemore and Strathskinsdale, parish of Clyne, Sutherland, in 1811. [SHS.8.91]

MUNRO, WILLIAM, in Dornoch, Sutherland, a sequestration, 1845. [NRS.CS279.1408]

MUNRO, WILLIAM, a merchant and draper in Dornoch, was accused of fraudulent bankruptcy in 1845. [NRS.AD14.45.124]

MUNRO, Colonel, in Pointzfield, tenant of Gruids, Lairg, in 1811. [SHS.8.57]

MUNRO, ..., born in Golspie, Sutherland, sister of William Munro a Lieutenant Colonel in Madras, India, wife of John MacKenzie, died in St Andrews, New Brunswick, in May 1822. [SM]

MURCHISON, DONALD, born in Bochearron, Ross-shire, emigrated to America in 1816, a merchant in Fort Clairborne, Mobile, and in Wilmington, North Carolina, died in Line Creek, Alabama, on 13 November 1819. [Camden Gazette, 30.12.1819]

MURCHISON, DUNCAN, born 1745 in Ross-shire, died in Lancaster, Upper Canada, on 3 June 1831. [Halifax Journal, 6.6.1831]

MURCHESON, JOHN, son of John Murcheson, [1779-1867], and his wife Eliza Mackenzie, [1786-1877], settled in Sommerville, Union County, Oregon. [Kishorn gravestone, Wester Ross]

MURDOCH, JOHN, was appointed master of the Adventure of Wick, Caithness, on 16 December 1794. [DCA.CE70.1.8/96]

MURRAY, A., born 1765, a soldier, with his wife and three children in Corgrain, Culmaily, Sutherland, in 1810. [SHS.1.14/15]

MURRAY, ALEXANDER, born 1784 in Rogart, Sutherland, a private of the 93rd Highlanders who served in St Kitts during 1827-1828. [NRS.RH2.8.97]

MURRAY, ALEXANDER, a joint tenant in Reisk, Lairg, Sutherland, in 1808. [SHS.8.229]

MURRAY, ALEXANDER, was granted a six-year lease of Aultendow, Sutherland, on 29 December 1812. [SHS.9.2/175]

MURRAY, ALEXANDER, joint tenant in Achunoluechrach, Rogart, Sutherland, in 1815. [SHS.8.232]

MURRAY, ALEXANDER, born 1763, a shoemaker, his wife Elizabeth born 1761, son James born 1799, son Donald born 1802, daughter Catherine born 1788, daughter Christian born 1790, daughter Isabella born 1797, from Sutherland, emigrated via Stromness on the Prince of Wales to the Hudson Bay Company settlement at York Fort on 23 June 1815, landed there on 26 August 1815. [PAC.M1659/61] [MG19.E4.1.165/8]

MURRAY, ALEXANDER, born 1794, from Siesgill, Sutherland, emigrated on the Prince of Wales in 1813, landed at Churchill in August 1813, settled on the Red River in 1814, moved to the Holland River in September 1815. [PACAN]

MURRAY, ALEXANDER, a labourer in Resolis, Cromarty, accused of mobbing and prison breaking in 1844. [NRS.AD14.44.443]

MURRAY, ANDREW, born 1765 in Sutherland, died at Cariboo Meadows, Nova Scotia, on 8 November 1841. [Halifax Journal, 13.12.1841]

MURRAY, ANGUS, son of William Murray and his wife Maria Murray, settled in Dunrobin Plains, Van Diemen's Land, [Tasmania], Australia, before 1841. [Clyne, Kirkton, gravestone, Sutherland]

MURRAY, ANGUS, born 1828, son of Robert Murray and his wife Margaret Gay, died in India on 19 November 1860. [Dornoch gravestone, Sutherland]

MURRAY, CATHERINE, in Dornoch, Sutherland, a victim of theft in 1829. [NRS.AD14.29.132]

MURRAY, DAVID, [1788-1844], and his wife Janet McDonald, [1789-1873], parents of Hugh Murray who settled in Ontario. [Loth, Brora, gravestone, Sutherland]

MURRAY, DONALD, born 1809, a mason in Resolis, Cromarty, accused of mobbing and prison breaking in 1844. [NRS.AD14.44.443]

MURRAY, DONALD, born 1849, son of Donald Murray and his wife Jane Munro, died in Quilchena, British Columbia, on 22 August 1897. [Dornoch gravestone, Sutherland]

MURRAY, HUGH, emigrated from Cromarty or Thurso aboard the Lady Grey bound for Pictou, Nova Scotia, in June 1841. [NRS.RH1.2.908]

MURRAY, HUGH, son of David Murray, [1788-1844], and his wife Janet Mc Donald, [1789-1873], settled in Ontario. [Loth, Brora, gravestone, Sutherland]

MURRAY, JAMES, tacksman of Greentoft, Eday, Orkney, versus Magnus Eunson a butcher in Kirkwall in 1810. [NRS.SC11.5.1810.4]

MURRAY, JANE, third daughter of Benjamin Murray in Thurso, Caithness, married John Oal a distiller, in Halifax, Nova Scotia, on 2 October 1846. [AJ.5156]

MURRAY, JEAN, born 1776, with family, from Sutherland, emigrated via Cromarty aboard the Ossian bound for Pictou, Nova Scotia, on 25 June 1821. [Inverness Journal.29 June 1821]

MURRAY, JOHN, born 1730, with his son born 1775, a weaver, and daughter born 1784, in Loanmore, Culmaily, Sutherland, in 1810. [SHS.1.14/15]

MURRAY, JOHN, born 1774, with his wife and five children in Culmaily, Sutherland, in 1810. [SHS.1.14/15]

MURRAY, JOHN, born 1792, brother Alexander born 1794, from Siesgill, Sutherland, emigrated via Stromness on the Prince of Wales to the Hudson Bay Company settlement at Fort Churchill on 29 June 1813. [PAC.M155.165-8]

MURRAY, JOHN, tenant in Balnadielson, Lairg, Sutherland, in 1815. [SHS.8.229]

MURRAY, JOHN, a merchant grocer and innkeeper in Thurso, Caithness, 1819. [NRS.CS223.SEQN.M2.52]

HARLES, a merchant and shipowner in Lerwick, Shetland, er Brown, son of Edward Brown formerly a farmer in Unst, later in Lerwick, re a violation of indenture in 1809. .1809.26]

RRY, a merchant in Lerwick, Shetland, in 1841. 1841.64]

N, of Quarff and Gossaburgh, born 1800, died 31 October k gravestone, Shetland]

GE, born 1836, son of George Oliver and his wife er, died in Australia on 8 December 1870. [Clyne Kirkton therland]

son of Thomas Oliver, [1797-1865], and his wife Hannah 0-1866], settled in New Zealand. [Tongue gravestone,

EW, born 1800, Sheriff Officer in Lerwick, Shetland, , husband of Elizabeth Hunter, born 1800, died 6 May avestone, Shetland]

a soldier of the Shetland Fencibles, versus Gilbert Delting, 1798, re the drowning of the petitioner's 98.31]

kipper in Stromness, Orkney, a sasine, 1792. -289]

stshore, Deerness, versus Thomas Cromarty in , re alimony, 1839. [OA.SC11.5.1839.74]

chant in Stromness, Orkney, 1805. 1]

ipmaster from Orkney, died 4 February 1829, idow of William McLeod Mackay a planter in H.1879]

Stromness, Orkney, relict of Charles Gregory a County, Virginia, a sasine, 1792.

MURRAY, JOHN, born 1797 in Sutherland, a carpenter, emigrated via Greenock to the USA, was naturalised in New York in 1827. [NARA]

MURRAY, JOHN, emigrated from Cromarty or Thurso aboard the Lady Grey bound for Pictou, Nova Scotia, in June 1841. [NRS.RH1.2.908]

MURRAY, JOHN, from Rogart, Sutherland, and Christy, daughter of Hugh McLeod of Hardwood Hill, Pictou, were married at Rogers Hill, Nova Scotia, on 9 January 1840. [Times, 28.1.1840]

MURRAY, JOHANNA, born 1828, daughter of Donald Murray and his wife Betsy Gordon, wife of Hugh McKenzie, died in Melbourne, Australia, on 5 November 1856. [Dornoch gravestone, Sutherland]

MURRAY, MARGARET, born 1780, with her daughter, in Sallichtown, Culmaily, Sutherland, in 1810. [SHS.1.14/15]

MURRAY, MARGARET, born 1791, with family, from Sutherland, emigrated via Cromarty aboard the Ossian bound for Pictou, Nova Scotia, on 25 June 1821. [Inverness Journal.29 June 1821]

MURRAY, MARGARET, a widow in Dornoch, Sutherland, letters by the Inspector of the Poor, 1845-1848. [NRS.SC9.74]

MURRAY, PETER, from Sutherland, settled in Earltown, Nova Scotia, in 1815. [History of Tatamagouche, 1917]

MURRAY, PETER, born 1826, son of Robert Murray and his wife Jane Munro, died in Pictou, Nova Scotia, on 16 November 1861. [Dornoch gravestone, Sutherland]

MURRAY, ROBERT, son of John Murray, [1780-1852], and his wife Betsy Murray, [1794-1875], settled in Marybank, Otago, New Zealand. [Dornoch gravestone, Sutherland]

MURRAY, ROBERT, a tailor from Sutherland, settled in Earltown, Nova Scotia, in 1815. [History of Tatamagouche, 1917]

MURRAY, ROBERT, born 1782 in Sutherland, a tailor in Charleston, South Carolina, was naturalised there on 8 February 1825. [NARA.M1183.1]

MURRAY, ROBERT, born 1784 in Sutherland, settled in Charleston, S.C. in 1819, died on 29 August 1831. [Unitarian gravestone, Charleston]

MURRAY, ROBERT, born 1785 in Sutherland, a tailor in Charleston, South Carolina, was naturalised there on 15 July 1831. [NARA.M1183.1]

MURRAY, ROBERT, in Edderton House near Tain, Ross-shire, versus Eagle and Henderson nursery and seedsmen in Edinburgh in 1820. [NRS.CS40.35.78]

MURRAY, ROBERT, born 1841, son of Robert Murray and his wife Isabel Allen, an employee of the Union Bank of Australia, died in Adelaide, South Australia, on 8 May 1877. [Golspie gravestone, Sutherland]

MURRAY, WILLIAM, from Sutherland, settled in Earltown, Nova Scotia, in 1815. [History of Tatamagouche, 1917]

MURRAY, WILLIAM, jr., a banker in Tain, Ross and Cromarty, trustee for Charles Smith in Golspie, Sutherland, in 1824. [NRS.CS96.1258]

MURRAY, WILLIAM, in Ardmore, Tain, Ross and Cromarty, letters, 1827-1828. [NRS.GD129.2.90]

MURRAY, WILLIAM, son of Robert Murray and his wife Jane Munro, a merchant in Halifax, Nova Scotia, who was drowned in the City of Boston off Halifax on 28 January 1870. [Dornoch gravestone, Sutherland]

MURSON, MARGARET, born 1812, a servant in Kirk Stile, Lybster, Caithness, accused of housebreaking and theft in 1828. [NRS.AD14.28.279]

NEALL, WILLIAM, with family, from Sutherland, emigrated via Cromarty or Thurso aboard the Prince William bound for Pictou, Nova Scotia, in 1815. [NSARM.mg100, vol.226.30]

NEVAN, ROBERT, of Windhouse, versus William Mouat, servant to Charles Scott, a merchant in Gardie, Mid Yell, Shetland, in 1792. [SA.SC12.6.1792.16]

NICOL, DAVID, tacksman of Duartman, versus John Reid a writer in Thurso, Caithness, 1803. [NRS.CS271.818]

NICOLL, JAMES, a house carpenter, builder, and contractor from Tain, Ross and Cromarty, settled in Canada by 1825. [NRS.242.70.2.283]

NICOLSON, GILBERT, born 1776, died
gravestone, Shetland]

NICOLSON, JAMES, a Captain of the
[NRS.R.S.Shetland.587]

NICOLSON, JAMES, born 16 June
wife Elizabeth Balfour, a Captain
19 February 1835 in Mussoorie,

NICOL, or NICOLSON, JAMES,
accused of taking part in the
[NRS.AD14.47.533]

NICOLSON, JOHN, a farmer
attempted with removal b
1820. [NRS.GD136.283]

NICOLSON, WILLIAM, a
Shetland, versus Capta
American ship George
1807. [SA.SC12.6.180

NICHOLSON, THOM
1856, father of Wil

NISBET, MAGNUS
Lieutenant Willia
1807. [SA.SC12.

NORN, SAMUE
Company Ser
1886. [Ross

OAL, DANIE
of Freswic

OAL, SIN
16 April

OAL, W
Sincla

OGILVY,
versus Pe
Shetland,
[SA.SC12.6

OGILVY, H
[SA.SC.12.6

OGILVY, JOH
1840. [Lerwi

OLIVER, GEO
Elizabeth Turn
gravestone, Su

OLIVER, JOHN,
Charleton, [179
Sutherland]

OLLASON, ANDR
died in May 1872
1882. [Bressay gr

OMAND, GILBERT
Manson in Quam,
dog. [SA.SC12.6.17

OMAND, HARRY, a
[NRS.R.S.Orkney.28

OMAND, JEAN, in W
Sty, Deerness, Orkne

OMAND, JOHN, a me
[NRS.CS230.SEQN.O.1

OMAND, MAGNUS, a s
father of Ann Omand,
the West Indies. [NRS.S

OMAND, MARGARET, in
skipper in Prince George
[NRS.R.S.Orkney.288-289

PATTON, ROBERT, a writer in Kirkwall, Orkney, day book, 1825-1827. [NRS.CS96.3794]

PATTON, WILLIAM, a baker in Kirkwall, Orkney, versus versus Reverend William Grant in Cross and Burness parish, Sanday, in 1825. [OA.SC11.5.125.71]

PAUL, JOHN, born 1788, died in Buckies on 25 November 1856, and his wife Margaret Henderson, born 1790, died 1 March 1878, parents of Margaret Paul, born 1836, died in Quincy, Gadsden County, Florida, on 7 September 1872. [Halkirk gravestone, Caithness]

PEACE, JAMES, in North Skaill, Burness, Orkney, a petition, 1801. [OA.SC11.5.1801.86]

PEACE, JOHN POLLEXFEN, and his wife Margaret Bell, were parents of Edward Peace, born 1859, died in Kalgoorlie, Western Australia, on 22 May 1924. [St Magnus gravestone Kirkwall, Orkney]

PEACE, JOHN POLLEXFEN, and his wife Margaret Bell, were parents of Williamina Bell Peace, born 1859, died in Kalgoorlie, Western Australia, on 22 May 1924. [St Magnus gravestone Kirkwall, Orkney], and of Williamina Bell Peace, born 1859, died in Perth, Western Australia, on 22 May 1924. [Lady gravestone, Stronsay, Orkney]

PEACE, WILLIAM, a bookseller and publisher in Kirkwall, Orkney, letter-book, 1863-1864. [NRS.CS96.4850]

PENANT, JANET, from Uyea Sound, Unst, Shetland a prisoner in Lerwick Tolbooth, petitioned to be banished rather than imprisonment in 1819. [SA.SC12.6.1819.22]

PENDRITH, DONALD G., son of Alexander Pendrith a farmer in Golspie, Sutherland, was educated at Marischal College in 1846, a Licentiate of the Royal College of Surgeons in Edinburgh in 1849, and a surgeon of the Royal Navy. [MCA]

PERRY, ISABELLA, born 1765, a midwife from Caithness, was naturalised in South Carolina on 19 March 1805. [NARA.M1183.1]

PETERKIN, JOHN, a house carpenter in Invergordon, Ross and Cromarty, dead by 1843, father of William Peterkin in America. [NRS.S/H]

PETTERSON, CATHERINE, born 1836 in Orkney, died in Victoria, British Columbia, on 19 February 1889. [Ross Bay gravestone, B.C.]

PETERSON, JAMES, a watchmaker in Lerwick, Shetland, a victim of housebreaking and theft in 1836. [NRS.AD14.36.4]

PETERSON, MAGNUS, tenant in Ham, Foula, Shetland, a summons of removal in 1804. [SA.SC12.6.1804.6]

PETTRIE, JOHN, a sailor in South Ronaldsay, Orkney, a sasine, 1795. [NRS.R.S.Orkney.350]

POLE, ROBERT, a merchant in Infield, Shetland, sederunt books, 1813-1815. [NRS.CS96.3498-3499]

POLLOXPEN, MARGARET, relict of James Stewart in Kirkwall, Orkney, a petition, 1803. [OA.SC11.5.1803.74]

POLSON, ALEXANDER, born 1779, a wheelwright, his wife Catherine Mathewson, born 1785, son Hugh born 1805, son John born 1810, son Donald born 1814, daughter Ann born 1808, from Sutherland, emigrated via Stromness on the <u>Prince of Wales</u> to the Hudson Bay Company settlement at York Fort on 23 June 1815, landed there on 26 August 1815. [PAC.M1659/61] [MG19.E4.1.165/8]

POLSON, DONALD, a tenant in Torrish, Kildonan, Sutherland, was accused of rioting, resulting from the removal or eviction of tenants in Kildonan in 1813. [NRS.AD14.13.9; SC9.7.64] [SHS.8.136]

POLSON, GEORGE, in Grudseray, was accused to rioting in Kildonan, Sutherland, in 1813. [SHS.8.136]

POLSON, JOHN, in Golspie, Sutherland, wrote to the Justice of the Peace recommending that William Matheson be appointed fox-hunter for the parishes of Clyne and Golspie, on 26 April 1804. [NRS.JP32.7.5]

POLSON, JOHN, joint tenant in Easter Aberscross, Golspie, Sutherland, in 1808, 1811, 1815. [SHS.8.89/226/227]

POLSON, WILLIAM, in Thurso, Caithness, a victim of theft in 1830. [NRS.JC26.1830.90]

POPE, ROBERT, tenant in Cain, Kilfedder, Kildonan, Sutherland, in 1808.and his heirs in 1815. [SHS.8.226/227]

POPE, WILLIAM, tenant in Culgower, parish of Loth, Sutherland, in 1808. [SHS.8.230]

POTTINGER, ARCHIBALD, a skipper in Stromness, a sasine, 1797. [NRS.R.S.Orkney.393]

POTTINGER, GEORGE, born 1823 in Westray, Orkney, a teacher who settled in Victoria, British Columbia, in 1864, died there on 15 December 1906. [Ross Bay gravestone, B.C.]

POTTINGER, ISABELLA, born 1828 in Kirkwall, Orkney, settled in Victoria, British Columbia, in 1864, died there on 24 May 1894. [Ross Bay gravestone, B.C.]

POTTINGER, WILLIAM, born 1814 in Westray, Orkney, a labourer in Hudson Bay Company Service who settled in Victoria, British Columbia, in 1851, died there on 19 March 1887. [Ross Bay gravestone, B.C.]

RAE, ISABELLA, former servant of Alexander McDonald a shepherd in Badnohacklash of Strathmore, Durness, Sutherland, was accused of child murder in 1816. [NRS.JC26.1816.8]

RAE, JOHN, of Gorseness, Orkney, died 6 October 1867, brother of Margaret Rae or Wygart and of Louisa Rae or Myrick both in Portland, Oregon, also of John Rae in North America. [NRS.S/H.1870]

RAE, WILLIAM GLEN, born 1812 in Stromness, son of John Rae in Wyre, Orkney, an employee of the Hudson Bay Company from 1827 to 1845, in Yerba Buena, California, in 1841, died in San Francisco on 19 January 1848, probate June 1849, PCC. [TNA][HBRS.4.355][SHR.153/144]

RAMSAY, ANDREW, son of Reverend David Ramsay in Mill Street, Kirkwall, Orkney, was accused of robbery and theft in 1838. [NRS.AD14.38.552]

RAMSAY, GILBERT, a tenant in Raefirth, Mid Yell, Shetland, summons of removal, 1800. [SA.SC12.6.1800.17]

RAE, WILLIAM GLEN, born 1809 in Stromness, Orkney, son of John Rae, a Hudson Bay Company employee from 1827 until 1845, he died in San Francisco on 19 January 1845. [HBRS.4.355]

RAMSAY, JAMES, a tenant in Gardie, Mid Yell, Shetland, summons of removal, 1800. [SA.SC12.6.1800.17]

RAMSAY, JOHN, born 1780 on Whalsay, Shetland, a Captain of the 21st Bengal Native Infantry, died at Brijetolla, Calcutta, India, on 20 August 1818. [BA.3.602]

RANDALL, HUGH, born 1803, a stonemason in High Street, Kirkwall, Orkney, with wife Margaret born 1803, emigrated to South Australia in 1848. [BPP.11.166]

RANNIE, JOHN, born 1829 in Walls, Orkney, son of John Rannie a schoolmaster, educated at King's College, Aberdeen, a minister in Ontario from 1859 to 1876, then a minister in British Guiana from 1876 to 1904, died in Essex, England in 1910. [F.7.673]

REED, DORA, youngest daughter of Ralph Reed in Skelpick, Sutherland, married Robert Forsyth, engineer to the Montreal Harbour Commission, at St Andrew's Church in Quebec on 10 September 1856. [AJ.5673]

REIACH, ALEXANDER, born 1753, tenant in Staxigoe, died 28 April 1819, husband of Margaret Craig, born 1756, died 9 November 1829. [Wick gravestone, Caithness]

REID, EPHEMIA, from Kildonan, Sutherland, married Robert Jardine in St John, New Brunswick, on 30 October 1834. [New Brunswick Courier, 1.11.1834]

REID, GABRIEL, applied for the lease of part of the Pollyour Lot in Sutherland in 1812. [SHS.9/2.175]

REID, GEORGE, an apprentice of William Burns a wright in Kirkwall, Orkney, accused of theft in 1820. [NRS.JC26.1820.101]

REID, JAMES, a shipowner in Stornaway, contractor for mail between Stornaway and Poolewe, Wester Ross, in 1829. [NRS.GD46.13.10]

REID, JAMES MURRAY, born 1803 in Orkney, in Hudson Bay Company Service from 1836, settled in Victoria, British Columbia Service in 1853, died there on 24 April 1868. [Ross Bay gravestone, B.C.]

REID, JEAN, tenant in Garth, Foula, Shetland, a summons of removal in 1804. [SA.SC12.6.1804.6]

REID, JOHN, a writer, cattle, fish, and victual dealer in Thurso, Caithness, in 1817. [NRS.CS227.SEQN.R1.37]

RENDALL, ANN, born 1824 in Orkney, died in Victoria, British Columbia, on 10 July 1908. [Ross Bay gravestone, B.C.]

RENDALL, JOHN, of Ingsay, sold Ingsay on Birsay, and Vestaben on Harray, to Mrs Christian Johnston, widow of John Robertson, a merchant in Stromness, Orkney, in 1819. [NRS.CS230.R8.47]

RENDALL, ROBERT SINCLAIR, born 1826 in Westray, Orkney, died in Victoria, British Columbia, on 29 January 1910. [Ross Bay gravestone]

RENDALL, WILLIAM, a merchant on Sanday, Orkney, versus Reverend William Grant in Cross and Burness parish, Sanday, in 1825. [OA.SC11.5.125.68]

RICHAN, WILLIAM, in Rapness, Westray, Orkney, versus Andrew Dreaver in Yarpha, Deerness, in 1801. [OA.SC11.5.1801.23]

RINDLE, JOHN, master of the Margaret of Kirkwall, Orkney, in 1797. [DCA.CE70.1.8/52]

RITCHIE, CHARLES, born 1848, a farm manager in Orkney, settled in Saltcoats, North West Territory, Canada, in 1888, [BPP.9.484]

ROBERTSON, ADAM, residing with Andrew Robertson in Trusta, Aithsting, Shetland, a victim of sheep-stealing in 1837. [NRS.AD14.37.471; JC26.1837.534]

ROBERTSON, ARCHIBALD, fifth son of Charles Robertson of Kindeace, Ross-shire, died in Demerara in 1795. [SM.57.133]

ROBERTSON, Lieutenant ALLAN, former Sheriff Clerk of Caithness, then Paymaster of the 2nd West Indian Regiment, died in Spanish Town, Jamaica, on 1 August 1849. [AJ.5307]

ROBERTSON, Mrs BARBARA OGILVY, wife of John Ogilvy of Quarff, Shetland, a contract with Olla Thomason, a sailor in Swarrister, Shetland, in 1839. [SA.SC12.250.1839.2]

ROBERTSON, DONALD, [1841-1882], and his wife Christine Fraser, [1843-1879], parents of Roderick Robertson who settled in Chicago, Illinois. [Dornoch gravestone, Sutherland]

ROBERTSON, DUNCAN, was a victim of rioting, mobbing, and assault at the Caledonian Hotel, Dingwall, Ross and Cromarty, in 1837. [NRS.AD14.37.36]

ROBERTSON, GILBERT, late in Demerara, son of Reverend Dr Robertson of Kiltearn, died in Edinburgh on 10 September 1839. [AJ.4784]

ROBERTSON, HENRY, a merchant in Voe, Walls, Shetland, versus James Robertson on Foula, a breach of contract, 1808. [SA.SC12.6.1808.33]

ROBERTSON, JAMES, of the Hudson Bay Company, a sasine, 7 October 1807. [NRS.R.S.Orkney.730]

ROBERTSON, JAMES, a tenant farmer on Hill of Fortrose, dead by 1832, father of John Robertson a baker in Philadelphia. [NRS.S/H]

ROBERTSON, JAMES, tenant in Lyking, Orkney, versus John Robertson of Ness, eldest son of Mrs Christian Johnston or Robertson, a ship agent in Stromness, a decreet, 1838. [NRS.CS46.1838.1/15]

ROBERTSON, or JAMESON, JOHN, born 1787, a fisherman in Aith, Aithsting, Shetland, was accused of theft from a stranded ship in 1816. [NRS.AD14.16.26]

ROBERTSON, JOHN, from Orkney a Hudson Bay Company employee from 1805 until 1830, then settled in Canada. [HBRS.2.239]

ROBERTSON, JOHN, born on Evie, Orkney, a Hudson Bay Company employee from 1805 until his death on the Berens River, Winnipeg, in 1828. [HBRS.2.240]

ROBERTSON, JOHN, late in Keanchilish of Coygash, tenant in Knockan, parish of Assynt, Sutherland, in 1808, and 1811. [SHS.8.48/216]

ROBERTSON, JOHN, a baker in Edinburgh, later in USA, a sasine, Fortrose, Ross-shire, 1832. [NRS.R.S.Fortrose.1/103]

ROBERTSON, MAGNUS, in Clusta, Aithsting, Shetland, a summons of removal in 1807. [SA.SC12.6.1807.16]; born 1776, a tenant farmer in Clusta, was accused of theft from a stranded ship in 1816. [NRS.AD14.16.26]

ROBERTSON, WILLIAM FORBES, born 1828, son of Reverend William Robertson in Rosehall, died in Montreal on 8 July 1849. [AJ.5301]

ROSE, ALEXANDER, a surgeon, son of John Rose the Customs Collector in Thurso, Caithness, died in Berbice on 23 August 1802. [EA.4066.02];

ROSE, ALEXANDER, son of William Rose in Dornoch, Sutherland, died in Darien, Georgia, on 20 May 1819. [S.131.19] [EA.5805]

ROSE, ANNE, second daughter of Edward Clouston in Stromness, married Augustus E. Pelly at York Factory, Hudson Bay, on 28 August 1849. [AJ.5324]

ROSE, DAVID, son of Ludovic Rose minister in Tain, Ross and Cromarty, was educated at Marischal College, Aberdeen, in 1844. [MCA]

ROSE, HUGH, son of John Rose of Ardnagrask, Ross-shire, settled in Demerara, died in North America in 1825. [S.593.591]

ROSE, JAMES H., second son of William B. Rose of Rhinie, Ross-shire, died in Markham, Upper Canada, on 28 March 1840. [EEC.20063]

ROSE, JOHN, from Petty, was educated at King's College, Aberdeen in 1840, later minister at Rosskeen, Ross and Cromarty. [KCA]

ROSE, MARGARET BAILLIE, born 18 July 1833 in Nigg, Ross and Cromarty, daughter of Reverend Lewis Rose and his wife Katherine Simpson, married Donald Archibald McLeod, died in Australia. [F.7.73]

ROSE, NANCY, from Caithness, married John Stirling from Halifax, Nova Scotia, there on 31 October 1825. [Acadian Recorder, 5.11.1825]

ROSE, PATRICK, a writer in Dingwall, Ross and Cromarty, versus James Alexander of Aignish, Isle of Lewis, 1839. [NRS.CS46.1839.7.204.1]

ROSE, ROBERT, son of John Rose of Ormly, died in Demerara on 11 January 1805. [SM.67.565]

ROSE, WILLIAM, tenant in Achinchanter, Dornoch, Sutherland, in 1815. [SHS.221]

ROSE, Mr, a storekeeper, a tenant in Cyderhall, Dornoch, Sutherland, in 1811. [SHS.8.61]

ROSIE, EDWARD, of Sucquoy, Sandwick, South Ronaldsay, Orkney, grandfather of Edward James Rosie in Norfolk, Virginia, a sasine, 1803. [NRS.R.S.Orkney.511]

ROSIE, LACHLAN, a fisherman at Duncansby, Caithness, was murdered in 1829. [NRS.JC26.1829.85]

ROSIE, MURDOCH, born 1791, from Bura, Orkney, emigrated via Stornaway on the Prince of Wales to the Hudson Bay Company settlement on the Red River in 1811. [PAC.M155.145]

ROSIER, or ROSS, EDWARD, in Sucquoy, South Ranaldsay, Orkney, dead by 1801. [NRS.S/H]

ROSS, ALEXANDER, born 1792 in Golspie, Sutherland, died at The Thicket, McIntosh County, Georgia, in 1819. [Darien Gazette, 24.5.1819]

ROSS, ALEXANDER, in Invergordon, Ross-shire, was a victim of rioting, mobbing, and assault at the Caledonian Hotel, Dingwall, in 1837. [NRS.AD14.37.36]

ROSS, ANDREW, a mailer in Tornabrock, Edderton, Ross-shire, accused of wilful fire-raising in 1822. [NRS.AD14.1822.138]

ROSS, ANGUS, in Golspie, tenant in Craggymore, Rogart, in 1811. [SHS.8.79]

ROSS, ANGUS, in Baderchuie, Sutherland, a victim of assault in 1829. [NRS.AD14.29.347]

ROSS, ANGUS BETHUNE, born 1812, eldest son of Reverend Donald Ross in Loth, Sutherland, died on Plantation Penitence, Demerara, on 9 June 1841. [AJ.4884]

ROSS, ANN, born 1807, daughter of William Ross and his wife William Cameron in Clyne, died in Quebec in 1868. [Loth, Brora, gravestone]

ROSS, or IRVINE, BARBARA, at Uyea Sound, Unst, Shetland, 1840. [NRS.CS279.1129]

ROSS, BATHEA, daughter of Donald G. Ross of Balmachore, Fearn, married a farmer in Lancaster, Canada, on 16 May 1851. [AJ.5401]

ROSS, CATHERINE ROSE, daughter of Hugh Rose Ross of Cromarty, married Thomas Knox Holmes, in Brussels, Belgium, on 17 July 1848. [AJ.5246][EEC.21686]

ROSS, CHARLES, from Alness, Ross and Cromarty, was educated at King's College, Aberdeen, in 1846, later a minister in Aberdeen and in Tobermory. [KCA]

ROSS, CHARLES, master of the Emerald Isle, fourth son of Charles Ross in Cromarty, died in Matantas, Cuba, on 15 October 1861. [S.1986]

ROSS, CHRISTINE, born 1801, from Sutherland, emigrated via Cromarty aboard the Ossian bound for Pictou, Nova Scotia, on 25 June 1821. [Inverness Journal.29 June 1821]

ROSS, COLIN, born 1800, a fisher in Ullapool, Wester Ross, was accused of rioting in 1833. [NRS.AD14.33.117]

ROSS, DAVID, a cooper in Pultneyton, Wick, died 23 May 1822, father of John Ross in New Brunswick. [NRS.S/H]

ROSS, DAVID, with family, emigrated from Rhilochan, Rogart, Sutherland, to Canada in 1829. [NLS.313.878]

ROSS, DONALD, born 1802, from Sutherland, emigrated via Cromarty aboard the Ossian bound for Pictou, Nova Scotia, on 25 June 1821. [Inverness Journal.29 June 1821]

ROSS, DONALD, born in Sutherland, a merchant in Halifax, Nova Scotia, a letter, 1865. [NLS.ms2626, fo.132]

ROSS, DONALD, born 1813, in Rosebank, Dornoch, Sutherland, was accused of forgery in 1844. [NRS.AD14.44.475]

ROSS, DONALD, was accused of cattle stealing from Alexander Craig's farms at Kirkton and Craigton, Golspie, Sutherland, was outlawed in 1829. [NRS.JC26.1829.77]

ROSS, DONALD, was found guilty of theft in Tongue, Sutherland, in 1830, and sentenced to seven years transportation but the sentence was remitted on 11 November 1830. [NRS.JC26.1830.90]

ROSS, DONALD, son of Reverend Thomas Ross and his wife Jane Mackenzie at Loch Broom, Wester Ross, died in New York on 8 January 1853. [F.7.159]

ROSS, DONALD, emigrated from Cromarty or Thurso aboard the Lady Grey bound for Pictou, Nova Scotia, in June 1841. [NRS.RH1.2.908]

ROSS, DONALD, a dyker on Hill of Fortrose, Ross-shire, dead by 1855, father of Roderick Ross in Canada. [NRS.S/H]

ROSS, DONALD, a cooper in Invergordon, Ross and Cromarty, died 12 September 1856, father of William Ross in Wilton, Waseca County, Minnesota. [NRS.S/H.1869]

ROSS, DUNCAN, born 1770 in Ross-shire, died at the West River, Pictou, Nova Scotia, on 25 October 1834. [Halifax Journal, 10.11.1834]

ROSS, DUNCAN, born 5 February 1831 in Contin, Ross-shire, son of Henry Ross and his wife Anne McKay, educated at King's College, Aberdeen in 1851, emigrated to New South Wales, Australia, in 1856, a minister there, died 10 January 1901. [F.7.597]

ROSS, FINLAY, born 1740 in Ross-shire, emigrated to New York in 1773, moved to Canada in 1783, died in Charlottenburg, Upper Canada, on 13 February 1830. [New Brunswick, Royal Gazette, 10.3.1830]

ROSS, GEORGE, in Dornoch Tolbooth, guilty of sheep stealing, was banished from Scotland for ten years in 1801. [NRS.JC11.45]

ROSS, GEORGE, a distiller at Culaig, later in Ullapool, Wester Ross, a tenant in Assynt, Sutherland, in 1811. [SHS.8.54]

ROSS, GEORGE, with family, emigrated from Achlomliny, Rogart, Sutherland, to Canada in 1829. [NLS.313.878]

ROSS, GEORGE, from Assynt, Sutherland, married Mary Sutherland, in Louisburg, Nova Scotia, on 3 September 1838. [AJ.4731]

ROSS, GEORGE, emigrated via Scrabster, Caithness, on board the Superior of Peterhead, bound for Pictou, Nova Scotia, landed there in June 1842. [Pictou Observer, 21.6.1842]

ROSS, GORDON, schoolmaster of Strathbrora, Sutherland, emigrated to Pictou, Nova Scotia, in 1820.

ROSS, HENRY, a writer in Lerwick, Shetland, dead by 1808, father of John Ross in Charleston, South Carolina. [NRS.S/H]

ROSS, HORATIO, in Tollie, Roskeen, was a victim of rioting, mobbing, and assault at the Caledonian Hotel, Dingwall, Ross and Cromarty, in 1837. [NRS.AD14.37.36]

ROSS, HUGH, joint tenant in Milnclaren, Lairg, Sutherland, in 1815. [SHS.8.229]

ROSS, HUGH, emigrated from Cromarty or Thurso aboard the Lady Grey bound for Pictou, Nova Scotia, in June 1841. [NRS.RH1.2.908]

ROSS, HUGH, and his wife Mary Forbes, parents of William Ross, born 1861, died in Hawaii on 1 April 1895. [Kincardine, Ardgay gravestone, Sutherland]

ROSS, JAMES, born 1785 in the Shetland Islands, settled in Charleston, South Carolina, was naturalised there on 25 March 1823. [NARA.M1183.1]

ROSS, Captain JAMES, born in Lerwick, a shipmaster in Charleston, South Carolina, since 1826, died in 1856. [Old Scots gravestone, S.C.]

ROSS, JAMES, from Burray, Orkney, a boatman in Hudson Bay Company service at Peace River in 1802. [OL.ms2e1.5]

ROSS, JAMES, of Quarff Lodge, Shetland, a bond of provision in 1805. [SA.SC12.50.1805.4]

ROSS, JAMES, second son of William Ross the tacksman of Duochorly, Ross-shire, died in Jamaica on 14 November 1822. [DPCA.1074]

ROSS, JAMES, son of John Ross, [1810-1867], a carpenter in Brora, Sutherland, and his wife Ann Ross, [1817-1898], died in New Zealand. [Invershin gravestone, Sutherland]

ROSS, JAMES, son of William Ross the tacksman of Knockshorty, Ross-shire, died in Jamaica on 4 November 1822. [DPCA.1074]

ROSS, JAMES, a tailor in Lower Lairg, Sutherland, was accused of rioting in 1821. [NRS.AD14.21.93]

ROSS, JAMES, a tenant farmer in Guids, Sutherland, was accused of rioting in 1821. [NRS.AD14.21.93]

ROSS, JAMES, emigrated from Cromarty or Thurso aboard the Lady Grey bound for Pictou, Nova Scotia, in June 1841. [NRS.RH1.2.908]

ROSS, JEAN, daughter of Donald Ross the Chief Factor of the Hudson Bay Company, married Reverend James Hunter of Cumberland Station at Norway House, Hudson Bay, on 10 July 1848. [SG.1766]

ROSS, JOHN, born 29 January 1729 in Tain, Ross and Cromarty, son of Murdoch Ross and Catherine Simpson his wife, emigrated to Philadelphia in 1763, a merchant, married Clementina Cruikshank on 8 December 1768, died in Philadelphia, Pennsylvania, on 8 April 1800. [AP]

ROSS, JOHN, born 1750, with his wife and three children, in Sallichtown, Culmaily, Sutherland, in 1810. [SHS.1.14/15]

ROSS, JOHN, born 1776, died in Nigg, Berbice, on 16 July 1807. [SM.68.958]

ROSS, JOHN, born 1783, son of Henry Ross a writer in Lerwick, Shetland, a merchant in Charleston, South Carolina, was naturalised there on 24 August 1810, there in 1818. [NARA.M1183.1] [NRS.S/H; CS17.1.38/359]

ROSS, JOHN, born 1739, son of Thomas Ross a shoemaker in Cromarty, a mariner, died on 26 February 1794. [Cromarty gravestone]

ROSS. JOHN, a tenant in Cloggin of Muy, Rogart, Sutherland, accused of sheep stealing in 1817. [NRS.JC26.1817.34]

ROSS, JOHN, was accused of cattle stealing from Alexander Craig's farms at Kirkton and Craigton, Golspie, Sutherland, was outlawed in 1829. [NRS.JC26.1829.77]

ROSS, JOHN, emigrated from Cromarty or Thurso aboard the Lady Grey bound for Pictou, Nova Scotia, in June 1841. [NRS.RH1.2.908]

ROSS, JOHN, a farm servant of Charles Hood at Inver Brora, Clyne, Sutherland, was accused of the culpable homicide of Elizabeth Gunn daughter of Donald Gunn, a carpenter in East Brora, Clyne, on the road from Golspie to Brora and Crakaig in 1847. [NRS.AD14.47.525]

ROSS, JOHN, and his wife Christian Mackay, parents of Thomas Ross, born 1853, died in Townsville, Australia, on 21 June 1886. [Lochinver gravestone, Sutherland]

ROSS, JOHN, in Honourable East India Company Service, surgeon to the British Residency in Baghdad, eldest son of Dr William Ross in Cambusmore, Sutherland, died in Baghdad, Iraq, on 19 June 1849. [AJ.531][EEC.21851]

ROSS, JOHN, born 1807 in Cromarty, son of Simon Ross a shoemaker, educated at Marischal College, Aberdeen, in 1825, a minister in Nova Scotia, and New Brunswick, from 1836 to 1867, died on 9 April 1871. [F.7.611]

ROSS, KENNETH, born 1763 in Tain, Ross and Cromarty, died in Charleston, South Carolina, on 13 December 1798. [Old Scots gravestone, Charleston]

ROSS, or GOW, MALCOLM, in Tain, Ross and Cromarty, was accused of sheep stealing and breaking prison in 1843. [NRS.AD14.43.12]

ROSS, MARGARET, daughter of Donald Ross, [died 1841], and his wife Jane Munro, [died 1843], emigrated to Australia. [Invershin gravestone, Sutherland]

ROSS, MARJORY, born 11 October 1782 in Logie Easter, Ross and Cromarty, daughter of Reverend John Ross and his wife Margaret Smith, died in Gibraltar in 1813. [F.7.69]

ROSS, MARJORY, daughter of Donald Ross, [died 1841], and his wife Jane Munro, [died 1843], emigrated to Australia. [Invershin gravestone, Sutherland]

ROSS, ROBERT, born 1745, in Balloan, Culmaily, Sutherland, in 1810. [SHS.8.14-15]

ROSS, ROBERT, and George Linklater, tacksmen of Northmavine, Shetland, versus Robert Wishart and Andrew Mouat in Bodigarth and Liascul in Northmavine, in 1802. [SA.SC12.6.1802.27]

ROSS, ROBERT, of Sound, George Linklater a merchant in Lerwick, and James Williamson in Murin, Northmavine, Shetland, versus John Potenger in Ustaness Whiteness, and John Doull in Unisfirth, Aithsting, in 1804. [SA.SC12.6.1804.32]

ROSS, ROBERT POPE, son of Hugh Ross a farmer in Edderton, Ross and Cromarty, was educated at Marischal College, Aberdeen, in 1844. [MCA]

ROSS, ROBERT, was commissioned as Captain of the 1st Cromarty Militia in 1860. [NRS.SC24.21.5]

ROSS, THOMAS, MA, son of George Ross the Customs Collector in Ullapool, Sutherland, emigrated in 1831, Rector of Kingstown Grammar School in Upper Canada, died on 17 November 1833. [AJ.4489]

ROSS, THOMAS, born 1853, son of John Ross and his wife Christine Mackay, died on 21 June 1886 in Townsville, Australia. [Lochinver gravestone, Sutherland]

ROSS, WALTER, tenant in Grinan, Clyne, Sutherland, in 1811. [SHS.8.92]

ROSS, WALTER, of Nigg, Ross and Cromaty, versus James Fraser of Pitcalzean in 1812. [NRS.CS42.5.71]; letters to Mungo Ross of Pitcalnie, from 1776 to 1809. [NRS.GD199.62]

ROSS, WALTER, from Tain, Ross-shire, in Pictou, Nova Scotia, married Elizabeth, daughter of H. Thorp, at the residence of William Anderson in Fredericksburgh, on 1 December 1845. [AJ.5115]

ROSS, WILLIAM, tenant in Proncycroy, Farr, Sutherland, in 1808. [SHS.8.223]

ROSS, WILLIAM, born 1760, with his wife and three children, in Sallichtown, Culmaily, Sutherland, in 1810. [SHS.1.14/15]

ROSS, WILLIAM, joint tenant in Achtomliny, Rogart, Sutherland, in 1815. [SHS.8.231]

ROSS, WILLIAM, with family, from Sutherland, emigrated via Cromarty or Thurso aboard the Prince William bound for Pictou, Nova Scotia, in 1815. [NSARM.mg100, vol.226.30]

ROSS, WILLIAM, schoolmaster in Durness, Sutherland, in 1826. [NRS.CS44.101.51]

ROSS, WILLIAM, born 1796, a shoemaker in Blackmuir, Roskeen, Ross-shire, accused of murder in Invergordon on 1830. [NRS.AD14.30.101A; JC26.549]

ROSS, WILLIAM, a shoemaker in Wick, Caithness, accused of mobbing and rioting in 1827. [NRS.AD14.28.279]

ROSS, WILLIAM, emigrated from Cromarty or Thurso aboard the Lady Grey bound for Pictou, Nova Scotia, in June 1841. [NRS.RH1.2.908]

ROSS, or COOPER, WILLIAM, in Ardgay, Ross-shire, 1844, nephew of James Ross or Cooper in St Mary's, Jamaica. [NRS.S/H]

ROSS, Dr, a tenant in Cambusmore, Dornoch, Sutherland, in 1811, and in Balvraid, Dornoch, in 1815. [SHS.8.64/221]

ROSS, Mrs, from Ross-shire, wife of Hugh Ross, died at Fishers Grant, Nova Scotia, on 25 November 1831. [Acadian Recorder, 10.12.1831]

ROSSIE, JOHN, a fish curer in Orkney, died 2 June 1856, father of William Sutherland Rossie in Illinois. [NRS.S/H]

RUGG, DAVID, born 1741, in Slickly, died 7 October 1820, wife Frances Sutherland, born 1757, died 31 December 1813, parents of David Rugg in Halifax, Nova Scotia. [Canisbay gravestone, Caithness]

RUDDACH, Reverend ALEXANDER, in Kirkwall, father of Thomas Ruddach a merchant in Tobago, a sasine, 1791. [NRS.R.S.Orkney.252]

RULE, GEORGE, of Cyderhall, Dornoch, Sutherland, a tack in 1823 [NRS.GD347.61]

RUSSELL, ANNABELLA, eldest daughter of Reverend James Russell in Gairloch, Ross-shire, wife of Roderick Matheson, died in Perth, Upper Canada, on 10 November 1854. [EEC.22688] [W.XVI.1619]

RUSSELL, JAMES, minister of Gairloch, Wester Ross, versus Sir Hector McKenzie of Gairloch in 1805. [NRS.CS271.56448]

RUSSELL, JOSEPH, born 7 October 1842 in Shetland, son of Walter Russell and his wife Ann Booth on Bressay, died in Yokohama, Japan, on 30 April 1879. [Banchory Ternan gravestone]

RYRIE, JOHN A., son of Magnus Ryrie in Wick, Caithness, married Lizzie Stanton in Alton, Illinois, on 29 December 1854. [Inverness Courier, 1945]

SABISTON, JAMES MCKAY, born 1838 in Stromness, Orkney, died in Nanaimo, British Columbia, on 18 October 1875. [Ross Bay gravestone, B.C.]

SABISTON, PETER, born in Stromness, Orkney, died in Nanaimo, British Columbia, on 29 September 1892. [Ross Bay gravestone, B.C.]

SAGE, Reverend, tenant in Kildonan, Sutherland, in 1811, 1815. [SHS.8.105/228]

SANDISON, JOSEPH, born 1811, an agriculturalist, with his wife Isabella born 1812, and six children, from Lothbeg, Golspie, Sutherland, emigrated to Australia in 1848. [BPP.11.216-217]

SANGTER, PATRICK, eldest son of John Sangster in Widewall, Orkney, died in Grenada in1817. [S.32.17]

SCARTH, ROBERT, of Binscarth, married Jemima Eliza Stevenson, youngest daughter of James Stevenson, late of Leith, at Rideau Cottage, New Edinburgh, Canada West, on 9 April 1855. [EEC.22732]

SCOBIE, ANGUS, son of Kenneth Scobie in Achmore, Assynt, Sutherland, died in Demerara on 11 December 1807. [SM.70.398]

SCOBIE, Captain JOHN, of the Sutherland Fencibles, tacksman of Ardvarr, Assynt, Sutherland, a bond of caution for David Nicol, tacksman of Duartman in 1803. [NRS.CS271.818]

SCOBIE, Captain WILLIAM, son of the late Kenneth Scobie in Auchmore, a tenant in Ardvar, Cromault, Little Assynt, and Aulnachie, in the parish of Assynt, Sutherland, in 1808, and 1811. [SHS.8.47/216]

SCOLLAY, ELIZABETH, and ISABELLA, heirs to their brother Thomas Scollay of Odness, in the lands of Trundershall, Stromsay, and in Papa Stronsay, Orkney, in 1805. [NRS.GD31.364]

SCOTT, CHARLES, of Gardie, Mid Yell, Shetland, versus his tenants in 1800, summons of removal. [SA.SC12.6.1800.17]

SCOTT, JOHN, of Scalloway, Shetland, agent for Captain Michael Teolcke late of the Columbus of Danzig, a petition dated 3 April 1800. [SA.SC12.6.1800.41]

SCOTT, JOHN, of Melbie, Foula, Shetland, versus various tenants in 1804, summons of removal. [SA.SC12.6.1804.]

SCOTT, JOHN, born 1781 on Ronaldsay, Orkney, a Hudson Bay Company employee from 1800 to 1825, returned to Scotland aboard the Prince of Wales in 1825. [HBRS.3.453]; in Stromness, a sasine, 1834. [NRS.R.S.Orkney.167]

SCOTT, OLIVER, a merchant in Kirkwall, Orkney, versus Andrew Munro jr. in Kirkwall, 1817. [NRS.CS42.17.78]

SEATTER, ANDREW, from Stromness, Orkney, emigrated to Canada in 1798, an employee of the Hudson Bay Company. [OM]

SEATTER, GEORGE, from Stromness, Orkney, emigrated to Canada, settled at the Red River in 1820. [OM]

SEATTER, JAMES, a shoemaker in Kirkwall, Orkney, died 1855. [NRS.S/H.1873]

SEATTER, THOMAS, from Orkney, emigrated to Canada, an employee of the Hudson Bay Company at York Factory in 1819. [OM]

SELLAR, PATRICK, in Culmoirly, Golspie, Sutherland, accused of culpable homicide and oppression in 1816. [NRS.JC26.1816.136]; letters, 1827-1828. [NRS.GD129.2.90]

SELLAR, THOMAS, born 12 January 1823 in Mowick, Shetland, a merchant in New York from 1840 to 1846, died in Cannes, France, on 22 October 1885. [ANY.2.239]

SHARPE, WILLIAM, lawful husband of Mary McFie in Redbanks, Washister, Rousay, Orkney, was accused of bigamy with Ann Marwick in Manners, Rousay, in 1843. [NRS.AD14.43.446; JC26.1843.505]

SHEARER, JOHN, jr., a merchant in Kirkwall, Orkney, sequestration, 1805. [NRS.CS236.S1617]

SHEARER, JOHN, a shoemaker or cartwright in Pultneytown, Wick, Caithness, accused of rioting in 1847, was transported to Australia. [NRS.AD14.47.533]

SIEVEWRIGHT, PETER, a baker in Lerwick, Shetland, versus William Black a merchant in Aberdeen, 1811. [NRS.CS36.2.62]

SIEVEWRIGHT, WILLIAM, born 6 October 1792, a writer in Lerwick, died 26 June 1870, husband of Jessie Spence, born 14 June 1801, died 5 June 1867. [Knab Road gravestone, Lerwick, Shetland]

SIM, WILLIAM, in Drummond, Kiltearn, Ross-shire, was a victim of rioting, mobbing, and assault at the Caledonian Hotel, Dingwall, in 1837. [NRS.AD14.37.36]

SIMPSON, AEMILIUS, born 1791, son of bailie Alexander Simpson of Dingwall, Ross and Cromarty, a Lieutenant of the Royal Navy, died at Nass on the Simpson River on the west coast of North America on 13 September 1831. [AJ.4406] [EEC.18876]

SIMPSON, ALEXANDER, tenant in Midgarty and Gartymore, Loth, Sutherland, in 1815. [SHS.8.231]

SIMSON, COLIN, born 1730, a skipper in Cromarty, died on 10 February 1803. [St Regulas gravestone, Cromarty]

SIMPSON, JOHN, from Orkney, was naturalised in South Carolina on 10 June 1823. [S.C. Circuit Court Journal, 9.295]

SIMPSON, JOHN F., emigrated from Cromarty or Thurso aboard the Lady Grey bound for Pictou, Nova Scotia, in June 1841. [NRS.RH1.2.908]

SIMPSON, THOMAS, born 1808 in Dingwall, Ross and Cromarty, was educated at Aberdeen University, settled at Hudson Bay in 1829, died at the Turtle River, Canada, on 28 June 1840. [GM.NS14.548]

SINCLAIR, ALEXANDER, born 1789 in Caithness, emigrated to USA in 1809, a mercantile clerk in Savannah, Georgia, by 1812, died there on 30 October 1813. [Savannah Republican, 2.11.1813]

SINCLAIR, ALEXANDER DOULL, born 15 September 1828, son of Alexander Sinclair and his wife Margaret Doull in Braemore, Berriedale, Caithness, a physician who emigrated to Boston, Massachusetts, in 1848. [SI.414]

SINCLAIR, ANDREW, a mariner in London, son of Edward Sinclair, portioner of Toft, and his wife Christian Fea, a sasine, 1791. [NRS.R.S.Shetland.238]

SINCLAIR, BENJAMIN W., third son of Alexander Sinclair, a merchant in Thurso, Caithness, married Susan C. Faries, second daughter of Major Faries of Savanna, Georgia, there on 24 November 1842. [AJ.4965]

SINCLAIR, BONAR, in Hascusay, Shetland, was accused of plundering a Norwegian shipwreck in 1803. [SA.SC12.6.1803.47]

SINCLAIR, DUDLEY, son of Sir George Sinclair of Ulbster, Caithness, died in Auckland, New Zealand, on 23 September 1844. [W.561]

SINCLAIR, GEORGE SUTHERLAND, of Brabster, Caithness, husband of Margaret Gibson, testament 1830, codicil, 1839. [NRS.GD139.81/82]

SINCLAIR, ISABELL, second daughter of William Sinclair of Tuswick, Caithness, married Thomas Cochrane Hume in Edinburgh in January 1836. [Acadian Recorder, 22.2.1836]

SINCLAIR, JAMES, at York Fort, Hudson Bay, a sasine in 1797. [NRS.R.S.Orkney.407]

SINCLAIR, JAMES, tenant in Semester, Reay, Caithness, late of the Caithness Fencibles, accused in 1802 of theft in Thurso in 1794. [NRS.JC26.1802.19]

SINCLAIR, JAMES, born 1783, from Thurso aboard the Elizabeth and Ann of Newcastle, bound for Prince Edward Island in 1806. [PAPEI]

SINCLAIR, JAMES, from Forse, Sutherland, in Jamaica, letters, 1803-1822. [NRS.GD139.390/499]

SINCLAIR, JANET, a prisoner in Lerwick Tolbooth, Shetland, a petition, 1799. [SA.SC12.6.1799.39]

SINCLAIR, JEROM, in Kellister, Sandness, Shetland, versus Peter Doull of Fogrigarth, Aithsting, re the illegal cutting of kelp in 1803. [SA.SC12.6.1803.31]

SINCLAIR, JOHN, a Customs House boatman in Stromness, Orkney, a sasine, 1791. [NRS.R.S.Orkney.257]

SINCLAIR, JOHN, in South Deal, Fetlar, Shetland, and his son Bruce Sinclair, a petition re plundering in 1794. [SA.SC12.6.1794.20]

SINCLAIR, JOHN, a Lieutenant, later Captain, of the 79th Regiment, letters, 1792-1815. [NRS.GD139.369]

SINCLAIR, Sir JOHN, in Thurso Castle, Caithness, a letter re mermaids seen on the coast of Caithness in 1809. [NRS.GD51.9.315]

SINCLAIR, LAURENCE, in Liabitten, a line manager on a whaler, versus Lieutenant William Wilson of the Impress Service in Shetland, a petition against impressment in 1810. [SA.SC12.6.1810.59]

SINCLAIR, PATRICK, a Captain of the Royal Navy, a sasine. 1789. [NRS.R.S.Caithness.130]

SINCLAIR, ROBERT, born 1792 in Orkney, a farmer who settled on Cape Breton in 1814. [1818 Census of Cape Breton]

SINCLAIR, ROBERT, [1767-1820], a Customs officer who died at Castletown, Caithness, husband of Williamina Barr Traill, [1787-1866], parents of Osborn Sinclair a merchant in Mitchell, Canada West. [Olrig gravestone, Caithness]

SINCLAIR, THOMAS, a merchant on Stronsay, Orkney, versus Peter Sinclair in Hercorn, Stronsay, in 1800. [OA.SC11.5.1800.54]

SINCLAIR, THOMAS, of Eastaquoy, Orkney, 1826, brother of William Sinclair of the Hudson Bay Company. [NRS.S/H]

SINCLAIR, WILLIAM JAMES, born 1753 in Forsenain, Reay, Caithness, settled in Anson County, North Carolina, before 1820, probate April 1824. [NCSA.2.13]

SINCLAIR, WILLIAM, a mariner from Orkney, a Hudson Bay Company employee from 1824 until 1834. [HBRS.3.456]

SINCLAIR, WILLIAM, of Freswick, versus James Traill of Hobbister in 1809, [NRS.GD136.217]; versus Dr Robert Groat a physician in Kirkwall in 1816. [NRS.CS40.21.6]; letters 1783-1835. [NRS.GD136.456]

SINCLAIR, W. J. J. A., of Freswick, attempted to remove any of his tenants who took part in the grain riots to prevent his grain being shipped from Wick, letters, 1847. [NRS.GD136.993] a petition

SINCLAIR, WILLIAM, from Caithness, married Elizabeth Wheston in Halifax, Nova Scotia, on 28 October 1843. [Times, 7.11.1843]

SINCLAIR, WILLIAM WATERS, second son of Alexander Sinclair a merchant in Thurso, Caithness, died in Bengal, India, on 26 July 1843. [AJ.5004]

SKETHAWAY, ROBERT, former schoolmaster of St Ola, Orkney, a summons of removal in 1800. [OA.SC11.1800.23]

SLEATTER, THOMAS, was indentured to William McGregor of Elwick a master mariner, on 26 September 1794. [NRS.NRAS.0627, box 25, bundle 1]

SMELLIE, GEORGE, born 14 June 1811 in the parish of St Andrew and Deerness, Orkney, son of Reverend James Smellie, educated at Glasgow University, minister of Lady parish from 1839 to 1843, married Margaret Lendrum Logie in 1843, emigrated to Canada, minister of Fergus, Ontario, died 22 November 1896. [F.7.265]

SMELLIE, JAMES, born in the parish of St Andrew and Deerness, Orkney, son of Reverend James Smellie and his wife Margaret Spence, died in Demerara in 1883. [F.7.212]

SMITH, ADAM, in Windbreck, Flotta, Orkney, versus Robert Harper and William Work, as he 'dreads bodily harm from them', 1801. [OA.SC11.5.1801.43]

SMITH, ADAM, in Gulberwick, Shetland, was accused of carrying off cattle in 1827. [SA.SC12.6.1827.72]

SMITH, ALEXANDER R., son of James Smith in Olrig, Caithness, was educated at Marischal College, Aberdeen, in 1849. [MCA]

SMITH, ANDREW, a merchant in Kirkwall, Orkney, 1804. [NRS.CS230.SEQN.S2.12]

SMITH, CHARLES, a merchant in Golspie, Sutherland, a sederunt book, 1822 – 1824. [NRS.CS96.1258]; sequestration, 1822. [NRS.CS234.SEQN.S4.18]

SMITH, GEORGE, fourth son of William Smith in Pennyland, Thurso, Caithness, died in Calcutta, India, in March 1845. [AJ.5081]

SMITH, GUSTAVUS, a labourer in Golspie, Caithness, accused of stealing sheep in 1833. [NRS.AD14.33.50]

SMITH, HECTOR WILLIAM POPE, son of James Smith in Caithness, was educated at Marischal College, Aberdeen, in 1854, later a sheep farmer in New Zealand. [MCA.II.568]

SMITH, HELEN, fourth daughter of Reverend Robert Smith in Cromarty, married John James Aitchison, MD, from Elmsley, in Perth, Upper Canada, on 28 October 1852. [W.XIII.1384]

SMITH, HENRY, and his daughter Philla Smith, in Tumbledown, Wester Quarff, Shetland, accused of 'carrying off doors' in 1802. [SA.SC12.6.1802.13]

SMITH, ISABEL GAIR ROSE, youngest daughter of Reverend Robert Smith in Cromarty, married Reverend George Romanes, in Beckworth, Upper Canada, on 2 August 1835. [AJ.4.578] [GA.XXXV,5123]

SMITH, JAMES, THOMAS, MAGNUS, and ROSS, in Aith, Bressay, Shetland, were accused of plundering the wrecked sloop *Polly of Dover* on Bressay in 1800. [SA.SC12.6.1800.27]

SMITH, JAMES, a merchant in Golspie, Sutherland, 1845. [NRS.CS280.7.63]

SMITH, JAMES, son of James Smith in Olrig, Caithness, was educated at Marischal College, Aberdeen, in 1847. [MCA]

SMITH, JAMES, a partner of Fraser and Smith in Thurso, Caithness,was accused of arson at Traill Street, Thurso, the property of Donald McLeod Smith in Golspie in 1848. [NRS.AD14.48.371]

SMITH, JOHN, his wife Mary, son John, daughter Jean, daughter Mary, from Asbus, Kildalton, Sutherland, emigrated via Stromness on the Prince of Wales to the Hudson Bay Company settlement at Fort Churchill on 29 June 1813. [PAC.M155.165-8]

SMITH, JOHN, from Caithness, died in St John, New Brunswick, on 17 December 1839. [New Brunswick Courier, 28.12.1839]

SMITH, JOHN, and Mrs Davidson, both from Sutherland, were married in Halifax, Nova Scotia, on 3 October 1842. [Acadian Recorder, 8.10.1842]

SMITH, MALCOLM LAING, son of Allan Smith, [died 1800], in Turmiston, Orkney, settled in Seaford, Van Diemen's Land, [Tasmania], Australia, before 1845. [NRS.S/H]

SMITH, ROBERT, in Buolfreich, Dunbeath, Latheron, Caithness, accused of rioting in 1829. [NRS.AD14.02.350]

SMITH, ROBERT, a tenant farmer in Daveckfin, Dornoch, Sutherland, 1849. [NRS.CS280.11.63]

SMITH, ROBERT, [1833-1903], a joiner in Duncansby, and his wife Elizabeth Robertson, [1825-1901], parents of Donald Smith, born 1858, died in Cincinatti, Ohio, on 25 August 1883. [Canisbay gravestone]

SMITH, WHITEFORD, from Orkney, was naturalised in South Carolina, on 17 October 1794. [S.C. Court of Wardens.y3.160]

SMITH, WILLIAM, son of William Smith of Furmiston, Orkney, died in March 1799, brother of Thomas Baikie Smith from Kirkwall then in Haiti. [NRS.S/H.1853]

SMITH, WILLIAM, in Unst, Shetland, an investigation into his death by shooting, possibly accidentally by Peter Smith a fish curer on Unst, a petition in 1820. [SA.SC12.6.1820.62]

SMITH, WILLIAM, son of James Smith in Olrig, Caithness, was educated at Marischal College, Aberdeen, in 1841. [MCA]

SMITH, ..., master of the Dublin of Lerwick from Lerwick, Shetland, to Leith in 1798. [AJ.2646]

SMYTH, WILLIAM, of Craigdarroch, Dingwall, Ross and Cromarty, versus Walter and Whitehurst coach and harness manufacturers in London, 1836. [NRS.CS46.1836.12.59]

SNODIE, ADAM, born 1783 in Orphir, Orkney, an employee of the Hudson Bay Company from 1801 to 1822, died in Stromness after 1832. [HBRS.2.242]

SNODY, JOHN, [1778-1850], husband of Janet Leith, [1750-1840], parents of Adam Snody, the Governor of York Factory at Hudson's Bay who died in Stromness on 20 December 1834. [Canisby gravestone]

SNODDY, JOHN, a farmer in Seater, Canisbay, Caithness, versus Alexander Lyle a tenant in Stroma, letters of poinding, 1806. [NRS.GD136.182]

SNODY, MORISON, a writer at Forter in Thurso, Caithness, trustee of Donald Campbell and Son merchants in Wick, Caithness, in 1815, [NRS.CS36.13.25]; versus William Manson in Halkirk, Caithness, 1832. [NRS.CS46.1832.14]

SPANKIE, DAVID, born 1774, a carrier in Golspie, Sutherland, was accused of the murder of Wilhelmina Grant a widow in Rogart at the Brora Inn, Clyne, Sutherland, in 1842. [NRS.AD14.42.454]

SPENCE, BALFOUR, a merchant in Lerwick, Shetland, a sederunt book, 1821-1822. [NRS.CS96.181]

SPENCE, DAVID, a Lieutenant of the Royal Navy, son of William Spence of Gardie, a sasine, 1806. [NRS.R.S.Shetland.512]

SPENCE, GEORGE, merchant in Stromness, Orkney, sederunt books, 1839-1841. [NRS.CS96.1050.1/2]

SPENCE, JAMES, a merchant in Kirkwall, Orkney, a decreet, 1820. [NRS.CS32.20.37]

SPENCE, JOHN, a merchant in Stromness, Orkney, died 30 December 1833. [NRS.S/H.1862]

SPENCE, JOHN, born 1798 in Stromness, Orkney, in Hudson Bay Company Service at Fort Vancouver in 1825, died in Victoria, British Columbia, on 29 September 1865. [Ross Bay gravestone, B.C.]

SPENCE, JOHN, born 1830 in Orkney, in Hudson Bay Company Service in British Columbia in 1852, died in Victoria, B.C. on 9 June 1897. [Ross Bay gravestone, B.C.]

SPENCE, NINIAN, of Howland, versus David Sinclair in Vigon, Shetland, in 1808. [SA.RH4.35.1.62]

SPENCE, PETER, born 1791, from Sandwick, Orkney, emigrated via Stornaway on the Prince of Wales to the Hudson Bay Company settlement on the Red River in 1811. [PAC.M155.145]

SPENCE, ROBERT MOIR, son of James Smith a silversmith in Kirkwall, graduated MA from Marischal College in 1842, later minister of Arbuthnott, Kincardineshire. [MCA]

SPENCE, THOMAS, in Fea, Birsay, Orkney, 1859, son of Nicol Spence of the Hudson Bay Company. [NRS.S/H]

SPENCE, WILLIAM, born 1830 in Stromness, Orkney, settled in Victoria, British Columbia, in 1852, husband of Jane Fraser, died at Salt Spring, B.C., on 24 July 1897. [Ross Bay gravestone, B.C.]

STALKER, HUGH, minister of Kirkwall, versus Henry Copland and John Mowat in St Ola, Orkney, in 1800. [OA.SC11.5.1800.9]

STANGER, JOHN, a shipbuilder in Stromness, Orkney, versus Izat Smith a pilot on Shapinsay, and Thomas Smith a skipper in Kirkwall in 1838. [OS.SC11.5.1838.22]

STEWART, ALEXANDER, born 1808, a tinker, and his wife Mary Fraser in Bogindoir of Allangrange, Kilmuir Wester, Ross-shire, accused of assault in 1828. [NRS.AD14.28.281]

STEWART, ALEXANDER, factor of Lewis, letters, 1828-1835. [NRS.GD46.1.530]; versus James Reid a shipowner in Stornaway, contractor for mail between Stornaway and Poolewe, Wester Ross, in 1829. [NRS.GD46.13.103]

STEWART, DONALD, shopkeeper in Maryburgh, Dingwall, Ross and Cromarty, was accused of rioting, mobbing, and assault at the Caledonian Hotel, Dingwall, in 1837. [NRS.AD14.37.36]

STEWART, ELIZABETH, second daughter of Major General Stewart of Strath, Caithness, and of Mount Pleasant, Bathurst, New South Wales, Australia, married Reverend Kirkpatrick Dickson Smythe, there on 14 July 1842. [SG.1152]

STEWART, JAMES BRUCE, of Symbuster, Shetland, versus John Bruce tacksman of Catfirth, Nesting, Shetland, a petition in 1796. [SA.SC12.6.1796.24]

STEWART, JAMES, a merchant in Kirkwall, Caithness, his trustees versus William Richan of Rapness in 1813. [NRS.CS42.8.106]

STEWART, JAMES, born 1802, a messenger-at-arms in Dornoch, Sutherland, was accused of oppression and assault in 1832. [NRS.AD14.32.151]

STEWART, JEAN, relict of Reverend Robert Scollay, in Stronsay and Eday, Orkney, versus Edward Robertson and John Robertson in Tenston, Sandwick, 1804. [NRS.SC11.5.1804.117]

STEWART, JOHN, son of Nigel Stewart a farmer in Wick, graduated MA at Marischal College, Aberdeen, in 1844, later a schoolmaster in Edderton, Ross and Cromarty. [MCA]

STEWART, MURDOCH, born 1809 in Contin, Ross-shire, was educated at Marischal College, Aberdeen, in 1834, minister on Cape Breton from 1843, died in Pictou, Nova Scotia, on 30 July 1884. [F.7.608]

STEWART, NEIL, born 1804 in Thurso, Caithness, died in Halifax, Nova Scotia, on 6 September 1834. [Acadian Recorder, 13.9.1834]

STOBBS, JOHN GARROW, born 1 July 1840 in Stromness, Orkney, son of William Stobbs, educated at Glasgow University in 1864, a minister in Melbourne, Australia, from 1875, died on 10 August 1882. [F.7.598]

STOCKAND, JAMES, born 1830 in Orkney, a carpenter in Hudson Bay Company Service, in Victoria, British Columbia, in 1852, died there on 9 December 1888. [Ross Bay gravestone, B.C.]

STOVE, HENRY, in Hascusay, Shetland, was accused of plundering a Norwegian shipwreck in 1803. [SA.SC12.6.1803.47]

STOVE, JAMES, a labourer in Kirkwall, Orkney, versus James Hourie, a farmer in Upper Stove, Deerness, in1802. [OA.SC11.5.1802.65]

STOVE, JANET, daughter of James Stove and his wife Jean Irvine in Deerness, Orkney, versus Robert Monceiff of Houston, re a marriage contract, 1823. [NRS.CS238.M11.41]

STRONG, LAURENCE, born 1782, a mariner from the Shetland Islands, was naturalised in South Carolina on 27 January 1804. [NARA.M1183.1]

SUTAR, JAMES, eldest son of Thomas Sutar the Sheriff Clerk of Ross-shire, died in Grenada in 1813. [EA.5192.13]

SUTHAR, FRANCIS, of Rhives, Golspie, Sutherland, letters, 1821. [NRS.SC9.96.5]

SUTHERLAND, ADAM, joint tenant in Bank, Rogart, Sutherland, in 1815. [SHS.8.231]

SUTHERLAND, ALEXANDER, from Sutherland, with for dependents, applied for a land grant in Nova Scotia on 6 October 1814, was awarded 300 acres. [NSARM.RG20. series A]

SUTHERLAND, ALEXANDER, born 1788 in Dunnet, Caithness, a former soldier, residing in Edinburgh, accused of housebreaking in 1833. [NRS.A14.33.9]

SUTHERLAND, ALEXANDER, born 1790, a labourer, from Sutherland, emigrated via Stromness on the Prince of Wales to the Hudson Bay Company settlement at York Fort on 23 June 1815, landed there on 26 August 1815. [PAC.M1659/61] [MG19.E4.1.165/8]

SUTHERLAND, ALEXANDER, tenant in Blarnafidoch, Golspie, Sutherland in 1811. [SHS.8.87]

SUTHERLAND, ALEXANDER, born 1789, with his brother William born 1794, and sister Katie born 1793, sister Hannah born 1795, sister Barbara born 1793 from Balnavaliach, Kildonan, emigrated via Stromness on the Prince of Wales to the Hudson Bay Company settlement at Fort Churchill on 29 June 1813. [PAC.M155.165-8]

SUTHERLAND, ALEXANDER, born 1771, with family, from Sutherland, emigrated via Cromarty aboard the Ossian bound for Pictou, Nova Scotia, on 25 June 1821. [Inverness Journal.29 June 1821]

SUTHERLAND, ALEXANDER, emigrated from Cromarty or Thurso aboard the Lady Grey bound for Pictou, Nova Scotia, in June 1841. [NRS.RH1.2.908]

SUTHERLAND, ALEXANDER, son of Donald Sutherland in Kelfederbeg, [1786-1841], settled in Ontario. [Sciberscross, Strathbrora, gravestone, Sutherland]

SUTHERLAND, ANDREW, joint tenant in Pittentrail, Rogart, Sutherland, in 1808,1815. [SHS.8.230/231]

SUTHERLAND, ANDREW, and family, from Craggybeg, Rogart, Sutherland, emigrated to Canada in 1829. [NLS.313.878]

SUTHERLAND, ANDREW, born 1783 in Ross-shire, died at St George, New Brunswick, on 22 Jun 1836. [New Brunswick Courier 23.7.1836]

SUTHERLAND, ANGUS, and Jean his wife, also their son Alexander Sutherland, in Rhiniskain, Clyne, Sutherland, accused of resisting officers of the law, failed to appear at his trial, and was therefore outlawed in 1821. [NRS.JC26.1821.9]

SUTHERLAND, ANN, born 1766, a widow with family, from Sutherland, emigrated via Cromarty aboard the Ossian bound for Pictou, Nova Scotia, on 25 June 1821. [Inverness Journal.29 June 1821]

SUTHERLAND, Mrs ANN, emigrated from Loch Laxford, Sutherland, aboard the Ellen of Liverpool bound for Pictou, Nova Scotia, on 22 May 1848. [PANS.257.110]

SUTHERLAND, ANN, emigrated from Loch Laxford, Sutherland, aboard the Ellen of Liverpool bound for Pictou, Nova Scotia, on 22 May 1848. [PANS.257.110]

SUTHERLAND, ANN WATERS, eldest daughter of David Waters in Brems, Caithness, wife of David Sutherland, Congregational Minister in Bath, New Hampshire, died there on 3 March 1852. [W.1309]

SUTHERLAND, ARTHUR SINCLAIR, from Forss, Caithness, settled in Verplank, USA, and Temperanceville, Canada, between 1837 and 1849. [NRS.GD139.469]

SUTHERLAND, Mrs BARBARA, wife of Donald Sutherland in Dornoch, died in Halifax, Nova Scotia, on 11 February 1832. [Acadian Recorder]

SUTHERLAND, CATHERINE, daughter of Donald Sutherland in Kelfederbeg, [1786-1841], settled in Ontario. [Sciberscross, Strathbrora, gravestone]

SUTHERLAND, CHARLES, son of Andrew Sutherland a merchant in Pittenrail, tenant in Rovy Kirkton, Rogart, Sutherland, in 1811, 1815. [SHS.8.70/231]

SUTHERLAND, CHRISTINE, daughter of John Sutherland, [1790-1875], and his wife Christine Mann, [1820-1868], settled in Embro, Canada. [Dornoch gravestone, Sutherland]

SUTHERLAND, DAVID SINCLAIR, possibly from Forss, Caithness, settled in Halifax, Nova Scotia, around 1830. [NRS.GD139.451.8/10]

SUTHERLAND, DAVID, from Reay, Caithness, was educated at King's College, Aberdeen, in 1847, later a MD in Thurso. [MCA]

SUTHERLAND, DONALD, born 1767 in Criech, Sutherland, settled in Nova Scotia in 1818, died 5 January 1841. [New Lairg gravestone, N.S.]

SUTHERLAND, DONALD, born 1782 in Lairg, Sutherland, emigrated to Canada in 1802, husband of Isabella Gordon, died in May 1848. [New Lairg gravestone, N.S.]

SUTHERLAND, DONALD, born 1787, a labourer, with two sisters and a brother's daughter, in Loanmore, in Culmaily, Sutherland, in 1810. [SHS.1.14/15]

SUTHERLAND, DONALD, a tenant in Ulbster, Kildonan, Sutherland, was accused of rioting, resulting from the removal or eviction of tenants in Kildonan in 1813. [NRS.AD14.13.9; SC9.7.64][SHS.8.136]

SUTHERLAND, or MCCARLISH, DONALD, in Achness, Clyne, Sutherland, accused of resisting officers of the law, failed to appear at his trial, and was therefore outlawed in 1821. [NRS.JC26.1821.9]

SUTHERLAND, DONALD, from Sutherland, married Elizabeth Merkel, in Halifax, Nova Scotia, on 10 January 1831. [Acadian Recorder, 15.1.1831]

SUTHERLAND, DONALD, born 1773 in Sutherland, died in Halifax, Nova Scotia, on 1 August 1834. [Acadian Recorder, 2.8.1834]

SUTHERLAND, DONALD, son of Donald Sutherland in Kelfederbeg, [1786-1841], settled in Ontario. [Sciberscross, Strathbrora, gravestone, Sutherland]

SUTHERLAND, DONALD, born 1771, with family, from Sutherland, emigrated via Cromarty aboard the Ossian bound for Pictou, Nova Scotia, on 25 June 1821. [Inverness Journal.29 June 1821]

SUTHERLAND, DONALD, [1764-1858], and his wife Rose Gordon, [1769-1849], parents of William Sutherland who settled in Australia. [Kildonan gravestone, Sutherland]

SUTHERLAND, DONALD, son of John Sutherland, [1790-1875], and his wife Christine Mann, [1820-1868], died in Melbourne, Australia. [Dornoch gravestone, Sutherland]

SUTHERLAND, DONALD, born 1775, with family, from Sutherland, emigrated via Cromarty aboard the Ossian bound for Pictou, Nova Scotia, on 25 June 1821. [Inverness Journal.29 June 1821]

SUTHERLAND, DONALD, emigrated from Cromarty or Thurso aboard the Lady Gray bound for Pictou, Nova Scotia, in June 1841. [NRS.RH1.2.908]

SUTHERLAND, Captain DUNCAN, tenant in Kinnauld, and Rhimusaig, in the parish of Dornoch, also part of the shealing of Craigasnarich, and Rhyline, Rogart, Sutherland, in 1811 also in 1815. [SHS.8.68/75/222]

SUTHERLAND, ELISABETH, born 1753, son Angus born 1793, and daughter Betty born 1795, from Auchriach, emigrated via Stromness on the Prince of Wales to the Hudson Bay Company settlement at Fort Churchill on 29 June 1813. [PAC.M155.165-8]

SUTHERLAND, ELLEN, born 1791 in Sutherland, died in September 1849, wife of John Graham, born 1791, died 1864. [Hill Cemetery, Pictou, NS]

SUTHERLAND, Colonel GEORGE, tenant of Rhearquhar etc in the parish of Dornoch, Sutherland, in 1811 and 1815. [SHS.8.68/222]

SUTHERLAND, GEORGE, born 1795, brother Adam born 1797, from Borrobal, Kildonan, Sutherland, emigrated via Stromness on the Prince of Wales to the Hudson Bay Company settlement at Fort Churchill on 29 June 1813. [PAC.M155.165-8]

SUTHERLAND, GEORGE JAMES, eldest son of Captain John Sutherland of Shorelands, Wick, Caithness, died in Bathurst, New South Wales, Australia, on 6 February 1851. [W.1245]

SUTHERLAND, GEORGE, born 1825 in Ross-shire, died at Owen Sound, Canada, on 1 January 1857. [EEC.21007]

SUTHERLAND, HECTOR, with family, from Achrinsdale, Clyne, Sutherland, emigrated to Canada in 1829. [NLS.Dep.313.878]

SUTHERLAND, HUGH, tenant in Ferranich, Kildonan, Sutherland, in 1815. [SHS.8.227]

SUTHERLAND, HUGH MACKAY, son of George Sutherland of Uppat, Sutherland, died in Washington, USA, on 26 October 1860. [S.1690]

SUTHERLAND, ISABELLA, born 1786 in Sutherland, wife of Donald Matheson, settled in Nova Scotia, died on 29 September 1850. [New Lairg gravestone, N.S.]

SUTHERLAND, JAMES, born 1737 in Caithness, joined the army in 1758, died on 26 April 1815 at Sheet Harbour, Nova Scotia. [Weekly Chronicle, 12.5.1815]

SUTHERLAND, JAMES, born 1760, a dyker, with his wife and four children, in Sallichtown, Culmaily, Sutherland, in 1810. [SHS.1.14/15]

SUTHERLAND, JAMES, born 1768, a weaver, wife Mary Polson, born 1767, son James born 1803, daughter Janet born 1799, daughter Catherine born 1801, daughter Isabella born 1800, from Sutherland, emigrated via Stromness on the Prince of Wales to the Hudson Bay Company settlement at York Fort on 23 June 1815, landed there on 26 August 1815. [PAC.M1659/61] [MG19.E4.1.165/8]

SUTHERLAND, JAMES H., born 1805, in Iver Lybster, died 4 November 1866, husband of Mary Sinclair, born 1805, of the Union Inn in Lybster, died 9 July 1893. [Old Latheron gravestone, Caithness]

SUTHERLAND, JAMES, in Crawsnest, Flotta, versus James Sutherland the principal tacksman on Burray, Orkney, in 1800. [OA.SC11.5.1800.56]

SUTHERLAND, JAMES, tacksman of Flotta, versus Thomas Johnston on Flotta, Orkney, summons of removal in 1803. [OA.SC11.5.1803.61]; versus Peter Wildridge in Westhope, Burray, a summons of removal in 1806. [OA.SC11.5.1806.44]

SUTHERLAND, JAMES, emigrated via Scrabster, Caithness, on the Superior of Peterhead bound for Pictou, Nova Scotia, arrived there in June 1842. [Pictou Observer, 21.6.1842]

SUTHERLAND, JAMES, son of Reverend William Sutherland, [died 23 June 1816], and his wife Catherine Anderson, [died3 October 1813], died in Baroda in the East Indies on 10 June 1840. [Wick gravestone, Caithness]

SUTHERLAND, JANET, a widow, with a son and daughter, from Sutherland, applied for a land grant in Nova Scotia on 6 October 1814, was awarded 200 acres. [NSARM.RG20. series A]

SUTHERLAND, JEAN, born 1799, with family, from Sutherland, emigrated via Cromarty aboard the Ossian bound for Pictou, Nova Scotia, on 25 June 1821. [Inverness Journal.29 June 1821]

SUTHERLAND, JOHN, born 1760, a dyker, with his wife and two children, in Sallichtown, Culmaily, Sutherland, in 1810. [SHS.1.14/15]

SUTHERLAND, Captain JOHN, tenant in Easter Kerrow, Rogart, and in Brora Easter, Sutherland, in 1811. [SHS.8.80/97]; possibly in Kinnauld, Farr, Sutherland, in 1808. [SHS.8.223]

SUTHERLAND, JOHN, born 1782, a merchant in Lybster, Caithness, died 10 October 1862, husband of Jane H. G. Sutherland, born 1787, died 9 September 1874, parents of William Sutherland, born 1815, died in Sydney, New South Wales, Australia, on 24 October 1842, and Donald Sutherland, born 1818, died in Montreal on 15 September 1850. [Old Latheron gravestone, Caithness]

SUTHERLAND, JOHN, son of Captain Sutherland in Shibercross, a Lieutenant of the 93rd Regiment of Foot, died at the Cape of Good Hope, South Africa, in 1812. [EA.5097]

SUTHERLAND, JOHN, joint tenant in Balquhairn, Lairg, Sutherland, in 1815. [SHS.8.229]

SUTHERLAND, or MILLER, JOHN, in Rhiniskain, Clyne, Sutherland, accused of resisting officers of the law, failed to appear at his trial, and was therefore outlawed in 1821. [NRS.JC26.1821.9]

SUTHERLAND, JOHN, born 1751, a miller, with family, from Sutherland, emigrated via Cromarty aboard the Ossian bound for Pictou, Nova Scotia, on 25 June 1821. [Inverness Journal.29 June 1821]

SUTHERLAND, JOHN, born 1761, [he died 2 September 1813], his wife Catherine born 1765, son George born 1795, son Donald born 1797, son Alexander born 1804, and daughter Janet born 1799, from Kildonan, Sutherland, emigrated via Stromness on the Prince of Wales to the Hudson Bay Company settlement at Fort Churchill on 29 June 1813. [PAC.M155.165-8]

SUTHERLAND, JOHN, [1790-1875], and his wife Christine Mann, [1790-1875], parents of Robert Sutherland who settled in Melbourne, Australia. [Dornoch gravestone, Sutherland]

SUTHERLAND, Sergeant Major JOHN, joint tenant of Doll, Clyne, Sutherland, in 1811. [SHS.8.90]

SUTHERLAND, JOHN, in Easter Brora, Clyne, Sutherland, a letter, 1812. [NRS.GD236.500]

SUTHERLAND, JOHN, in Keanakyle, Kildonan, Sutherland, was accused of rioting there, in 1813. [SHS.8.116/136]

SUTHERLAND, JOHN, with family, from Farlary, Golspie, Sutherland, emigrated to Canada in 1829. [NLS.313.878]

SUTHERLAND, JOHN, born 1737 in Sutherland, died in Earlstown, Nova Scotia, on 18 July 1840. [Halifax Journal, 10.8.1840]

SUTHERLAND, JOHN, born 1790 in Sutherland, emigrated to Nova Scotia in 1833, settled in New Lairg, died in September 1838. [New Lairg gravestone, N.S.]

SUTHERLAND, JOHN, emigrated from Cromarty or Thurso aboard the Lady Gray bound for Pictou, Nova Scotia, in June 1841. [NRS.RH1.2.908]

SUTHERLAND, JOHN, son of Elizabeth Sutherland, [1792-1821], settled in New South Wales, Australia. [Clyne, Kirkton, gravestone, Sutherland]

SUTHERLAND, JOHN, born 1834, son of John Sutherland and his wife Margaret McPherson, died in Kinloch, Ontario, on 6 May 1914. [Navidale gravestone, Sutherland]

SUTHERLAND, JOHN, born 12 August 1830, a schoolmaster and Inspector of the Poor, died on 1 August 1892, husband of Henrietta Manson, born 1832, died 18 June 1916. [Canisbay gravestone]

SUTHERLAND, JOSEPH, son of George Sutherland, tenant in Scollag, Watten, Caithness, accused of rioting in 1821. [NRS.AD14.21.82]

SUTHERLAND, MARGARET, born 1802, a farm worker in Wester Abercross, Golspie, Sutherland, was accused of fraud and swindling in 1818. [NRS.AD14.18.99]

SUTHERLAND, MARGARET, born 1815, a domestic servant in Lothbeg, Golspie, Sutherland, emigrated to South Australia, in 1848. [BPP.11.216]

SUTHERLAND, Mrs M., tenant in Cambusavie, etc, Dornoch, Sutherland, in 1810, also in 1815. [SHS.8.62/221]

SUTHERLAND, Captain ROBERT, applied for the lease of part of the Pollyour Lot in Sutherland in 1812. [SHS.9/2.175]; tenant in Drummuy, Golspie, Sutherland, in 1815. [SHS.8.225]

SUTHERLAND, ROBERT, born 1765 in Sutherland, emigrated to Nova Scotia in 1833, settled in New Lairg, died 26 April 1843. [New Lairg gravestone, N.S.]

SUTHERLAND, ROBERT, [1777-1863], a farmer in Duncansby, and his wife Elizabeth Lyall, [1783-1871], parents of John Sutherland who settled on Prince Edward Island. [Canisby gravestone, Caithness]

SUTHERLAND, ROBERT, born 1796, from Borrobal, Kildonnan, Sutherland, emigrated via Stromness on the Prince of Wales to the Hudson Bay Company settlement at Fort Churchill on 29 June 1813. [PAC.M155.165-8]

SUTHERLAND, ROBERT, a tenant in Coul Eachter, Dornoch, Sutherland, in 1811, and 1815. [SHS.8.65/221]

SUTHERLAND, ROBERT, tenant in Kintraid, Rogart, Sutherland, in 1815. [SHS.8.231]

SUTHERLAND, ROBERT, born 1776 in Dunrobin, son of Robert Sutherland and his wife Elizabeth Baillie, settled in St Vincent in 1796, of late of St Vincent, West Indies, and Millmount, Ross-shire, died in Hastings, England, on 31 November 1828. [EA.6777.719] [NRS.RS54.PR216/228; 1910][Inverness Journal, 7.11.1828]

SUTHERLAND, ROBERT, born 1805, in Ross-shire, son of George Sackville Sutherland, [1772-1858], and his wife Jean Mackay, [1772-1858], settled in St Vincent in 1821, a stipendiary magistrate, died in London on 7 March 1883.

SUTHERLAND, ROBERT, in Achskeiriglet, Halkirk, Caithness, a former drummer of the Ross-shire Militia, and of the 78th Regiment, was accused of house-breaking and theft in 1829. [NRS.AD14.29.132]

SUTHERLAND, ROBERT, [1], a pensioner, with family, emigrated from Backies, Golspie, Sutherland, to Canada in 1829. [NLS.313.878]

SUTHERLAND, ROBERT, [2], with family, emigrated from Backies, Golspie, Sutherland, to Canada in 1829. [NLS.313.878]

SUTHERLAND, ROBERT, born 1817 in Reay, Caithness, son of John Sutherland and his wife Margaret McLeod, educated at Marischal College, Aberdeen, in 1838, a minister in Australia from 1854 to 1876, died in Reay on 31 August 1880. [F.7.599]

SUTHERLAND, ROBERT, a tenant farmer in Daveckfun, 1849. [NRS.CS280.11.63]

SUTHERLAND, ROBERTA, eldest daughter of George Sackville Sutherland of Uppar, Sutherland, married Alexander McLeod from St Vincent, West Indies, in Tain, Ross-shire, on 26 September 1823. [DPCA.1107]

SUTHERLAND, SPENCER, born 1798 in Sutherland, a railway contractor, died 4 March 1874 in Shubenacadie, Nova Scotia. [S.9567]

SUTHERLAND, SUTHERLAND, a shoemaker in Dornoch, Sutherland, was accused of forgery in 1844. [NRS.AD14.44.130]

SUTHERLAND, WILLIAM, son of Donald Sutherland, [1764-1858], and his wife Rose Gordon, [1769-1849], settled in Australia. [Kildonan gravestone, Sutherland]

SUTHERLAND, WILLIAM, born 1791, his wife Margaret born 1798, and his sister Christian born 1789, from Borrobal, Sutherland, emigrated via Stromness on the Prince of Wales to the Hudson Bay Company settlement at Fort Churchill on 29 June 1813. [PAC.M155.165-8]

SUTHERLAND, WILLIAM, joint tenant in Kinbrace and its mill, Lairg, Sutherland, in 1808. [SHS.8.229]

SUTHERLAND, WILLIAM, born 1761, a weaver, wife Isabella born 1765, son Jeremiah born 180, son Ebenezer born 1804, son Donald born 1808, and daughter Helen born 1809, from Sutherland, emigrated via Stromness on the Prince of Wales to the Hudson Bay Company settlement at York Fort 23 June 1815, landed there on 26 August 1815. [PAC.M1659/61] [MG19.E4.1.165/8]

SUTHERLAND, WILLIAM, was granted a six year lease of Gailable, Sutherland, on 29 December 1812. [SHS.9/2.175]

SUTHERLAND, WILLIAM, a tenant in Baliavalich, Sutherland, formerly a servant to Mr Sage in Kildonan, was accused of rioting, resulting from the removal or eviction of tenants in Kildonan in 1813. [NRS.AD14.13.9; SC9.7.64] [SHS.8.136]

SUTHERLAND, WILLIAM, born 1803 in Lairg, Sutherland, emigrated to Nova Scotia in 1818, died 30 November 1874. [New Lairg gravestone, N.S.]

SUTHERLAND, WILLIAM, and family from Helmsdale, Loth, Sutherland, emigrated to Canada in 1829. [NLS.313.878]

SUTHERLAND, WILLIAM, in Halkirk, Caithness, died 10 November 1841, father of George Sutherland in New York. [NRS.S/H.1865]

SUTHERLAND, WILLIAM, from Dornoch, Sutherland, was educated at King's College, Aberdeen, in 1840, later a minister in Dornoch. [KCA]

SUTHERLAND, Colonel, of Rhiarcher, tenant in Dalmore, Rogart, Sutherland, in 1811. [SHS.8.72]

SUTHERLAND, Lieutenant Colonel, tenant in Brae Grudy, Rogart Sutherland, in 1811, and in Pitfure, Rogart, in 1815. [SHS.8.80/231]

SWANNY, PETER, a merchant in Thurso, Caithness, sequestration, 1811. [NRS.CS236.S.18.9]

SWANSON, ALEXANDER, in Louisburgh, Port Dunbar, Bay of Wick, Caithness, a victim of housebreaking in 1832. [NRS.JC26.1832.132]

SWANSON, THOMAS, born 1777, Lieutenant of the 42nd Royal Highlanders, died at Heathfield House, Dunnet, on 31 March 1866. [Olrig gravestone, Caithness]

TAIT, GILBERT, in Watthersta, Delting, Shetland, and his son Hugh Tait, versus James Anderson in Wathersta, a petition, 1800. [SA.SC12.6.1800.23]

TAIT, JAMES, from St Olla, Orkney, a seaman aboard HMS Captain, died in Boston, Massachusetts, probate, 1799, Prerogative Court of Canterbury. [TNA]

TAIT, THOMAS, in Houster, Aithsling, Shetland, summons of removal in 1807, [Shetland Archives.SC12.6.1807.6]

TAIT, WILLIAM, of the Hudson Bay Company in Stromness, Orkney, died 5 October 1826, father of Catherine Tait, wife of John Garrioch a carter in Kirkwall, Orkney, and Jean Tait, wife of John Barron a, plasterer in Stromness. [NRS.S/H.1861]

TAIT, WILLIAM, an employee of the Hudson Bay Company, later settled at the Red River, a sasine, 1834. [NRS.R.S.Orkney.167]

TARRAL, WILLIAM, a tenant in Gardie, Mid Yell, Shetland, summons of removal, 1800. [SA.SC12.6.1800.17]

TATE, JOHN, from Orkney, settled at Fort Vancouver, Oregon, probate 1855, Prerogative Court of Canterbury. [TNA]

TAYLOR, ALEXANDER, emigrated from Cromarty or Thurso aboard the Lady Grey bound for Pictou, Nova Scotia, in June 1841. [NRS.RH1.2.908]

TAYLOR, BENJAMIN, born 1830, died in Christchurch, New Zealand, on 18 August 1877. [South Walls gravestone, Shetland]

TAYLOR, D. and F., tenants in Ferryoons, Golspie, Sutherland, in 1811. [SHS.8.82]

TAYLOR, GEORGE S., a writer and burgess of Dornoch, Sutherland, in 1820. [NRS.GD347.38]; a writer in Golspie, a book inventory, 1847. [NRS.GD347.65]

TAYLOR, JAMES, in Cromarty, trustee of William Junner a merchant in Cromarty in 1813. [NRS.CS36.8.69]

TAYLOR, WILLIAM, a writer and postmaster of Dornoch, Sheriff Clerk of Sutherland, a letter, 1793. [NRS.GD347.33]; a writer in Dornoch versus William Johnstone a writer in Edinburgh, on 2 October 1820. [NRS.CS42.22-28]

TAYLOR, WILLIAM, tenant in Evelix, Farr, Sutherland, in 1808. [SHS.8.223]

TAYLOR, WILLIAM, a tenant in Little Garvary, Dornoch, Sutherland, in 1811. [SHS.8.65]

TAYLOR, WILLIAM, a joint tenant in Milnton of Evelix, Dornoch, Sutherland, in 1811 and in 1815. [SHS.8.67/222]

TAYLOR, WILLIAM, a merchant in Dunnet, Caithness, a lease, 1817. [NRS.GD136.259]

THAIN, JOHN, manager of the Thurso Tanning Company, a trustee of Peter Swany a merchant in Thurso, 1811. [NRS.CS36.3.105]; a letter 1824. [NRS.GD136.554]

THOMASON, HELEN, wife of Fraser Williamson a tenant and fisher on Foula, Shetland, an inventory, 1834. [SA.SC12.6.1834.117]

THOMASON, HENRY, in Roemarlands, Grooten, Fetlar, Shetland, versus Andrew Gordon, son of Reverend James Gordon on Fetlar, Shetland, 1800. [SA.SC.12.6.1800.5]

THOMASON, OLLA, a sailor in Swarrister, Shetland, in 1839. [SA.SC12.250.1839.2]

THOMSON, ALEXANDER, born 1841, a farmer in Orkney, settled in Saltcoats, North West Territories, Canada, in 1888. [BPP.9.484]

THOMPSON, JAMES, born 1732 in Tain, Ross and Cromarty, died in Quebec on 25 August 1830. [New Brunswick Courier, 11.9.1830]

THOMPSON, JAMES, born 1799 in Ross-shire, died in Halifax, New Brunswick, on 16 June 1832. [Acadian Recorder, 23.6.1832]

THOMSON, JOHN, born 1808, a schoolmaster, died in Aithsetter on 21 October 1886, husband of Joan Inkster, born 1808, died at Aithsetter on 24 January 1892. [Cunningsburgh gravestone, Shetland]

THOMSON, MACKAY, born 11 December 1784 in Durness, Sutherland, son of Reverend John Thomson and his wife Mary Robertson, died in Kingston, Jamaica, in 1803. [F.7.102]

THOMSON, ROBERT, in Carnachy, Farr, Sutherland, a victim of housebreaking in 1824. [NRS.AD14.24.118]

TOLMIE, JOHN, from Duirinish, Ross and Cromarty, was educated at King's College, Aberdeen, in 1849, later a minister at Strontian Contin. [

TOMISON, WILLIAM, Chief Factor at York Fort, Hudson Bay, a sasine in 1805, [NRS.R.S.Orkney,632]; later in South Ronaldsay, Orkney, dead by 1838. [NRS.S/H]

TRAILL, GEORGE, versus John Harvey, re sale of the Ellen of Kirkwall, in 1829. [NRS.AC9.6108]

TRAILL, HENRY WILLIAM, of the Public Land Office at Kangaroo Point, Brisbane, Queensland, Australia, in 1848, son of John Heddle Traill. [NRS.NRAS.9110.53]

TRAILL, ISABELLA, relict of Christopher Thuring in Helsingfors, Sweden, in 1839. [NRS.GD31.513-514]

TRAILL, JAMES, of Ratter and Hobbister, a letter to Robert Heddle of Melsetter, Orkney, in 1836. [NRS.GD263.183]

TRAILL, JOHN HEDDLE, and his wife Eliza Dunbar in Saville, Sanday, Orkney, a letter re their elopement, in 1841. [NRS.GD263.94]

TRAILL, ROBERT, born 29 April 1744, son of Reverend Thomas Traill of Hobbister and his wife Sibella Grant, settled in Philadelphia, Pennsylvania, died 31 July 1816. [F.7.264]

TRAILL, THOMAS, in Duoro, Ontario, son-in-law of Patrick Fotheringham in Kirkwall, Orkney, a letter 1836. [NRS.GD26.64.6]

TRAILL, WILLIAM, of Frotoft, a shipowner in Kirkwall, Orkney, 1836-1850, sederunt book. [NRS.CS96.4261-2]

TROTTER, ALEXANDER, born 1759, died 6 May 1817, husband of Jane Sinclair, born 1777, died 8 February 1867, parents of William Sinclair in New Zealand. [Dunnet gravestone, Caithness]

TUACH, ALEXANDER, and DONALD TUACH, tenants in Ardterach, Contin, Ross, were accused of assaulting Revenue officers and breaking prison in 1818, trial papers. [NRS.JC26.1818.11]

TULLOCH, ARTHUR, in Fetlar, Shetland, was accused of plundering a Norwegian shipwreck in 1803. [SA.SC12.6.1803.47]

TULLOCH, JAMES, born 1836, son of Reverend George Tulloch and his wife Mary McIntosh Clark, an assistant surgeon of the Black Watch, died at Murree, Punjab, India, on 16 July 1867. [Scourie gravestone, Sutherland]

TULLOCH, WILLIAM, born 1801, Excise Supervisor, died at Fortrose, Ross and Cromarty, on 12 June 1883, husband of Elizabeth Urquhart, who died on 17 May 1862. [Fortrose gravestone]

TWATT, HENRY, in Setter, Walls, Shetland, Jerom Yell in Deal, Sandness, and William Moffat in Melby, were accused of frightening James Man in Truligarth, Shetland, so severely that he died in 1831. [SA.SC11.5.1831.9]

TWATT, MAGNUS, a Hudson Bay Company employee at York Fort, Hudson Bay, sasines 1806-1807. [NRS.R.S.Orkney. 695/715]

URQUHART, Reverend ALEXANDER, tenant of part of Balintample, Rogart, Sutherland, in 1811. [SHS.8.72]

URQUHART, CHARLES, born 1785 in Ross-shire, a factor in Charleston, S.C., was naturalised there on 30 March 1814. [NARA.M1183.1]

URQUHART, COLIN, born 1804, a carrier in Dingwall, Ross and Cromarty, accused of assault in 1827. [NRS.AD14.27.221]

URQUHART, DONALD, from Dingwall, Ross and Cromarty, married Catherine Bryant in Kingston, Canada, on 20 December 1834. [AJ.4545]

URQUHART, DONALD, born 1811, a quarrier in Cullicudden, Cromarty, accused of mobbing and prison breaking in 1844. [NRS.AD14.44.443]

URQUHART, ELIZABETH TRAILL, in Elsness, Sanday, Orkney, versus Alexander Fairweather in Silverhall, Sanday, a summons of removal in 1801. [OA.SC11.5.1801.32]

URQUHART, GORDON, born 23 February 1788, son of Reverend Thomas Urquhart and his wife Johanna Clunes in Rosekeen, Ross and Cromarty, a Lieutenant of the 96th Regiment, died in St Croix, West Indies, on 5 September 1808. [F.7.68]

URQUHART, or BELL, ISABELLA, born 1809, in Raddy, Rosemarkie, was accused of theft and fraud in 1836. [NRS.AD14.36.2]

URQUHART, JAMES, born 18 August 1794, son of Reverend Thomas Urquhart and his wife Johanna Clunes in Rosskeen, Ross-shire, died in St George, Grenada, on 8 April 1823. [DPCA.1095][F.7.68]

URQUHART, JESSIE, youngest daughter of Reverend Thomas Urquhart, minister of Rosskeen, Ross-shire, married John McLean from Carriacou, near Grenada, in London on 2 April 1812. [SM.74.398]

URQUHART, JOHN, born 1815, a quarrier in Cullicudden, Cromarty, accused of mobbing and prison breaking in 1844. [NRS.AD14.44.443]

URQUHART, MURDOCH, born 1803, a fisher in Ullapool, Wester Ross, was accused of rioting in 1833. [NRS.AD14.33.117]

URQUHART, ROBERT, born in Cadboll, Ross-shire, died in Charleston, South Carolina, on 11 August 1800. [GM.70.1107]

URQUHART, THOMAS, a quarrier in Cullicudden, Cromarty, accused of mobbing and prison breaking in 1844. [NRS.AD14.44.443]

VALES, ELIZABETH, born 1807 in Cromarty, residing in Old High School Close, Canongate, Edinburgh, accused of housebreaking ad theft, 1833. [NRS.AD14.33.439]

VINCENT, THOMAS, in Innertown, Stromness, Orkney, dead by 1839, father of John Vincent at Hudson Bay. [NRS.S/H]

WALKER, THOMAS, born 1852, son of John Walker and his wife Mary Williamson, died in Jackson, USA, on 24 May 1893. [Clyne gravestone, Sutherland]

WALLACE, JOHN, in Borgie, Langwell, Latheron, Caithness, a victim of rioting in 1829. [NRS.AD14.29.350]

WALLS, WILLIAM, born in Orkney, a Hudson Bay Company servant, settled in Victoria, British Columbia, in 1859, died there on 3 January 1862. [Ross Bay gravestone]

WARDS, JOHN, a farmer in Goodwalter, Rendall, Orkney, died 6 January 1869, father of James Wards in Ontario. [NRS.S/H.1882]

WARES, ALEXANDER, son of Donald Wares a farmer in Hempriggs, Caithness, married Jessie Fraser, third daughter of John Fraser a seaman in Leith, in St John's, Newfoundland, in 1872. [S.9022]

WATERS, ANN, eldest daughter of David Waters in Brems, Caithness, wife of David Sutherland a Congregationalist minister, died in Bath, New Hampshire, on 3 March 1852. [W.1309]

WATERS, JAMES, born 1840, died in Boston, Massachusetts, on 26 November 1912. [Lady gravestone, Stronsay, Orkney]

WATER, MATTHEW, a miller in Dun, Watten, Caithness, accused of rioting in 1821. [NRS.AD14.21.82]

WATERS, WILLIAM, in Scalesburn, Port Dunbar, Bay of Wick, Caithness, a victim of housebreaking in 1832. [NRS.JC26.1832.132]

WATSON, ALEXANDER, a mason in Fortrose, Ross and Cromarty, husband of Isabella Fowler, born 1749, died 25 December 1795, parents of John Watson, born 1770, late of Trelawney, Jamaica, died in

Fortrose on 5 December 1810; Colin Watson, born 1771, died in Jamaica in June 1793; and Andrew Watson, born 1776, died in Jamaica in April 1805. [Rosemarkie gravestone, Ross and Cromarty]

WATT, JOHN, in Kirkbuster, Orkney, died 21 January 1872, uncle of William Watt in Chicago, Illinois. [NRS.S/H]

WATT, WILLIAM, in Skaill, Orkney, a letter to William Sinclair, a writer in Kirkwall, re Odness and Papa Stronsay, in 1804. [NRS.GD31.459]

WEBSTER, DAVID, from Fearn, Ross and Cromarty, was educated at King's College, Aberdeen, in 1845, later minister of Fetlar. [KCA]

WHITE, ARTHUR, tenant in North Berwick, Tingwall, Shetland, was accused of stealing floss in 1832. [SA.SC12.6.1832.96]

WHITE, JAMES, of Trusta, Aithsling, Shetland, versus Robert Ross of Sound, re the division of the runrig lands of Trusta in 1806. [SA.SC12.6.1806.43]

WHITE, JAMES, in Tumbline, Aithsling, Shetland, summons of removal in 1807, [Shetland Archives.SC12.6.1807.6]

WHITE, PETER, in Trusta, Aithsting, Shetland, a victim of sheep-stealing in 1837. [NRS.AD14.37.471; JC26.1837.534]

WILLIAMSON, ANDRINA, in Nether Sound, Weisdale, Aithsting, Shetland, a victim of sheep-stealing in 1837. [NRS.AD14.37.471; JC26.1837.534]

WILLIAMSON, BARBARA, tenant in Colliesburgh, Bressay, Shetland, a summons of removal, 1800. [SA.SC12.6.1800.59]

WILLIAMSON, ELIZABETH, a merchant and fish curer in Latheronwheel, Caithness, an act and decreet, 1821. [NRS.CS44.761]

WILLIAMSON, GILBERT, tenant in Melbie, Foula, Shetland, a summons of removal in 1804. [SA.SC12.6.1804.6]

WILLIAMSON, JAMES, tenant in Croon, Nesting, Shetland, summons of removal in 1803. [SA.SC12.6.1803.13]

WILLIAMSON, JAMES, born 1816 in Caithness, settled in Greenvale, Australia, died in London on 10 August 1854. [Dornoch gravestone]

WILLIAMSON, JOHN, tenant in Melbie, Foula, Shetland, a summons of removal in 1804. [SA.SC12.6.1804.6]

WILSON, ANDREW, born 1787 in Orphir, Orkney, an employee of the Hudson Bay Company until he drowned in Lake Winnipeg in 1835. [HBRS.3.461]

WILSON, DANIEL, born 1820 in Stenness, Shetland, an employee of the Hudson Bay Company from 1842 to 1857, later settled at the Red River. [HBRS.16.378]

WILSON, WILLIAM, a shepherd in Aucorn, Wick, accused of sheep stealing in 1847. [NRS.AD14.47.128]

WISHART, EDWARD, in Oback, Orkney, dead by 1864, uncle of John Wishart a carpenter in Portsmouth, Canada West. [NRS.S/H]

WISHART, JAMES, from Kirkwall, Orkney, was educated at King's College, Aberdeen, in 1849, later a minister in Liverpool. [KCA]

WISHART, WILLIAM, in Thurso, Caithness, a victim of theft in 1830. [NRS.JC26.1830.90]

WOOD, Reverend ALEXANDER, born 1785, died 8 January 1874, husband of Agnes Walker, born 1792, died 27 March 1861. [Rosemarkie gravestone, Ross and Cromarty]

WOOD, Major ANDREW, born 1770, died 20 July 1834, husband of Kennethina Wood, born 3 December 1795, died 29 January 1878. [Rosemarkie gravestone, Ross and Cromarty]

WOOD, ANN BAILLIE, born 19 June 1782 in Rosemarkie, Ross and Cromarty, daughter of Reverend Alexander Wood and his wife Janet Houston, married John Watson in Jamaica in 1805. [F.7.23]

WOOD, CECILIA, wife of William Loutit in Rendall, versus Thomas Garioch in Ness, Stenness, Shetland, in 1802. [SA.SC11.5.1802]

WOOD, JOHN, a skipper in Stromness, Orkney, a sasine 1795. [NRS.R.S.Orkney.357/478]; master of the brigantine Royal Recovery of Stromness was stranded in the Sound of Islay, Argyll, in 1798. [NRS.NRAS.0627.box 10, bundlle 6]

WOOD, JOHN, eldest son of Reverend Alexander Wood in Rosemarkie, Ross-shire, died in Trelawney, Jamaica, on 3 May 1811. [GM.81.88]

WOOD, JOSEPH, brother of Reverend Alexander Wood in Rosemarkie, Ross-shire, died in Jamaica in March 1819. [GM.89.472]

WOOD, JOSEPH, born 29 July 1770 in Rosemarkie, Ross-shire, son of Reverend John Wood and his wife Sophia Irvine, emigrated to Jamaica, died on 21 February 1811. [F.7.23]

WORK, WILLIAM, a Customs House boatman in Kirkwall, Orkney, in 1801. [OA.SC11.5.1801.94]

YONSON, JOHN, a tenant in Nether Sound, Weisdale, Aithsting, Shetland, accused of sheep stealing in Shetland, was sentenced to transportation for ten years in 1837. [NRS.AD14.37.471; JC26.1837.534]

YORSTON, ANDREW, in Aith, Bressay, Shetland, was accused of plundering the wrecked sloop Polly of Dover on Bressay in 1800. [SA.SC12.6.1800.27]

YORSTON, ROBERT, son of Robert Yorston a farmer in Harray, an employee of the Hudson Bay Company at York Factory, Hudson Bay, a sasine 1810. [NRS.R.S.Orkney.789]

YOUNG, WILLIAM, a tenant in Rhives, Golspiemore, Sutherland, in 1815. [SHS.8.225]

YOUNG, or PEARSON, MARGARET, in Natal, South Africa, a sasine, 7 March 1854. [NRS.RS.Fortrose.1.250]

EMIGRANT SHIPS FROM NORTHERN SCOTLAND

ADMIRAL OF GLASGOW, from Stornaway to Quebec in 1851

AIMWELL OF ABERDEEN, from Thurso to Halifax in 1816

ALEXANDER, from Stornaway to Pictou in 1803

ANNE OF NORTH SHIELDS, from Stornaway to Pictou in 1811

ANN, from Stornaway to Cape Breton in 1828

BARONET, from Cromarty to Quebec in 1831

BLANCHE OF LIVERPOOL, from Stornaway to Quebec in 1852

BOWES, from Cromarty to Quebec in 1834

BRITISH KING OF DUNDEE, from Cromarty to Pictou and Quebec in 1826

CANADA, from Cromarty to Pictou and Quebec in 1830

CLEOPATRA, from Cromarty to Quebec in 1831

CORSAIR, from Cromarty to Cape Breton and Quebec in 1825

CRUICKSTON CASTLE, from Stornaway to Cape Breton and Quebec in 1839

DEVERON, from Lochinver to Pictou and Quebec in 1830

EDDYSTONE, from Stornaway to Hudson Bay in 1811

EDWARD AND ANNE, from Stornaway to Hudson Bay in 1811

ELIZABETH AND ANN OF NORTH SHIELDS, from Thurso to Charlottetown in 1806

ELLEN OF LIVERPOOL, from Loch Laxford to Pictou in 1848

EMPEROR ALEXANDER, from Cromarty to Cape Breton in 1823

ENERGY, from Stornaway to Quebec in 1838

FAVOURITE OF KIRKCALDY, from Isle Martin to Pictou in 1803

GEORGE OF DUNDEE, from Cromarty and Thurso to Pictou and Quebec in 1841

GREENOCK, from Loch Laxford to Quebec in 1848

HARMONY, from Cromarty to Pictou in 1822, and from Stornaway to Halifax and Quebec in 1827

HEDLEYS, from Cromarty to Quebec in 1832

HEROINE, from Stornaway to PEI and Quebec in 1840

HIGHLANDER, from Cromarty to St John, Halifax and Quebec in 1817

HOPE OF LOSSIEMOUTH, from Isle Martin to Pictou in 1801

INDUSTRY, from Cromarty to Pictou and Quebec in 1831

JANE KAY, from Cromarty and Thurso to Pictou and Quebec in 1833

JOSEPH GREEN, from Cromarty, Thurso, and Lochinver to Quebec in 1842

LADY EMILY, from Cromarty, Thurso and Loch Laxford to Pictou and Quebec in 1842

LADY GREY, from Cromarty and Thurso to Pictou and Quebec in 1841

LISKEARD, from Stornaway to Quebec in 1849

LOUISA, from Stornaway to Canada in 1816

MARGARET BOGLE, from Thurso to Pictou and Quebec in 1824

MARQUIS OF STAFFORD, from Stornaway to Quebec in 1851

NORTHERN FRIENDS OF CLYDE, from Stornaway to Charlottetown in 1805

OSPREY, from Cromarty and Thurso to Pictou and Quebec in 1840

OSSIAN, from Cromarty to Pictou and Quebec in 1821

OUGHTON, from Uist to PEI and Quebec in 1803

PACIFIC, from Cromarty and Thurso to Pictou and Quebec in 1835

PANAMA, from Loch Laxford to Quebec in 1847

PEKIN, from Stornaway to PEI in 1839

Foreword

Have you ever wanted something so earnestly but underestimated the effort needed to maintain your desire? Now imagine the devastation of a premature separation from that desire because you neglected to prepare properly. Unfortunately, this disparity is all too common for those longing for marriage and companionship without considering the short and long-term investments.

In an age where dating apps, imposture syndrome minimize biblical courtship, and consensual sex involving complete strangers. The sacredness of marriage is compromised by a generation of lustful men, women, and those contemplating their sexual orientation. The sense of entitlement for temporary pleasure that prompts a husband or a wife to walk away from a covenant made to a Holy God has not only destroyed families but has brought about a demonic division that continues to impact the family unit to the 3rd and 4th generations. It is sad to say that we've emerged as a society who at one point made a conscious effort to flee fornication in an attempt to escape a burning hell to a generation who credits freedom to an act of divorce.

You may have heard that no book can teach you how to be married. I beg to differ, so long as the author is willing to speak from a place of genuine transparency. Tamora writes from both experience and passion, sharing some of her most intimate experiences, learned through her transition from a young, naive girl who grew into a seasoned wife, to a divorced spiritual midwife who unapologetically advocates for God-ordained and God-sustained marriages.

She challenges both the love bird new to what appears to be a promising relationship and the self-sabotaging vulture that has become disengaged in his or her marriage to adopt a set of policies and procedures that will inevitably guard the love required to sustain a healthy marriage. Whether you are celebrating your 20th wedding anniversary or two months into a monogamous relationship, this book offers the tools and resources to glorify God in your relationship.

Dr. Kristal Walker

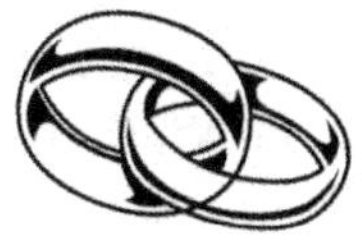

Policies & Procedures: What is the Point?

I know that you are asking, "Why do I need to follow policies and procedures?" Trust me! As you read each policy, you will understand that I was once where you are, but without the manual. I sort of felt my way through my dating process, my engagement period, and most of my marriage. However, once I learned what the design for marriage was, I agreed to adhere to it and put it into action.

I decided to be what I needed to be for my marriage. You will read some of my experiences as we cover each policy. I chose to share some experiences (lessons) to help you understand and connect the importance of why the policy is necessary. There are no big "I's" and little "you's" in this book, nor is it finger-pointing. Ultimately, you will see that when you design a plan and execute the plan, your relationship and marriage can thrive.

When adhering to the policies, you will receive clarity on the expectations and duties for both parties to follow or refer to them during your marriage.

Accountability for both husband and wife will be made clear once reading and understanding what is expected. What is most important when using the policies is that you are both on one accord. Being on one accord in a marriage guarantees a successful and thriving relationship. It does not necessarily say that you will always agree. However, expressing your differences and coming to an agreement for the sake of the marriage is the goal.

Knowing that we are going to have different opinions, yet we are committed to making it work for the union, is what being on one accord looks like. By following the policies, you commit to using them as standards for the union, and for you as an individual. The procedures or specific methods that are used to express the policies will serve as your day-to-day way of operation for the RISE of your union. I am attempting to be (for you) what I needed before I said, "I do," and when I was in the valley of my marriage.

Although this book came after my divorce, it is something that God planted in my spirit three years prior. Never did I think that the seed planted would blossom into this flower to be considered "*The Blueprint to a Thriving Marriage*." As I have had to recall and ultimately relive so many experiences that I share in this book to be clear about why policies and procedures are essential, I know now that it was necessary! I do not regret anything that I was chosen to experience.

Policies and procedures are used in business for the same reason they are needed in marriage. The Marriage Policies & Procedures (MPP) are used as a sense of structure in the boundaries of a relationship. As an employee, you agree to adhere to the policies that the company has deemed as a set of directives that will keep and continue to enhance the integrity of the company mission and vision. When employees are out of compliance, there are consequences and discipline to follow. Policies and Procedures provide a roadmap to the day-to-day operation and give guidance for proper decision-making. As it is with marriage, if we are committing to follow a set of rules that have been designed for our union, what happens when one chooses to step outside of the realm of what we said "I do" to? There is a price to pay. Not necessarily money, although if this leads to getting some type of counseling, it might. Take it all into consideration, before stepping on the other side of what you have said "I do" to.

I will never forget the day that I began to connect my everyday work with marriage. I first thought it was a bit funny that I connected the two until one day I read a "discipline letter" at work that I completed and began to insert my name where it stated "you." There was a section that said, "You have brought embarrassment to yourself and the department," and I remember feeling like, geesh, when we make decisions, not only are you affected, but those who we are committed to are affected as well. It was then that I began to toy with the thought of the MPP. Years later, my marriage began to crumble, and I was reminded of how not following what we have committed to, even if it were one party, the union would have to face the consequences.

When in a marriage, and actions are not parallel to what the MPP's state, embarrassment, and dishonor are brought to the union and the integrity of what marriage was designed for is lessened. It is about being proactive and not reactive. This manual will serve as a guide of where the relationship is, and where the union can be – all by design.

THE POLICIES

Everyone has a story, whether we talk about it or not. Our story is a direct reflection of why we say what we say and do what we do. The MPP's will allow you and your spouse to be intentional about being on the same page and understanding why you both do what you do.

There are 17 MPP's in this book to encourage you as you are building or rebuilding your solid foundation. At the end of each policy, you will have an opportunity to answer questions that will help you in creating the blueprint to your thriving marriage. Do not be afraid, to be honest, and candid for the best results. This book should not be viewed as just something to read, but something to implement into your relationship and marriage. This book is a tool…It is time to build!

You will benefit from the MPP's if…

- You have a ring on your left finger, accepted the challenge by saying, "I will marry you," but have not said, "I do."

- You think you know what marriage is, but have not walked a mile in the shoes of a wife or husband...yet? So, you ask yourself, "Do I really know?"

- You are looking for a plan that keeps a marriage thriving.

- Growing up, you were given an example of marriage, that you know today was not the best example, and you are ready to learn the correct design.

- You have not seen any healthy marriages in your community and want to be the change.

- You are ready to be equipped with the necessary tools to have a thriving marriage.

- You are not sure if this is the person that you should marry, although you are in love.

- You want to say, "I do," but honestly you are scared as hell because you do not know what you do not know.

- You have witnessed healthy marriages and want to know the tools that they used to get there.

- You have said "I do" already but need to press reset to renew and revive the relationship to thrive.

- You have said "I do," but never committed to the commitment. You only committed to love.

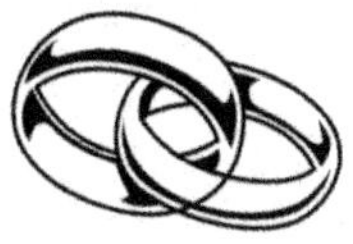

The Vow

Before we get into the MPP's, I want to encourage you to consider *The Vow*. The marriage vow sets boundaries before making the commitment. These vows hold you accountable to do just what is stated and serves as a reminder to stay committed to the commitment. If we were to dissect the traditional vow, line-by-line, here is what it may look like.

If you are married, did you realize that you were committing to ALL of this? If you are not married yet, please consider what you are committing to. Most people are not quite ready to say "I do" to ALL of this.

I_____, take you ______, to be my wife/husband, to have and to hold from this day forward for better, for worse, for richer, for poorer, in sickness and in health, to love and to cherish, till death us do part, according to God's holy law, in the presence of God I make this vow.

- ✓ **To have and to hold**
  Ok, this is a pretty easy one. We all want to be "had and held," BUT…

- ✓ **From this day forward**
  How far out is "forward?" This is where things begin to get questionable, but usually we are still good to go.

- ✓ **For better or for worse**
  We are rolling with *better*, but what does "worse" look like?

- ✓ **For richer or poorer**
  I have not met one person who has willingly said, "If we reach poorer, I'm still in 100%," before saying "I do." It is usually not a conversation that we have. We do talk about the "richer," hence prenuptial.

- ✓ **In sickness and in health**
  We *think* healthy living, even when we are not living it. Yet sickness never crosses our mind. If we think of sickness, we are usually thinking of sickness that we can see. We do not think about the illness that comes in forms of addictions, i.e., pornography or masturbation. You know things that people cannot look at you and immediately see as an addiction or vice.

- ✓ **To love and to cherish**
  Ok, we can do this. Loving and cherishing someone that you *love* is easy, but it's work when you don't, particularly *like* your spouse. FYI...there will be days that you WILL NOT like your spouse.

- ✓ **Til death do us part**
  Who gets married with the end (death) being on their mind? No one!! If you go in thinking about the end (death), saying "I do" would not be an option. However, one has to go before the other. There is no way around it.

This is the vow. Did you consider these things BEFORE you said, "I do?" Are you ready to say, "I do" for the first time or again as a recommitment?

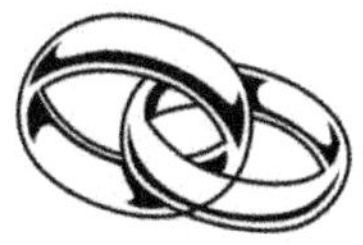

Definitions & Acronyms

It is important that you understand me clearly as you read and use this Marriage Policy and Procedures book. I have listed a few terms and definitions for you, that are included in the following policies so there is no misunderstanding.

DWAP - Dating with a Purpose; Collecting data to broaden your scope of knowledge about the person that you are dating; Understanding the end goal to be till death do us part, is knowing that you should (whether married or headed that direction) be the student and teacher simultaneously.

Marriage Toolbox - Where your strategies, and applicable principals are housed and describes all that we have been equipped with to build a thriving marriage.

Policy - Standards that you agree to adhere to on the journey as you date with a purpose or commit to the commitment that will or has led to "I Do."

Procedure - An established or official way of doing something.

R.I.S.E.- Rebuild Intentionally & Strategically for Effectiveness; Derived from Make it R.I.S.E., The ministry and organization founded by Tamora Johnson.

The "D"- Divorce

The RISE - Continual growth as you design what you desire for your relationship and marriage. There is only one way to measure your growth, and that is being in a position to do the design.

Umbrella - The husband. The covering and protector of the wife.

Year-End Review - In your marriage will you discuss what worked well, not well, and not at all in the previous year. Although you can set this to be at the beginning of the year, a birthday, or any other holiday, I recommend it be done on the anniversary. The anniversary is the day when you should be celebrating or recognizing that you' have made it through the year. Why not agree on what will continue, do more, less, or not at all in the upcoming year.

Note: At the end of each policy, there is a reflection section titled Reflect & R.I.S.E. Use this section to add any thoughts, notes, and ideas you have about the preceding policy.

The Policies

1.1

THE COMMITMENT

I did not have a plan for marriage. I figured growing up in the home with both parents; it would just happen. All I thought about was dancing. Dancing was what I would have considered "marrying" at the time. I loved it and was sure that I would spend the rest of my life doing it.

I did not grow up thinking of the dream wedding. I never wanted to be Cinderella, and I did not have Prince Charming all put together in my mind. Unlike many little girls, it never crossed my mind to be married. What was that about? I did not say things like, "My husband will be..." It just was not on my radar. I was not thinking about a husband; I was not thinking about a wedding. My parents did not say things to me like, "When you get married," until I was a sophomore in high school.

I remember signing up for an automotive class and sharing this with my dad once I got home from school. He told me that I had to drop the class because there was no need for me to learn anything about fixing a car. "Why?" was my question, and his response was, "You have me, and when you don't have me, you will have a husband for all of that." I was confused and upset at the same time. He burst my bubble.

My dad is no longer here, and I have on many occasions, said in my head, "Dad, you were wrong. I do not have you any longer and I do not have that husband you told me I would have." I chuckle when saying it, but it is my truth. "Dad, you set me up."

I was with my first husband for 18 years. We were married 14 of the 18. We were separated for 14 months before facing the "D!" For those who do not get it, "D," is for *divorce*.

When I began to think about what type of man I wanted to marry, he was the spitting image of my dad. Not necessarily his looks, but my dad was the husband that took care of his wife. He was a praying man, a hard worker, brought the money home for the bills to be paid, did things around the house, washed the cars weekly, took the car to get gas and made sure that he was active in our lives. He even helped with homework, and I felt like my dad was the smartest man on earth. I truly did. There was no question that I could ask that he did not have an answer for.

One day I asked him, "What does promiscuous mean?" He looked at me and said, "I don't know." I was shocked. I remember looking at him as he washed a few dishes thinking, "Wow, that must be a hard one if he didn't know." He was not willing to have that conversation with his elementary-aged baby. I cannot remember why I asked him, but I was so disappointed because he did not have the answer for me.

All these things that I saw my dad do and be were how I built my imaginary husband once I got to that point. But then, something happened. Maybe it was reality shows I watched, that led me to start thinking about getting married, but not once thinking about the lifetime commitment. No one told me the importance of knowing the difference between the two – not even my dad.

Dad protected, provided, and prayed, but he never gave me too much on what to watch for in a man once I began to date. The most he said about that was regarding one of the boys that went to church with me. This young man had already gotten someone pregnant. He said, "You know he's having sex, and you aren't, right?"

My only response was, "I know," and that was it. Leading and teaching, by example, may have been his way of showing me what a good man with good morals, good qualities, integrity, that loved God looked like. I wish he had sat me down and had "the talk" with me before I began dating, but especially before the proposal!

He proposed! Once the proposal happened, I was on with the planning. My focus was on the wedding and not the marriage commitment. Having a nice ceremony is great and there is nothing wrong with it, but I had my focus completely wrong. Not once did we think about pre-marital counseling. I never thought about the challenging part of the vow showing up. I definitely did not think about how we would respond when it did. What I agreed to commit to did not play a part in my thoughts at all.

Having a wedding and spending thousands of dollars to make the people happy, is not ok, especially when we have not spent an hour sitting and making sure that we genuinely understand what committing to the vow entails, the possibilities of what's to come, and how to handle them. We spend months and months planning for everything but how to adhere to the marriage commitment. My commitment was more about the planning of the wedding, and not the commitment to the marriage vows. It is easy to love, but it takes work to commit. You must do the work that keeps you committed.

The Policy: *Plan Your Marriage Commitment*

Have a plan and design for your marriage. Be sure that your time and energy goes into what will sustain and maintain the relationship. You must be willing to dedicate time to designing your union. You have to be available to make changes.

Two people who have taken the vow to honor, love, and cherish each other, during the good the bad and ugly, are going to run into times where they disagree. Both parties go into this commitment blind, not knowing exactly what to expect. At this point, we are assuming that it will be what we've seen or learned growing up or read in a book. However, we never know what our "good" is, we can never pinpoint what our "sickness" may be, we can't prepare for our "poorer," and we definitely can't predict "until death do us part!"

Planning the commitment for your marriage will assist in continual growth. You will R.I.S.E (*Rebuild Intentionally and Strategically for Effectiveness).* Committing to what you said "I do" to, and having a plan for your marriage, will keep you from violating this policy and the following policies.

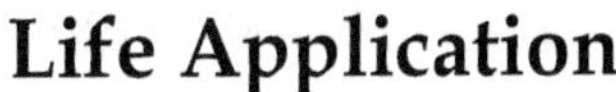

Life Application

- Discuss what the commitment is: Design your marriage.

- Have a plan to reach what you have designed and committed to.

Be sure to have the same understanding of what the commitment is and what it will look like for your marriage. There is no way to move forward with this policy and be effective if your commitments are different. Do not be afraid to talk about those differences. Ask questions that will paint a clear picture of what the expectation is. Give examples of what you define as commitment and begin to create what you will be committed to as a couple.

Once you have the solid meaning of what you are committing to, create a design for your marriage. What would you like to see in your marriage? Is it quality time? Clear communication? Sex often? Set date nights? Having the answer to this will assist in getting what you design.

It is said that life and death are in the power of the tongue, which means that you have the power to say what you want and expect that it will happen if you are doing the work. Life and death are in the power of the tongue. Plan the journey and understand that things will happen that you could not plan for, while on the journey. Just as we may have directions to a place that we are driving to, we are not always aware of the traffic, maintenance needed on the road and even traffic lights being out. We should be leaving to get there with time built in for any unexpected occurrences. Building in a piece in your relationship that protects you from the hiccups is best. Reaching what you are committing to is why designing your marriage is so important. It is tailor-made to what you want to see.

If there is not a plan to reach the design and commitment, there will not be clarity for the goal. Have a vision that is clear to you both and write it down. Having a vision that both parties can see holds you accountable for doing the work to get to the design.

Building YOUR Policy

What are you committing to?

____

____

____

What does the design of your marriage look like?

____

____

____

What are a few steps that you will need to take, to execute the desired design?

____

____

____

____

____

____

Name a time that you've had to prove your commitment to your relationship.

____

____

____

____

____

____

Once you understand the importance of planning your commitment, you are ready to do the work that it takes to stay committed. It will not always be easy to serve your spouse, but when you are committed, you will be willing to jump over hurdles, and do the work necessary to be effective in doing so.

Reflect &R.I.S.E.

1.2

SERVING YOUR SPOUSE...CLASS IS IN SESSION

After only a few years of being a wife, I thought that I knew my husband better than ever. "I'm married now!" I know him like the back of my hand. The biggest mistake I could have ever made was thinking that I knew him like "the back of my hand."

I set myself up by assuming that the person that I said, "I do" to on June 5, 2004, was still the same. I wasn't the same person, so why would he be? There had been so many changes, additions, etc. to our lives and the experience of those changes shifted our paradigm.

While I continued to serve the need of the man that I said "I do" to, things had become a bit different. Not to say that it was a bad thing, but the bad thing is that I was stuck serving the need(s) of the fiancé and not the husband that he had grown to be. We were new parents, he had a new job, we were now in a different home, and we were now operating in new roles, as husband and wife. So, to say the least, things had shifted. Everything had shifted, except my way of serving him.

Although we had already crossed the line of premarital sex, as a wife I was withholding sex from my husband. I had not considered the biblical principle that my body was no longer my own. Honestly, I never thought about what God said about this. That was definitely before learning to do marriage according to how it was originally designed. There is a time when it's ok to withhold sex and it's essential that as a married couple you know when that time is. We will get into that later.

The Policy:
Serve Your Spouse

Serve your spouse with an attitude of gratitude, while being a student available to adjust to their growth. Always be a student and teacher of your spouse. As time continues to move, different experiences are encountered, and growth on both parts will occur.

As we change, things in our lives are adjusted and shifted. If you are not both a student and a teacher, there cannot be growth. When the relationship is stagnant, you are not receiving any of the benefits that come with what you could get when operating in the relationship to its fullest capacity.

You have been built to handle all that comes with your mate. It is not to say that it will not come with working to use what you were built for, but you have what it takes. There will be some stretching involved as a result of doing the work, but it will assist you in being greater for the union as you do so.

Life Application

- Have a mindset to serve your spouse.

If you are not willing to serve your spouse, it is time to shift your mindset. When you are prepared to serve the needs of your spouse, you are also preparing yourself to be served by your spouse. Remove the focus off yourself when you are in the role of the student. You cannot be selfish when you are learning your spouse.

Having the mindset to serve your spouse keeps you available to see, hear, and adjust to what changes are necessary to be a star student. This is when allowing your marriage to be a mirror and not a window takes place. Looking into a mirror allows you to reflect on who you are but looking out the window at your spouse puts you in a finger pointing position.

- Stay available to learn new things about your spouse.

You must keep an open mind and heart to receive growth and change. Your spouse will not have the same mindset, after saying, "I do." In most cases, you will not know it is happening. Your spouse's mindset will shift, and you will not be able to see it. However, know that it will happen. There may come a time when you expect a particular response, and it will be something different. Why? Because the shift has occurred, and your spouse is evolving.

- -Be willing to teach your truths that may be new and understand that you may have to reteach the lesson sometimes for clarity.

You too will have changes as you grow, and the expectation is that your spouse will adapt and grow with you. In this instance, you must put on the hat of a teacher. Class is in session! This is why being willing to teach or reteach your truths that may be new, is important. Have those conversations that allow for "make up" work when the lesson was not executed properly. The goal is that you can teach it for your spouse to understand and pass the test when given.

Building YOUR Policy

Is it easier for you to be a teacher or a student? Why?

Which hat have you worn the most in your relationship? The teacher or the student?

Intentionally take the time to teach your spouse a new lesson about you. Teaching could be done on a date night. Once you have given the lesson, ask a question to see how your spouse received it, and if corrections are needed, make them for clarity.

Now that you have completed this policy, I am certain that the following policy, *Effective Communication* will come in handy in delivering your lesson and receiving from your spouse. These two policies work great when paired together.

Reflect &R.I.S.E.

1.3

ARE YOU A GOOD LISTENER, HEARER, & DOER? (THERE'S A DIFFERENCE)

He listened, but he did not hear me. I would express my feelings, thoughts, and emotions to my ex-husband, and he would disregard what I was saying, or at least that is how I felt. Just because you are quiet does not mean you are listening and hearing. Now, I had become the nagging wife, and we all know that a nagging wife is like a leaking roof in a rainstorm.

I always thought, "If I am repeating myself (nagging)," you must be repeating the action, which is causing me to nag. I learned to stop reacting to the action, instead of responding to the action, give it to God and focus on something beneficial. More prayer and focus on how I could be a better wife, or a better listener were needed.

I was not successful at this until I listened to God and heard His instructions. Listening to someone does not take energy or work. Hearing, however, is putting what you have listened to, into action by doing the work. There is a difference!

Effective communication in a marriage is when both parties are clear about the message being delivered and received. The style of communication may not be the same for both parties, and this is most important to know when communicating effectively. Verbal and physical communication are both included. To get a clear understanding, you must first know the language. When speaking to someone who was raised to speak a different language than you were raised to speak, there could be a language barrier. You may initially attempt to make out what is being said, but it will definitely be a struggle. You may never understand what is being said, and this is when we seek assistance.

Marriage works the same way. We may not consider it to be a language barrier, but that is precisely what it is. Therefore, learning your spouse's primary language will be a helpful tool to keep in your marriage toolbox. Fluently speaking what is understood, is appreciated.

The Policy:
Communicate Effectively

Know your love language before requesting your spouse to speak it. It will require you to become bilingual if your language is different than theirs.

Life Application

- -Learn the language of your spouse.

The love languages are defined in the book, "The Five Love Languages," by Gary Chapman. They include: 1) words of affirmation, 2) quality time, 3) receiving gifts, 4) acts of service, and 5) physical touch. Depending on the individual, you could very well speak multiple languages. Strive to stay away from speaking "your" language only, to your spouse, expecting him or her to respond clearly.

Just as your language has to be studied and learned before it's spoken to you, you must do the same for your spouse. Compromising becomes a major factor. It is easier for us to speak the language that we are accustomed to, but this will require you to step outside of your box and speak their love language, even if it is uncomfortable.

- Speak the language.

Once you are willing to learn their language and communicate their way, they are more open to communicate your way. Listen to what they are asking but remember that there is always a piece that you must listen to that they are not saying. Who knows, at some point, you may both agree on one style of communicating that works for not one or the other, but the union. Listen, hear, and do!

Building YOUR Policy

What is your communication style? Do you know your mates love language?

____

____

____

____

____

Your spouse may be bilingual. Does more than one communication style describe their love language?

____

____

____

Use the online 5 Love Languages Quiz at 5lovelanguages.com to find out your love languages and discuss them. Before taking the quiz, list what you both would say your love languages are. After taking the quiz and getting the correct answers, if they were different, explain why you chose the language(s).

This policy should have shed light on the effective way of getting points, messages, and requests across. Use this policy to determine how you will design the roles and assignments for your marriage and decide who will be expected to do what? The following Policy 1.4 *Be Clear About Roles and Assignments* will help you get there.

Reflect &R.I.S.E.

1.4

ROLE PLAY .... THE ROLES JUST GOT REAL!

Two months before saying, "I do," my husband lost his job. For me, I was not worried. We were just about done paying the balance for everything. My family really stepped in and played a major part in the entire process, i.e., decorating, cooking, coordinating, and the planning in general. We did not take a big hit financially. Although I was going to work daily, he was home cooking, cleaning and once I had the baby, taking care of her. That helped out a lot. It kept the cost of childcare down, and I was actually able to come home and relax since he was handling things at home.

Periodically, I thought, "He needs to go to work," because of what I was raised to see and believe. "A man doesn't work; a man doesn't eat." Plus, growing up, my father was the breadwinner. My mom worked, but only because she chose to. Now, was that the truth? Probably not, but that was my truth, and what I believed it to be. But in my attempt to show what marriage "really is" and support my husband, many times I would not mumble a word about what I truly felt. I would not suggest doing this. It is the opposite of "effective communication."

I thought he should have worked harder to find a job, allow me to stay home with the baby, do the cleaning and cooking etc., because that is the role of a man. That is what I thought at the time. It is funny how we create a role according to our experience, as opposed to communicating what actually works for the union.

At this point, I was all over the place emotionally about him being a stay at home dad. My own opinion was shaped by the views of others. If I spoke with someone that gave him praise for doing all that he did, I was on the bandwagon with them celebrating him. If I spoke with someone who thought that we were doing it backwards, I totally agreed with them. It took some time for me to get grounded.

What is getting grounded? Great question. Getting grounded is knowing what works for your marriage and effectively communicating with each other, how it will be executed. Remember, what may work for one couple, may not work for another. This is a tailor-made deal.

Most importantly, I had to realize that I was still allowing other thoughts, opinions, and experiences to sway mine. Who says that because things worked in one home, that it would work in mine? I mean, after all, it was a temporary situation. He was looking for work, but being home was also beneficial.

It is funny how when he got what I was so pressed for him to have (a job), the roles began to change slowly. Now, I had to pick up the baby from childcare, grab my oldest from school, cook dinner for the family, assist with homework, spend some time with him, and make sure that the girls were good for the evening. Then, I had to get them to bed, wash clothes when needed, get myself together for bed, and most nights wake up to a tap on the shoulder, or other places, and be *ready*. "I'm married, now," and the roles just got real!

The Policy:
Be Clear About Roles and Assignments

Have a clear understanding of who will be held accountable to do what. Build-in areas of this policy that will allow for roles to be interchangeable when it works best for both parties, and ultimately the union. Your role and assignment have an umbrella effect when you allow it to. The umbrella effect builds in the sense of safety, protection, and covering. When the design is agreed upon, your roles and assignments are contingent on what works for your home. The overall design for man and woman does not change and has no room for alterations.

As the man, your base role is to protect, provide, and love your wife. Protection comes in many forms and once you have become a student of your wife, you will learn what she needs your protection for, and what you need to provide. The woman's base role is to submit and reverence her husband. Her behavior and inner beauty should speak louder than her outer beauty and be an encouragement for him to love her as he has been designed to do.

These are both "serving" roles. Learning to serve your spouse need is half the battle. Not that it is a battle, so to speak, but it is definitely work. There should never be downtime for learning and teaching. Unlike work, we do not get to put in for vacation when married or in a committed relationship. Sick days do not exist. When you are sick, there's still work to be done, and you surely do not get an option of transferring to another unit or job just because you are tired of this position or location. If you are not ready to serve, you are not ready to say, or should not have said "I do!"

Life Application

- Know the need for what your marriage requires for roles and assignments to be completed.

The work to be done can only be determined based on what the need is. Have you already established what your desire for your marriage is? If not, set things aside and make it a priority to get it done. Now is the time to say how you will reach it. Doing things that bring results for another area of your marriage is a prime example of using the wrong tools from your marriage toolbox. For example, you may assist in picking up dry cleaning for your spouse on Fridays, and it's appreciated, but what they are really asking you to do is help out with dinner on Tuesdays because that may be the day that they're most exhausted due to scheduled weekly meetings. Either cook a meal or go grab dinner. Knowing the need is important.

- Do the work to get it done.

What is the goal? What do you want to accomplish in your marriage? You cannot sit and stare and wish upon a star to get results. Doing the work that it will take to receive what you are looking for is imperative. Once the need is communicated effectively, it is time to get busy and execute. As a team, you can achieve the dream, and therefore doing the work together is important.

- Use the correct tools in your marriage toolbox.

You have been equipped with the proper tools in your marriage toolbox to build and continue to build. Your tools, i.e., effective communication, laughter, supporting and encouraging your spouse, prayer with and for your spouse, sex, and quality time, to name a few, will guarantee the R.I.S.E in your marriage when appropriately used. Many times, we are aware that we have the tools, but we have not been taught when and where to use the tools. Using the wrong tool in the wrong area of your marriage will damage the area. Therefore, it is essential to use the tools in your marriage toolbox, in the correct area.

For instance, using the tool of effective communication, when only prayer is needed, is not so effective. We must be wise enough to discern or determine where to use the tool. However, there may be a time where your spouse may need that encouragement and support to motivate, reassure, and confirm that they are in the right place and making the right move. Know the difference; it will make the difference.

Building YOUR Policy

Do you believe in assigning roles and sticking to them, even when a little change would make it easier for your spouse?

List your reasons why? Selfish and Selfless...two words to take into consideration when answering this question.

Trade roles periodically. Give your spouse duties that you would do in a day's work and talk about it the following day. What roles and assignments will you trade? Make a list below and follow up on a designated day.

Does it seem that your role is appreciated more after this assignment? Trading roles is one way of finding the need.

As important as it is to solidify the need for the marriage and choose roles and assignments for each other, it is equally important to find the time to do so. Quality time can be used for things such as this — a time where you are both focused on each other and the growth of the marriage by design. The next policy will lay out what quality time is for and why it should be used wisely.

Reflect &R.I.S.E.

1.5

WHEN YOU DON'T INTENTIONALLY CONNECT, YOU AUTOMATICALLY DISCONNECT

What kind of schedule is this? He worked graveyard (5 pm – 5 am), thirteen days on, twelve hours a day, and three days off (Saturday, Sunday, Monday). I worked dayshift (7 am - 3:30 pm), five days a week, eight hours a day, and two days off (Saturday, Sunday). For the most part, it worked, until for me, it just did not work anymore.

When the kids were younger and involved in different activities and needed to be picked up from here and there at a specific time, he was available, and it worked. I was able to get them to practice and or games etc. and it worked. But as they got older and became a bit more independent, I had a change of heart. I wanted more. I needed more. I desired more of his time. Quality time.

The more I thought about the importance of connecting with your spouse, the more I wanted it. I was the "if there's more to get, let's get it" type, while he was the "if it's not broke, why fix it" type. Granted, there is nothing wrong with either of those philosophies. However, we were not on the same page, and that is what made it wrong.

You know women, we are usually the ones to try to make it make sense. My suggestion was that on his Mondays off, he would come to the job and we could have lunch together. Honestly, I was not asking for every Monday that he was off, but once a month would have sufficed. Yes, there were weekends when he was off that we did things. Sometimes with the kids, sometimes with friends, and other times just the two of us. His reasoning for saying "no," was because he would have dinner cooked (most times) when I got home, as to say, it was taking a load off once I got home. Thank you, thank you, thank you, and it was always appreciated. Lunch once a month was just something that I wanted to incorporate into our intentional connecting.

Spending time together with the kids and friends was not like spending time alone. Maybe I was a bit hyper-sensitive in this area because I was teaching it in my ministry. And maybe there were times that I even used some of what I wanted as a case study, but it was all genuine, and I was certain that it would help more than hurt the marriage, so why not? If we can have more, let's get it.

Intentionally connecting is a part of being a student and teacher in your marriage. It provides the opportunity to learn what is shifting, what needs to shift, what is doing good right where it's at, any adjustments needed, etc. Not that it has to be a heavy encounter each time but learning by action is a great teacher as well. Having fun together is connecting. Laughing is connecting, and all of this reminds us of why we said, "I do." When these things are not being intentionally done, changing as individuals, which affects the marriage, automatically occurs. Be aware of what is happening in the union, on purpose!

The Policy: *Schedule Quality Time*

Make attainable goals to spend the time that will serve as an opportunity to pour into each other, love on each other, be a student and teacher and execute anything that will help the marriage RISE!

Quality time is the time spent in giving your spouse undivided attention to strengthen the relationship. With the everyday jobs that both parties have, it is imperative that time is taken to spend together without any distractions. Focusing on your spouse reminds them that they matter, they are important, needed, and nothing or no one comes before them. We are usually not given an option to focus on what we are working on solely. We are encouraged to balance it all. When balancing time with your spouse, it says that everything stops except what "we" are doing, it speaks volumes about your order of importance.

Life Application

- Intentionally discuss schedules.

Your schedule and all that you do is important to share with your spouse. Your spouse should know what you have on your calendar or have access to it. When the schedule is discussed, adding your quality time date on the calendar becomes an easy task. If both parties are aware of what is happening, choosing a realistic time is simple and a success. It is vital to intentionally discuss each other's schedules.

- Assign a set time to spend quality time with your spouse.

Having a weekly and maybe a monthly activity or vision board available to refer to will help with avoiding double booking or becoming frustrated because you are trying, but there seems to never be any time. Scheduling a set date night, lunch, or quick getaway would also be a great idea. This is imperative if you want to make sure that the time is set.

- Put it on the calendar.

Whatever you do, be sure to put yourselves on your calendar of things to do. Too often, we place our marriage on the back burner because we believe that they will understand and will always be there. While there may be some truth to it, things like this tear away at the relationship and not intentionally connecting becomes the norm. Eventually, you will automatically disconnect. You will be left asking, "How did we get here?" Therefore, putting yourself, and your marriage on the calendar is important.

- Try to avoid having to reschedule set quality time and dates, but if there is no way around it, immediately do so and do not consider it a loss.

If for some reason something comes up that you cannot avoid, and are forced to cancel your quality time date, reschedule immediately. Do not push it off and assume that it is ok to wait until the next scheduled quality time. Place yourselves back on the calendar. This time is still necessary to spend. When your spouse feels like other things and people come before them, this could cause a problem. Therefore, I encourage you to reschedule and put it back on the calendar immediately but do not make it a habit.

Building YOUR Policy

What does quality time look like for you?

____

____

____

____

How often will you connect for quality time? Will it be weekly, bi-weekly, or once a month? The more you connect, the less chance of disconnecting will occur in your marriage.

____

____

____

____

Choose date night together and place it/them on the calendar monthly. List some of your favorite places to go with each other or create a list of places to go or things to do that neither of you has done before.

How do you choose your date night or quality time spent?

____

____

____

____

____

____

Quality time is one of the best opportunities to let go of the everyday hustle and bustle and just enjoy each other. Life has so many twists and turns, ups and downs and ultimately stressors. Some that we can avoid or quickly fix, and others that we have no choice but to ride the wave until it is over. Designating quality time will always have its advantages because you get to choose what you will do. Quality time can sometimes even lead to what is behind the next policy door: SEX! Knowing that you will have each other all to yourselves can ignite a little foreplay that can end in a bit of fun throughout this set time. Let us talk about sex, baby, in the next policy!

Reflect & R.I.S.E.

1.6

SEX...THE TOOL THAT'S OFTEN USED THE WRONG WAY

I have heard so many things about a woman and her "Hakuna Matata" (vagina). For example, I have heard, "No woman should be broke when you are sitting on a gold mine." Is that what it is come to? While I understand the statement, I do not quite agree with it. That is unless I am selling it.

If he is my husband, it gets deeper than what is between my legs. My chaste attitude and my inner self will override any outer adornment that he sees. Yes, every man wants the eye candy, but a husband looks for and desires a wife that is able to take care of business, manage the home, take care of the kids, cook a good meal, and be a good steward over everything that not only God has blessed her with, but the things that he has blessed her with.

It takes a wise man to receive that and allow it to mean more than sex. I believe that with providing all the necessary things that a wife should offer, we would consider it ongoing foreplay. Sex is inevitable. You will get it either way.

I recall when I used this tool for all the wrong reasons. Somewhere in those 18 years, there were times when I truly believed and lived by the attitude "if he's not acting right, he ain't getting none of this." Wrong attitude, but it was my attitude. Nights or mornings that my husband would come in after a time I thought was inappropriate, and he did the "tap tap" (wake up) method, I would place him on punishment. BOY BYE! You do not get to stay out until the early hours of the morning and think it is about to go down. Nope...not with me.

I was a mess for that. But on the flip side, which was still considered using the tool the wrong way, I gave it up more when there was something that I needed or wanted. I was taught wrong. I knew that it was a tool but never taught how to use it properly. Sex is not a tool to use for punishing your spouse. Sex is to be enjoyed and not used as a weapon or withheld as a punishment. Sex became my weapon, however.

Never did I give any thought to changing my mentality about sex. Withholding sex definitely did not help with getting my husband to come home earlier. What point does this prove? Although sex should not be used as a game, I used it as one, and I never won! This game went on for quite some time, and I cannot remember what the turning point was for me, but I sure had a change of heart at some point.

As far back as I can think, I know that it took a little time to retrain myself and my belief system regarding sex. At the time, I did not have wise counsel. Hell, at the time, I did not have any counsel. I was too busy wearing the mask. The mask that said we had it all together. Eventually, pieces of the mask began to fall off and as I attempted to catch each piece and glue it back in place, the mask became weaker and weaker. Cracks began to appear even when they had been glued. I had no choice but to remove the mask, but because of fear that our true identity would be revealed, somehow, I found another one and replaced it for as long as I could.

The Policy: *Know When it is Ok to Withhold Sex*

Be available for the sexual needs of your spouse. The act of sex is a manifestation of one flesh. Neither husband nor wife have authority over their own body. We are not to deprive one another, except perhaps by agreement for a limited time, that you may devote yourself to prayer, but then reconnect to keep the tricks of the mind and world from slipping in and out.

Sex is a tool and should not be used as a weapon. Weapons are designed to inflict bodily harm or physical damage. Tools are used to assist in completing something that is being built for enhancement. Sex can be used either way, but your mindset will be a significant factor in how you choose to use it. It is up to you.

Life Application

- Only withhold sex when both agree, and this should only be done for a short period.

Withholding sex is WRONG! Once you commit to be the husband or wife, you no longer have authority over your own body, but you must now yield it to your spouse.

- Give your spouse full access sexually.

Because of the authority that your spouse has over your body, he or she now has full access sexually to it at their leisure. Giving your spouse full access to your body is not the easiest at all times, but the importance of trusting your spouse not to take advantage of the authority comes to play at this point in the marriage.

- Come together often.

Work, kids, and the everyday hustle and bustle sometimes put a strain in this area of the marriage, but it is essential to come together often, as this is another form of *communicating*. *Communicating* in this manner as often as possible is healthy.

- Do not use withholding sex as a punishment.

Your spouse is your spouse and not your child. Withholding sex as a form of punishment is never the answer to fixing a problem. Not speaking to your spouse about a situation because you are angry does not solve a problem, just as withholding sex does not solve a problem.

Do not withhold sex as a form of punishment. It will only make matters worse. Who's winning? Honestly, withholding sex will only push or encourage your spouse to do what you are "trying" to ask them not to do.

 Building YOUR Policy

When would it be ok to deny your spouse of his or her sexual needs?

____

____

Have you ever used sex as a weapon against your spouse?

____

____

The build-up to the actual act begins before it happens. Try having conversations throughout the day that can be used as a vehicle to get to the main event. What are some things that prepare you for sex?

____

____

____

____

Make a list of things that you would consider foreplay, that your spouse may not know you consider as foreplay.

____

____

____

____

____

____

Sex...the tool that feels good to use. Most tools don't necessarily feel good when using, but they are necessary to use when fixing something that may be broke or may need a bit of enhancement. This tool has its benefits and creates communication within the marriage that provides a very intimate way of delivering it. When using the tool, the husband enters a conversation that will never end mentally as the wife receives every word spoken and feels covered in the process. The following *Understand the Effect of Being the Covering* describes the benefits when the policy is properly executed. When a wife is assured that she is being covered, she will be vulnerable.

Reflect &R.I.S.E.

1.7

COVERING IN THE STORM

What is that feeling? Why do I feel so vulnerable? Why does it seem like I am being attacked in so many areas of my life now? These are the questions that I asked God, and it took a minute for me to hear his response clearly. It is not that I was not listening for the answer, but my emotions were speaking louder than He was.

This reminds me of when a baby is crying or throwing a tantrum. I am not having a yelling match with my child. It is not happening. Go ahead and get it out, and once you realize that the response you thought you would get isn't happening, you will calm down. At that point, the child will then be able to hear what I was saying all along. God will allow us to be so emotionally drawn into the circumstance, that He is spiritually drowned out, and He is not competing with that.

The day that my ex-husband decided to remove the "umbrella," I felt it. I felt the rain. I felt the wind. I was in the storm. God allowed my covering to be removed so that I could experience what being covered really felt like. You never know what you have, until you do not have it anymore. Although I did not ask for the umbrella to be removed, it was a part of my journey and on this journey, I had to experience the storm in this way.

It was no secret that I was experiencing things that had always been there, but I had been protected from it by my ex-husband as he covered as best he could. I was so vulnerable. It felt like every wind that blew; I could tell you it's direction and the speed. I felt every raindrop individually, and when it hailed, the pain that I experienced was unspeakable.

During this time, I thought to myself, "*Wow, the importance of the covering is not talked about enough. Men need to be aware of what danger they place their wives in.*" But I also thought this is my time to use the tools that God had given me as a Christian to go to war. It was not time to stop, drop, and roll. I had to fight! Then, I felt Gods covering.

What a difference in the covering. From being covered by God (before marriage/wisdom) to being covered by my husband. Then, being uncovered and in the battle, which felt as if I was alone, back to being covered by God and having the wisdom and knowing the difference now. I'm covered!

The Policy: *Understand the Effect of Being the Covering or Being Covered*

Husbands be the protector and covering. Your covering will be her comfort and security in the marriage. This particular covering and protection is felt whether you are in her presence or not. Just as an umbrella shields from the rain, the husband does the equivalent when the wife needs to be shielded, protected, and covered from the different things that occur in life. This covering should be felt whether he is near or far. The spiritual aspect of covering and being covered is an act of protection.

As the wife, there are some things that she should never feel the complete blow from, and as the husband, he should work for this to be the goal. There will be some things that both will have to address, but the wife shouldn't feel the bulk of the responsibility because she knows that her King will handle it, yet she will hold the umbrella up (support his moves) as needed.

Life Application

- Cover her in prayer daily.

To protect and cover your wife, is to spiritually stay connected to the Creator so that He can cover you and that will be the example of how to cover her. Speak life over her daily and summons things that will enhance who she is as a woman and wife, which will benefit the marriage

- Listen, hear, and address her concerns.

Listening is having the ability to hear, but hearing is putting action to what has been said. It should always be your desire to hear and move on what has been said, especially when it is beneficial to the marriage. Once you have heard her, decide on how you will address what she is sharing and move on it.

- Confirm your love for her.

Acting on what her concerns are confirms your love and respect for her. There will be times when you may not agree, however, effectively communicating that is another form of confirming your love for her. She will appreciate you communicating with her for understanding even when you do not agree.

- Be attentive and always be a student of hers.

Pay close attention to what is needed or requested. Your wife is teaching you who she is. Being attentive is a sure way to receive the same in return. When you permit yourself to be attentive, you are also constantly being a student of hers and learning who she is and who she is becoming. With time and different experiences, change is inevitable, and having the ability to adjust and address the new things will be necessary in order to continue to be the umbrella that you were designed to be, covering and protecting her.

Building YOUR Policy

Husbands, did you know that you are the umbrella for the elements that will be inevitable?

____

____

____

What are a few things that you expect to be her covering for? Wives, what are some things that you expect him to cover you from?

____

____

____

____

Have you considered the danger that she is vulnerable to when the umbrella is removed?

____

____

____

____

After reading this policy, will you make changes with how you cover her?

____

____

____

This policy was geared for the men, but there was definitely a portion for the women to take in and appreciate. Many times, there are standards and things that the husband is held accountable for that we aren't taking into consideration. It may come across as being unappreciative. It is our job to express our appreciation and honor his works. Doing this shows our support to what he is doing for the sake of covering. The following Policy 1.8 *Support Each Other* gives a clearer picture of how support is necessary, and very important when working as a team.

Reflect &R.I.S.E.

____

____

____

____

____

____

____

____

____

1.8

SPOUSAL SUPPORT

Make it R.I.S.E was born in 2015. As I fed my ministry, my baby, I knew that I would need the support of my husband (the baby daddy). I was afraid and felt unqualified, but I soon came to realize that you are automatically qualified if it is your purpose and you do the necessary work to accomplish the goal of the purpose. Honestly, I was not certain in the beginning that it was my purpose, but I was certain that what I was offering was needed. People were hurting in marriage and that was due to the lack of knowledge, encouragement, and transparency of others. I would say that it took me about a year before I began to truly believe that advocating for healthy marriages was my purpose.

My husband and I had been through some tough times and I kept being nudged to share some of the things that we had encountered, but like anyone else, I did not want to expose what we had gone through. I felt like some of it was embarrassing and most of it no one had a clue about, so I did not want to remove the mask that I was wearing. I wasn't ready. As time went on, and I continued to get *the nudge* I had to answer the call.

Answering the call consisted of me getting my husband's approval to share some of our trials as I spoke with and advocated for healthy marriages. Unsurprisingly, he said he did not mind. I explained what my vision and mission was, and he was still ok with it. As I created my platform for Make It R.I.S.E, there came times when I had to speak to wives and husbands and include my personal story. He was okay with that.

There were times when I needed his assistance to set up at different workshops that I was hosting, and he would assist me. He gave me support in these areas. I appreciated it, but this was the surface support. The support that the world saw and created a grand story about.

The support that I NEEDED was the behind the scenes support. I needed prayer (with me) for the ministry and each workshop, event, and anticipated attendees. I needed and desired prayer over our marriage because the enemy would have to stop the deliverer for the message to be intercepted. There were also times that I needed a male point of view on a topic or something that I would be addressing at a workshop. Sending it to him for review or his opinion was like pulling teeth. These were the things that were most needed as spousal support during the journey of building Make It R.I.S.E. and advocating for healthy marriages.

The Policy: *Support Each Other*

Learn the weight of what your spouse is doing. Bear part of the weight with your spouse and hold him/her up. Your spouse should never feel alone. In any situation, whether they choose to get your opinion or support for something, there should not be a question. The greatest feeling is knowing that what makes you sad, makes them sad; what makes you laugh, makes them laugh; what concerns you concerns them; But most importantly, what disappoints you and makes you want to give up, they empathize but motivate and encourage you to keep going.

Your spouse is your biggest cheerleader. They are the ones closest to the court when you are playing the game. They will be the ones who will have access to you when or if needed while the fans sit in bleachers and watch from afar. They pay attention when they choose to and cheer if they feel like it. Your spouse was hired to do the job, and there is an expectation that it will get done.

Life Application

- Have an understanding of what the task is.

You must first know what your spouse is working on. Asking questions and how you can serve is important to get an understanding of what the task is. Your interest in what they are doing is the start of you supporting them.

- o Learn the needs of the task and all that it would take to execute it successfully.

The journey to getting the task done is where help will be needed. We all have goals but doing the work during the journey is what gets us there. Lend a hand where it's needed to execute the task successfully.

- o Offer your assistance.

Ask your spouse how you can help. Even if there isn't much for you to do with the particular task, offer your help in another area. Maybe you can have lunch or dinner prepared and brought to them. A simple kiss and I love you is also appreciated.

- o Be proactive when possible.

It is impressive and appreciated when you are proactive and not reactive. Knowing the goal and the journey is half the battle. Being proactive and moving towards the goal when you can, instead of being reactive helps get to the intended goal quicker. Being a team player goes a long way.

Building YOUR Policy

Are you current with your spousal support, or are you playing catch up?

____

____

____

____

What do you consider supporting your spouse and what is an example of that?

____

____

____

____

When is the last time you offered your support to your spouse, and what did you do?

____

____

Ask your spouse if you could be a part of one of their projects after reading this policy. Once you assist them, ask how it made them feel and return to this policy to add the emotion, words, and body language seen at that time.

Supporting your spouse is a tool that will always make them feel appreciated and loved. Wanting to lend services where you can is a true testament to what teamwork looks like and how it can be an asset to the marriage when consistently done. To make it a consistent practice, you must intentionally do it on purpose. Nothing will become second nature if we aren't. Pay close attention to our next Policy 1.9 *Have A Strategic and Intentional Marriage*. Do it on purpose!

Reflect & R.I.S.E.

1.9

DO IT.... ON PURPOSE

Whether I wanted us to be or not; we were an example of "what marriage is" on display. I realized that anytime you profess to stand for something, folks will watch to make sure you are lining up with what you are standing up for. The day I posted my acceptance to advocating for healthy marriages and doing business as "Make It R.I.S.E," the light became brighter, the judgment became louder, and the enemy became stronger. I had just silently said, "Hey, y'all look at us with a fine-tooth comb."

Initially it was no problem, but when he began to come home and say, "I ran into one of your little followers," I knew that we had come to a place that was a bit uncomfortable for him. I was absolutely fine with it. I knew the attention it would bring, and I also explained this to him before committing to make clear what it REALLY look like.

****

"The Dating Game" couples' event that I organized and put on was a hit. It was a sold-out event, and every couple in attendance came with an open mind, ready to have some fun. It was exactly what I fasted and prayed for leading up to the event.

I wanted the couples to show up and be available for the fun, but the lesson as well. The game was fun and interactive. We had wine, we had food, and we had prizes. The event ended and we packed up and went home. We got home at about 10 pm and I was dog tired, but as usual, I was ready to review and get a little feedback from the Mr. To my surprise he wanted to step out and hang...with friends. I thought it is not the time for that and stated it as well. He insisted and he left. Let's say that I was not happy, at all. That is not how I expected the night to end.

The next morning, I decided to press reset and let it go. "Good Morning, are we going to church?" I asked. He answered, "No, not today," but not once looking at me. "Are you ok?" I asked. He nodded his head and said, "Yes." I then asked, "Are WE ok?" He looked at me and said without hesitation, "No, I don't want to be married anymore."

Wait…what?

The process of getting him to hear God about this decision that he was making truly was not very hard. Three weeks had passed, and he was still set on not wanting the marriage anymore. I told him a few times that God had not given me the approval to stop being his wife, so until then, I will be the wife, which I did. At the time, my ankle was broken, and there was only so much that I could do psychically, but I was obedient to God. I operated as if he had never said that he did not want the marriage anymore. Obedience is better than sacrifice.

A few weeks later, he attended a men's conference with the church, and God specifically told me what would happen. He said: 1) *he will contact you and express how much he loves you, 2) I will meet him there, and 3) when he returns he will be a different man, and he will express his sincerest apologies like never before.* Everything that God told me would happen happened. It blew my mind. All of this was a result of my obedience and continuing to be the wife with purpose. It would have been easier just to say *ok* and throw in the towel. It was not our first rodeo. We had been at these crossroads before. Do not get me wrong; I was not a saint. I cannot say that he was always the cause of our chaos. It was not until I allowed God to heal me of my insecurities that I realized enjoying attention from other men wasn't the antidote to getting more attention from the man I wanted more attention from…my husband.

For the next few months, things were extremely sensitive, but he said that God met him at the conference and told him what he needed to do and that he was committed to doing it. I trusted his word because it was confirmation to what God had told me. The missing part to this was there was no written vision, but we attempted to do everything on purpose and intentional. Making each other aware of our growth became common. We were very proud. We discussed in detail what we wanted in the marriage, where we would go from there and how we would get there, and we moved on it.

Things were great, as long as we stayed committed to strategizing and being intentional about doing the work. When work slowed down because we got comfortable, things began to change, and our way of handling disagreements evolved as well. I would ask if he noticed that we had gotten a bit comfortable and he did not agree, so many things that I would bring to his attention felt like I was the "nagging wife." No one wants that lady in their house. These were the times that I realized that he was the "if it's not broke don't fix it" type of thinker, while I was the "there's more/better to get, let's get it" kind of thinker. Neither being wrong or right, but if we were not strategizing and intentionally doing one or the other together, it was wrong and did not help the marriage thrive.

The Policy:
Have a Strategic & Intentional Marriage

Identify the overall aims, interests, and the means of achieving them. Be deliberate about your goals for your marriage, and effectively communicate them. What do you consider to be a successful marriage? These are the things that you and your spouse must agree to and create a plan that leads you directly to it. Build-in space for hiccups because they will happen. Your aim may change or shift periodically. Make yourself available to adjust to the changes.

Life Application

- Be aware of what has not worked and what has worked in the marriage.

Your experience is important. There is a saying that we've all heard, that tells us not to beat a dead horse over the head. If the horse is dead, why continue to beat it? In other words, if you have tried something that does not work, do not keep trying it. Move on to the next thing. A person that continues to do the same thing, but expect a different result is considered to be a fool.

- Strategize as a team to accomplish the goal.

Teamwork makes the dream work. Discuss how you plan to get to your destination in marriage. Strategize and design your marriage the way you want it.

- Do it on purpose...work the plan.

Write the vision and make it plain. Once it is written, work it. Do it on purpose. Nothing gets done just because it is written for you to see. Writing it down only sets it in place as a reminder and to hold you accountable to what you have planned to do.

Building YOUR Policy

When something does not benefit the marriage, how will you handle it? Will you repeat it, or will you remove it from the table of "how to handle it?"

____

____

What are the benefits of being intentional in the marriage?

Make a list of what you consider to be successful in a marriage?

It's no secret that when we fail to plan, we plan to fail. This policy lays out the importance of having a plan and executing it. In marriage, as a team, the two of you now become one, which is much more powerful. Bringing all that you have together and blending it as one to make it work for the union is what will take your marriage to a higher level. Your next task in the following Policy 1.10 *Do the Work for the Two to Become One,* will encourage you to be powerful by bridging everything together. Allow what is being shared to resonate with you while you do the work needed to make the two become one.

Reflect & R.I.S.E.

1.10

1+1=1 -ARITHMETIC IN MARRIAGE

Couples' bible study was the dopest for those that were married, engaged, or DWAP. Many times, I went alone because of his work schedule. I understood that even if I were going with him, it still began with me as an individual, which would ultimately benefit us as a couple. Yes, I would have loved for him to be there with me each time, but it was not possible. The Pastor over the ministry would explain things very clearly, and I always left understanding the true meaning of "the two becoming one." I read many things about the what's, why's and how's in a marriage but the delivery from Pastor and the input from the attendees was amazing. There was always a sense of, "Ok, I'm not in this by myself." It is incredible how hearing other points of view regarding the exact topic can change your opinion and create paradigm shifts for the better when you permit yourself to do so.

I knew what the scripture said and I had an idea of what it meant, but it wasn't until I had to make decisions that included my husband that made it come to life and I completely understood it. Something that I should have always been doing, but I wasn't. I considered how he would think or feel about certain things, but I never felt obligated, until the end of our 18 years, to ask his opinion or how he thought things should be done.

He never questioned things that I did and at the time, I assumed it was because I did things the way he liked. It wasn't until our later years that I realized that we hadn't been doing that part of marriage correctly. After reading about marriage the way that it was designed to be, hearing stories about what worked and what didn't, coupled with our bad times, I had an "aha moment." Of course I attempted to rectify what looked like no problem at all to him because it was working. However, it was not working, and it never will if the two aren't becoming one in their decision making.

One of the biggest things that I did without getting his opinion or approval before doing it is an example of what "two becoming one" is not. I purchased a car. Not an outfit, but a $27,000 car that I did not second guess when I bought it. I got in my old car with my baby girl and said to her "We're about to buy a new car. I don't have the money for a down payment, but I'm trusting God on this one."

Sure enough, I did not have to put any money down, and I was out the door with a new car (and bill) before I knew it. We stopped and grabbed a bite to eat at Buffalo Wild Wings, and I remember it raining a bit. The parking lot was not as crowded as usual, so I parked the car away from others. I did not want anyone to bump my new baby with their door. I took a picture of the car and sent it to him letting him know that I had just made this purchase. His response, as usual, very lackadaisical, said "It's nice, how much did it cost and where did you get it." He also asked when I decided to buy a new car, but that was the extent of it. What does this tell you? There clearly was not a shared account that this money was going to come from (two still haven't become one), and this is not to say that two can't become one if they do not have a joint account, that is far from the truth. However, there was no plan, nor communication regarding finances. When two become one, they become one heart, one home, and one mind, as they lay aside their individualism and selfishness. Expressing your individual opinion is always important but remember that ultimately the decision has to be what's best for the union.

The question that is most asked is, *how does two become one*, and does this discard your individuality. Of course not, but becoming one is permitting yourself to be open and ready to combine or bridge thoughts and ways that will benefit the union. You can no longer think about "what works best for me." You are becoming one.

As the husband, your role is to be her prophet, priest, and king. You are held accountable to be her umbrella. Cover her, protect her, pray with and for her. You are the head and you ultimately make all decisions. Her opinion may be the answer to the question or used, but you (King) decide that as well. I know, that can be a lot of pressure. But she, your Queen, your softer side, your rib, has her primary job. She is keeping her head on a swivel as she submits and respects her King. She too has a protecting job. As the King is hard at work for his family, she is making sure that nothing gets in the marriage that shouldn't be there and nothing is allowed out that is needed to continue the RISE of the union. She is virtuous and does her King good all the days of her life. She is trustworthy and a helpmate. She is constantly at work doing these things, which builds the marriage. There's work to do and marriage works when we do the work! The two must become one.

The Policy:
Do the Work for The Two to Become One

Release what you have been taught as a child, or previous relationships and take on a new responsibility of becoming one flesh with your spouse. Have a mindset of it being a union of mind, body, and spirit to reflect the original design for marriage. A husband should leave his mother and father and hold on to his wife to become one. As one, you may be overpowered, but two can defend themselves. Your mother is no longer the leading lady in your life. Everyone has their rightful place, but the wife has now taken precedence over everyone but God. If she is now you, you are now one.

Boundaries must be established. There are times when we have given a part of ourselves to others before saying "I do," and the expectation from others after we've committed to the commitment is that we will continue to serve and consider them as we did before. There is no way around changing after saying, "I do." There is power in the two becoming one.

Life Application

- Work together, no matter how hard the job is. You can do it as a team.

If you plan to do the work, understand that you cannot accomplish the duties unless you work as a team. There may be some jobs that are harder than others but, doing it together will make the difference.

- Have sex, consummation connects you as one.

The act of sex is the manifestation of "one flesh" physically and metaphorically. Do it often...become one over and over again!

- Come together as a unit to continue maintenance in the marriage often.

Continuing maintenance in your marriage will require an open line of communication that allows both to be clear and direct about likes, dislikes, understandings, and misunderstandings. Consistent maintenance is a tool used that may not always be the first to be picked up. It may not always feel good. It may not be most desired, but it is one that will bring great results when two are becoming one.

- Be patient. This is not an overnight process.

Becoming one with another individual takes intentional work. You must first understand the importance of becoming one. Doing the work to become one will consist of setting aside any selfish desires that can hinder the two becoming one. You will now have to train yourself to have a mindset that considers more than yourself when making decisions. Training your mind to consider your spouse will go against everything that you were raised to do. We were always taught self-preservation, but no one ever considered our lives as married adults. You may not get the art of becoming one at the same time, and this is where patience has to be present. If you get it first, be the example. Show your spouse how it is done. Just do it!

Building YOUR Policy

Prior to reading this policy, how would you define "two becoming one"?

____

____

____

____

____

____

Are you willing to set aside what works for you as an individual to gain in areas where your marriage is built?

____

____

Share tools that you believe will assist in building the union to become one.

____

____

____

____

____

____

____

____

It's not easy to set aside what you want, to pick up what's best for the union, but it is necessary. If you desire a thriving marriage, there is no way around doing the work to become one. You will always have your individuality. You will never be robbed of your individual opinion. Be open to share what your thoughts and wants are even when they are not in alignment with what your spouse shares. If ideas and desires are not agreed upon, and you can't come to a common ground, getting wise counsel is always healthy. Policy 1.12 *Seek Counsel That Will Help Solve the Problem*, will encourage you to understand why you should and when you should invite a third party to help.

Reflect &R.I.S.E.

1.11

INVITING A THIRD PARTY IN

"I need to get your opinion on this. My parents are separated, and I feel horrible." That is how I started the conversation with "that loud guy" that is now my Pastor. We worked together and I was told that he was a Pastor, but never knew him personally. Our offices were near each other's in the basement, and I would hear him EVERYDAY coming in singing some love song. His voice is extremely deep, so it carried throughout the hall. He was always in the best of moods each time I saw or heard him.

One day, I got bold and said, "Sir, if you have a minute, can I get your opinion on something?" His response was, "Sure, go for it." He walked into my office, sat down and I began to tell him that my parents are separating, and I felt horrible about it. His question to me was, "Why? Why do *you* feel horrible? Separation is a decision that they have made that must be best for them, and it has nothing to do with you." He asked again, "So, why do *you* feel horrible?" I explained how at the age of nine years old my mother took me into the bathroom and we sat on the edge of the tub while she broke the news about her and my dad separating. I was devastated and I cried extremely hard. My mom made sure that I knew that it was not my fault, and the love that they had for me would never change. I made like I understood, but honestly, I did not. Here I was 32 years old, sitting in my office talking to a complete stranger about my parents. He still could not understand why I felt so bad. I continued and told him that nothing came from that talk. My parents never separated. I felt that if I had not been such a brat when my mom gave me the news, they would have separated and lived a happy life with someone that would make them happy. I imagined they stayed together because of me.

At this point, I thought my parents had lived over 20 years unhappy, or in that space, trying to make me happy. I felt so guilty. He had me look at it from a different angle. He said, "As parents, we make sacrifices for our children to protect them and to keep them happy. They loved you so much that they were willing to put their personal situation aside to make sure you were ok." Hearing that lightened my heart, even if it was not the truth, I felt better. This led me to talk about some of the things that I was currently experiencing in my marriage. He gave his advice but offered to sit with us both. I was not sure how that was going to go, because most men that I knew were not open to marital counseling, but I suggested it to my husband and to my surprise, he agreed.

We scheduled our meeting and we met with him at his church soon after. I'll never forget seeing him at work in the office before the first meeting and hearing him say "T, I was up at 4 am praying for y'all and I haven't gotten a bad feeling about this. God usually let's me know. Things are going to be all right girl, just keep doing what you're supposed to do." I was not convinced, but I smiled and said, "Ok, thank you."

We began counseling sessions and they were beneficial. Each session we left with an exercise that encouraged us to focus on each other, not the initial problem that led us to where we were. We talked about that in the meeting and there was no need to go backward.

After we completed counseling with him, I realized that all his techniques worked. They were not necessarily techniques, they were tools that we had stored in our marriage toolbox, yet we had not used in years. He simply coached us, encouraged us to get back to the foundation of our marriage, reminded us why we said "I do," told us to lay aside the weight that was so easily besetting us, and to get back to enjoying each other. We had to reaffirm the union. Each session got better. Our responses during the sessions became happier and we eventually were back where we belonged.

The Policy: *Seek Counsel That Will Help Solve the Problem*

Look for wise counsel (advise) that will assist in the area that is needed. Respect each other's time and sit with counsel that will be of assistance in getting you through the hiccup that you are in, whether it's a verbal opinion only, or actionable advice to guide you to the next stage.

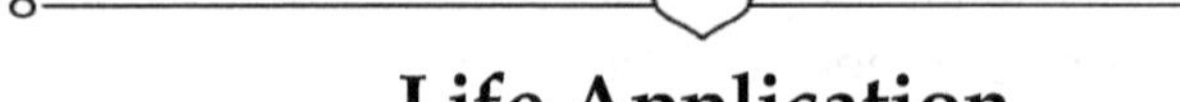

Life Application

- Seek wise counsel and instruction.

Spending time with others for counsel that is not an asset, is a waste of time. One thing that you will never get back is time. Opportunities come and go, but the time to get it and move to the next place that has been prepared for you will never come again. This is why seeking wise counsel is important – no time to waste.

- Be wise and listen more than you speak.

When you are having a conversation with your spouse that cannot be solved or agreed upon with only the two of you, be careful to listen more than you speak. Listen to more than the words. Listen to the body language and the things that are not being said to determine what is needed to correct the situation. Many times, verbalizing our true feelings are hard. Repeating what you heard and received is always good so that your spouse can agree or disagree with that being the message that they are trying to convey. For example, "What I hear you saying is..." and repeat what you heard. Emotions have a very strong and powerful voice, and sometimes the actual message gets lost in translation as a result.

- Be careful who you listen to.

If you need a third party, be sure that it is unbiased counsel. You should always want to hear from someone that will side with the truth, no matter who it is NOT coming from.

Who you listen to is important if you desire to come to a middle ground that you can build from. Having a set person that you both agree to call in, for this reason, is best, and should be done prior to needing the counsel. Be proactive and decide before you are put in a position to quickly find someone. Your judgment may be off because of the emotion that will undoubtedly linger.

- Listen to understand and not to defend.

When we are in the midst of a disagreement, our sole purpose sometimes can be to get our point across and defend ourselves. Listening to understand and fix your part in it is the goal. When both are listening to defend, there will never be resolve, and it will be an ongoing problem that could be fixed quickly.

Building YOUR Policy

Do you have someone that you have both agreed on to be your counsel? Be proactive and not reactive. Handle this before you need it.

____

____

When will you know that it is time to invite the third party in for counsel? You have been equipped with everything that you need inside of you, or it is right at your fingertips. Know when to reach within, or when to reach out.

____

____

____

____

Did you have pre-marital counseling and if so, would you consider using the same person for counsel?

____

____

What is a technique that you can use during the time of a disagreement that will encourage each spouse to listen to understand and fix, instead of listening to respond and defend?

____

____

____

____

This policy should have confirmed that wise counsel will steer you in a positive direction that can only reach a positive conclusion. Having counsel that has the best interest of the union in mind will always foster and require you to shift the mindset to *WE* over *ME*. The following Policy 1.12 *Speak Life Not Death* describes using the proper words when discussing your differences or disagreements and using the appropriate tone knowing when to speak about a particular topic. This is mandatory. The wrong words will only ignite a bigger fire that could possibly delay extinguishing the differences.

Reflect & R.I.S.E.

____

____

____

____

____

____

____

____

____

1.12

THE TONGUE

I have heard many times in my life how powerful the tongue is, but never did I think I would have to remind myself of it. Time and time again, I wanted to share, or maybe talk about what we were going through in our marriage. This is not to say that I never did it, because I had not always had the wisdom that told me to shut my mouth. I allowed my emotions to speak out. Then, after speaking death to my marriage, I thought about how bad of an idea it was to say some of the things that I had said.

Quite a few times I would only say the negative to those that I knew would feed that with "Girl, I understand because I...," and "If I were you..." The biggest one was the encouragement to give him a taste of his own medicine. I fell for the okie doke, and I allowed myself to fall in the trap of speaking death and not life to my marriage. I knew who to go to if I needed some encouragement, but truthfully, I was tired of being encouraged, only to end up back where I was. I could say it was out of frustration and the world may even say that I had every right to be upset and man bash, but it is never ok.

Speaking death and not life was not my practice, but I had times that I got stuck in that box - the box that said "I'm not going anywhere, but this is what he's doing," or, "Woe it's me," or, "You get to do this since he's not doing that." I found myself in a box with a lid that I did not know I could stand up and push off until I got under wise counsel.

Wise counsel reminded me that I had the power to remove the lid and step out of the box if what I wanted for my marriage did not fit. Wise counsel told me that it was ok to speak to what you want before you see it. Wise counsel taught me that a change in mindset would change the words that I used to describe my husband and marriage. I began to speak things that would help and not hinder my marriage and as I did so things began to line up. I began to realize that the saying I had heard all my childhood life became real. Life and death really are in the power of the tongue.

As long as I spoke death (nothing positive) about my marriage, things stayed the same or got worse. As soon as I began to speak life (positive), things that were dead began to wake up. We hold the power to which direction our marriage can go, and it is done with one of the smallest members on our body – the tongue.

The Policy:
Speak Life Not Death

Allow yourselves the capacity for growth, reproduction, functional activity, and continual change preceding death. Feed what will grow in your marriage and bury those things that will not. Death is the end of life. Choose to live in your marriage.

There will be things that you say and may not consider as a death agent. Ask yourself how it will breed more life to the marriage. If your answer is "it cannot," this a tell-tale sign that it is death. If it is not living, it is dying.

Life Application

- Never speak negatively about your spouse.

Speaking negatively about your spouse to others can sometimes curve their thoughts or respect. We are usually speaking out of anger, and will soon forgive our spouse, but forgiveness may be far from the mind of those that you are sharing with.

- Be mindful of what you are sharing, when just sharing.

Everyone does not deserve every intricate detail of your marriage. Some things are better left unsaid. In most situations, it is a moment that should never be talked about. Talking about it only feeds it and gives it an opportunity to grow and continue to live.

- Do not say something about your spouse to others, that you haven't said to them.

You cannot make the change if you are not communicating with the person that needs to make the change. Telling a friend, family member, your Pastor, etc., does not encourage action for your spouse to fix the issue. The first to hear what you would like to see done differently should be your spouse. Give them a chance to do it differently, and even if things are not completely done the way that you would like, be careful with sharing it. What good does it do to share something with others if they cannot give a positive response that could possibly help?

- Consider your tone when you are speaking to your spouse.

It is not what you say, it is how you say it in most cases. What you are saying could be correct, but your delivery can make it wrong.

Building YOUR Policy

What situation would you consider it to be sharing and not talking about your spouse or the marriage?

____

____

____

____

____

____

What are some affirmations that you can say to your spouse daily that will build them or the marriage?

____

____

____

____

____

____

____

Name a few things that your spouse could say in different tones that would change the meaning or how you would receive a message. Speak them out loud to hear the difference.

____

____

____

____

____

Knowing the mindset of your spouse when having a conversation is important. Using the tool of knowing when it is a good time to share with your spouse, and choosing to wait when it's not, is wise. Remember, in this policy the tongue is the smallest part of the body, yet it has a mighty force and ability to be used in different ways. As previous policies have ushered us to this policy by telling us how to listen before speaking, and how to communicate effectively, and knowing who to speak with if counsel or an opinion is needed, we will now use the following Policy 1.13 *Schedule Mandatory Me Time,* to put them all to use.

Reflect & R.I.S.E.

1.13

ME ME ME ME ME!

I came back on fire for him! "I missed you while I was gone," is what I said to him. I did not usually do things solo, but when I was away from doing the usual daily routine, I considered it "me time."

Taking the time to recharge was always important to me. Everything gets worn out if we do not take a proper break from it. Being a wife, mother, active member of different organizations, mentoring, coaching, etc., will drain you. Though you can never take a break from being a wife, you must include "me time" in your schedule.

I never really took advantage of what I would consider "real me time." There was always someone there with me, whether it was the nail shop, the hair shop, or the mall, etc. I did not permit myself to celebrate me. I had days where I would go and do things alone, but not with the intention of it being "me time." I heard time and time again the importance of intentionally getting away for myself, by myself, not taking the kids, not including the friends, no hubby, but only me.

It was not until the separation that I took "me time" serious. It should not have taken separation for me to realize the importance of it. I felt overwhelmed with trying to be all that everyone needed me to be for them, that I had to step away so that I could be everything that I needed me to be for myself. With the timeshare that we both owned, I booked a weekend stay in Cathedral City, California. Cathedral City? Who would have ever known that I would take a drive out by myself to get some much needed "me time?" I was a bit leery because he had full access to see exactly where I would be. Not that I thought he would show up and do anything crazy, that was out of his character. It was just weird. Both of our names were on the property, but I did it anyway. The drive alone was so freakin' freeing. I put a playlist together, I threw on my shades, opened the sunroof, and coasted to my home for the weekend. Once I got close, I stopped at the grocery store and grabbed some wine and a few items for me to snack on and cook, and continued to the timeshare and checked in.

I did everything that I wanted to do...NOTHING! Hung out by the pool, ate some good food, drank some excellent wine, wrote in my journal, rested, regrouped, reflected, and recharged. This was the best three-day stay that I had ever imagined. I remember playing Franky Beverly and Maze while I danced in the middle of the floor feeling free as a bird. I felt the weight of everyone's issues were gone, and I had an opportunity to see mine for what they were.

It was not as bad as I thought. It was just facing my truth. This trip came a few weeks after attempting to give him another chance to love me the way I deserved or hurt me again. Sometimes when you are not sure if you are sure, you make yourself available for clarity. Boy was I clear at this time.

The Policy:
Schedule Mandatory Me Time

Give yourself an opportunity to regroup, recharge, and revive yourself, so that you can be what's needed in your marriage. Intentionally pressing reset for yourself is an automatic reset for the marriage. Resetting your marriage is a direct reflection of the "me time" that you gave yourself permission to have.

Life Application

- Focus on yourself.

Do you love you? Give yourself permission to focus on what you need to do, to be a great you.

- It is ok to say no to others so that you can say yes to yourself.

You cannot obligate yourself to others when you lack some things for yourself. At some point, you will be no good to others if you have not poured into yourself or allowed someone else to pour into you. Anything that you once used to build others up will be depleted if you are not replacing it.

- Give yourself permission to be selfish; your spouse will thank you later.

When you get away for "me time," returning home with a regrouped, recharged, and revived energy, your husband will appreciate the time spent alone. Your mindset will be free to receive and dictate from a safe space and not just space to get an answer out. We are so accustomed to having the answer that in some instances, instead of asking for a little time to get an answer, we just answer without thought.

Building YOUR Policy

Before reading this policy, did you consider "me time" as being important?

____

____

How do you feel about telling yourself that it is time to be selfish?

____

____

____

____

____

____

In the past, what have you done that you consider "me time?"

____

____

____

____

Write a list of "me time" activities or outings that you can begin to incorporate into your life. Be specific.

____

____

____

____

____

____

____

Ultimately, when practiced, this policy will keep you mentally healthy. You are not the best you for yourself or your spouse when you are not allotting time to free space to pour and receive again. Every tool that you have been equipped with will require your best when executing, and the following Policy 1.14 *Know Each Other's Finance Beliefs* will be no different when attempting to understand and combine finance beliefs. This policy will be a vehicle to getting your family financially comfortable and free.

Reflect & R.I.S.E.

1.14

C.R.E.A.M.
(CASH RULES EVERYTHING AROUND ME)

I did not have the slightest idea about how we should handle our finances "together" because I believe we were both taught different (wrong) rules about our money. I wanted to have an account that we were both on, but, not really. I spoke about it a lot but, I knew that he did not want to (either).

I could be wrong, but just like me, he never pressed the issue. I listened to my friends who had shared account discussions about "the bills getting paid late." Or how he overspent this month or how she overspent in general. On top of what I had already been conditioned to believe, I was thinking, *"Hell no. I'm good."*

At the beginning of the year, we talked about our goals and budgeting was thrown in. I recall thinking, *"This will never happen, but for giggles, let's entertain it."* We never opened an account. We never saved together, and we did not make a big fuss about it. There were no secrets with how much we made. I knew his salary and he knew mine, but for some reason, we would not collaborate with our monies.

Now that I think about it, it is a little weird. Clearly, we did not have a plan for our money. It was a "what's mine is mine" relationship, and we thought it worked. Had it worked we would not have lived paycheck to paycheck. We both made good money, but again, when you don't have a vision for your money, your money doesn't work for you, and when the two aren't becoming one not much will work for you as a union. Keep in mind that money was created as a resource for access. It should never be a resource that causes division.

The Policy:
Know Each Other's Finance Beliefs

Have the money conversation to gauge each other's finance beliefs. Approach the conversation with honesty and transparency to assure that you are on the right road to bridging your finances together. Money is one of the three known reasons for disagreement in marriages, that can lead to the "D." Do not be a part of the statistic. Prove the system wrong and do it the righteous way.

Life Application

- Effectively communicate what works best for your union financial and where bank accounts are concerned.

The love of money is the root of all evil. Decide what works best financially for the union. Attempting to keep the "what's mine is mine, and what's yours is yours" mentality is a setup for failure. Transparency, including your money, is a tool that must always be used to continue growth in areas that it will affect.

- Track the money that is coming in and how you are spending it.

Know what is coming in and what is going out monthly. It is fair for both parties to know how the money is being spent.

- Talk about financial priorities and then create your own.

Know the importance of prioritizing financial obligations. Talk about what is most important to the least important to avoid any misunderstandings on what should be paid and in which order. You can not only assume that it is obvious or "common sense."

Build YOUR Policy

Who taught you how to handle your finances?

____

____

____

Compare your financial beliefs without making a judgment and create one that lines up with your design as a union.

Create a spreadsheet that includes all monies coming in and itemize what is going out to begin an open conversation about your finances.

After reading this policy, I am sure you can related to it somehow. Whether you believe like I did and hold tight to your money, or you have already begun walking in all that is mentioned in the Life Application section, I encourage you to use money as a resource for access and do not allow it to divide you and your spouse. You can also use the upcoming Policy 1.15 *Control Outside Influences* in this area of marriage. When we allow money to divide the union, we have given it power, just as we do with any other outside influence.

Reflect & R.I.S.E.

____

____

____

____

____

____

1.15

IF IT'S NOT INSIDE THE MARRIAGE, IT'S OUTSIDE THE MARRIAGE.

Why in the world would I think that getting advice from them or these resources was going to help me? In hindsight, I am thinking, *"They aren't married," "They're married, but hell, they are struggling, too," "She's bitter, so her point of view should never be considered," "He's flirting with me, and wants to give me what I'm saying my husband isn't," "This book, well, that's just it. It is a book. Something that someone only wrote for sales, possibly and I didn't feel anything authentic about this read."*

I had itchy ears and was desperate to get answers on how to make this thing called marriage work. I gave everything mentioned an opportunity to provide me with answers. At the time, I never referred to the manufacturer who knows exactly what is needed to fix what is broken or breaking. It is totally different now.

When you know better, you should do better. My references never led to a RISE in my marriage, and I suffered from the consequences. It felt like I was on a merry-go-round. I was repeating the same thing over and over, again. It was just a different day, but the players were the same....my husband and me. He would reach out to others, as well, for their opinions. The funny thing is that most of who he talked to would call and tell me what he said, or their version of what he said. Getting this information would make me extremely upset, although we were doing the same thing. I felt like those that I reached out to were "more qualified," than those he reached out to. Boy was I wrong. They were all giving their opinion, according to their experience.

The Policy:
Control Outside Influences

Do not allow others the opportunity to influence the character, development, or behavior of your decisions concerning your marriage. Be mindful of the wise counsel when you invite third party opinions to assist in any area of the union. Opening the door for some to hear the story, when not requesting an opinion is still considered outside influence. Venting can many times become bashing. Be careful.

Life Application

- Have a plan on how you will reach your calm center before having the "how to fix it" conversation with folks outside of the marriage.

Remember, when speaking to friends, family, etc., about your encounters inside of your marriage, they will give you their opinion according to their experience. This is why having a plan to reach a calm center is essential. It is also a reason why having a set person that you seek wise counsel from is important as stated in Policy 1.11 *Seek Counsel That Will Help Solve the Problem.*

Build YOUR Policy

When would you consider yourself to be most vulnerable to adhering to outside influence?

____

____

____

____

Are you venting to outsiders?

____

____

Who or what would you consider to be outside influences?

____

____

____

____

____

____

At what point do you throw up the red flag that says, "It's time to bring in counsel" versus talking to family or friends just to get it "off your chest?"

____

____

____

____

This policy will take practice. Many times, we are comfortable with sharing what is happening in our marriage with friends, family, co-workers, etc., to release the thought and sometimes to get their point of view. These are usually people who we see and talk to daily, so there is a sense of trust there, but we are not taking into consideration the impact or influence that it may have on our decision making - decisions that could create a bigger issue than is warranted.

How often are we sharing and not receiving a response? Not too often. Discipline your "just need to get it out " chatter and use that energy for things in your marriage that will catapult you to another level, as the next Policy 1.16 *Dating With A Purpose* will lay out for you.

Reflect & R.I.S.E.

1.16

DWAP (DATING WITH A PURPOSE)

My best friend and I were both single and ready to mingle. We went to Sky Sushi Night Club, and there he was, on the dance floor with one of the young ladies that we went to high school with. I walked through the crowd, but before passing, I spoke, "Hey you, it's good seeing you here," I made a hand gesture as if I were asking if he and the young lady that he was dancing with were together. She answered with her nose turned up, still smiling, "Not anymore," and he shook his head "No." I thought to myself, "Ok, ok ok."

He and I had seen each other on a few occasions at different parties and each time we were both in a relationship, so this was music to my ears because I always had a crush on him. Even in school, I thought he was a cutie, and his meek, humble spirit was attractive to me. I was the total opposite. I was nowhere near quiet, and I do not think I would have considered myself to be a humble young lady at the time, but I was still sweet as pie.

My girlfriend and I continued moving through the crowd. It was scorching and crowded, so we decided to first go to the ladies' room to check ourselves out. It was just what I wanted. Going on the other side of the club allowed me to walk around once we came out to see where he was sitting. I spotted him, and it was no big thing to linger around in the area that he was in so that I could hopefully make eye contact with him. "Dude, would you look over here?" I said out loud, but not loud enough for him to hear. Only my girlfriend. We chuckled and walked around the club. Eventually, I ran into a friend of his that he was there with and I didn't want to take a chance at not giving him my number so I gave it to his friend, and asked if he would give it to him.

My girlfriend and I hung out for another 30 minutes before we left to go and grab a bite to eat. I did not think he would call me that night because it was late. I assumed he would call within a few days. Well to my surprise, I got the call that night. I guess we could say that this was the beginning of our 18 years.

We saw each other every day from that point and seemed to be inseparable. We dated, but I'm not sure we had a purpose attached to our dating. It was fun. He was cute. Why wouldn't we date? But the bigger question is, why weren't we dating with a purpose? Was it because no one taught us what that was? Was the true purpose of dating to collect data and eventually marry each other, or just for fun?

Why did he talk with my dad to tell him what his intentions were with his baby girl? Why did he buy the ring? Why did he get on one knee in front of my entire family and ask me to marry him? What was the purpose? I had questions.

When there is no purpose while dating, the decisions made are usually based on emotions. There is no real intent. Many times, it is what feels good, what "the people" want you to do, or what you have witnessed being done in relationships that you've been around. You may have an idea of what you want but not necessarily know how to get there. I believe that was my case. Being raised in a two-parent home, I knew that I wanted that for my family, but neither of us knew the steps to getting there and staying there. We never talked about how to get there, but we talked about wanting to be there. Hence the engagement.

We had our good and we had our bad while dating and throughout the marriage, but never did I think it would end with the "D." Each time we experienced a hiccup, and we fixed it, I thought, *"We've learned, and there is nowhere else to go but up,"* especially once we joined our church. Our Pastor always spoke about the importance of family. He was an advocate for men standing and answering the call of duty that he felt was given to them. He encouraged them to stand as a man of valor for the family while protecting and providing. He encouraged the women to submit to their husbands and reverence them. They are our Kings and we are their Queens.

Men were challenged to be active fathers and the example for the family. I was certain that we were being led by a shepherd who was not only talking the talk but walking the walk – great examples of what healthy dating and marriage were given to us. I cannot say that we immediately put the lessons into action, but they were lessons that we were able to use later once we grew and disciplined ourselves to do so.

As a married couple who is DWAP, there is a slight difference in the data that you are collecting. However, the result is the same. You are learning more about your spouse that may not have been required to learn earlier in your relationship. As stated in Policy 1.2, *Serve Your Spouse*, you and your spouse will change. There will be unexpected changes and intentional changes that you will now need to know how to navigate and adjust. You cannot expect your spouse to stay the same, and you will not stay the same.

What does *dating with a purpose* truly look like? DWAP is collecting data. It is getting to know the person by asking questions, paying attention to actions, reactions, and responses. Body language is another factor in learning. You will never know everything about your spouse but know as much as possible to determine who he or she is or has grown to be. You too are being held to all these standards. You are being watched, you are being judged, and you are being questioned, as well.

Be honest. Be transparent and be available and present for them to conclude how you desire and need to be served. Too often we are not available to teach what we need, yet we require it. The purpose in your dating process should not come with any reservations when sharing your do's and don'ts. Remember, you must begin and remain the student and the teacher. Being a student and teacher in your relationship is a tool that you will always need to continue the R.I.S.E.

The Policy:
Date with a Purpose

Know what you want when dating and pursue it. Even in marriage, you must continue to date with a purpose and knowing what you want will also apply.

You may both desire the same outcome but understand that you will probably have two different routes of getting there. Dating is collecting data, which is done before and during the marriage. While dating, you should collect data and continue collecting data after marriage. Intentionally get to know who you are sitting across the table from, whether you are dating with a purpose or already married. It is imperative to do this when you are getting to know a person, but it is most important when you want to continue to know your spouse.

Life Application

- Ask the question that you are afraid to hear the answer to.

In many cases, when dating before marriage, we are not asking questions that will define their belief system. There is never a question that is too much or too soon to be asked when it will help describe their character, integrity, or morals. If you are dating with a purpose, asking the hard questions is necessary. For example, we need to know the background of the person that we are dating. However, being more specific with your questions will help cut to the root. Many of our characteristics or habits derive from childhood. As a woman, we may want to know who taught him how to be a man. We know how we desire to be loved and treated, and if you have not been given a great example or proper tools, it could show up in the relationship.

Men who are dating with a purpose look for key things in a woman, as well. A nurturing and loving woman is desired to balance the relationship, and if she was not nurtured or loved properly, nor taught at some point, it will be evident. Ask for the information you want to know. Be specific! This applies after saying "I do" as well. Ask questions geared as a student of your spouse. Things change and just because you have said "I do" does not mean that they have not.

- Be prepared to answer any question that you ask.

If you ask a question, there is a great possibility that it will be reversed for you to answer. Be available and transparent when answering. Your truths are your realities that cannot be changed. What you do with your experiences is what matters the most.

- Keep an open mind, after all, your gender difference comes with a difference in point of views.

As important as it is to become one, it is inevitable to consider one of the most important differences, which is gender. One will respond from a male point of view and the other from a female point of view. We were created differently. Because of these differences it is important to keep an open mind. When we are available to receive another point of view, it opens the doors to agree on what works best for the union, and not the individual.

- Take on the spirit to serve.

If you are not able to provide the needs of your spouse, you are not ready for marriage. Taking on the spirit of serving is required.

Building YOUR Policy

Do you think *Dating with a Purpose* is important?

____

____

What is your dating purpose?

____

____

____

____

____

Have you created a journey to reaching your dating purpose?

____

____

What are some of the harder questions you have asked?

____

____

____

____

In everything that you do in the relationship, do it with purpose. You should have ultimately completed this policy, understanding that there are layers in relationships and to unwrap each layer, you must be willing to be present and available for the work that it will take in getting there. In new relationships, it is a bit more challenging to be transparent because the "love and trust," which is our next policy, has not been established. For those that have already said "I do," if you are adhering to Policy 1.3, *Communicate Effectively*, being vulnerable to get results while you are DWAP, will be less challenging

Reflect & R.I.S.E.

____

____

____

____

1.17

I LOVE YOU, BUT I DON'T TRUST YOU

I did it all because of love. *"I forgive you because I love you. But do I trust you? Do I trust myself? Bigger than that do I trust God? I do trust God, and that's why, although I want to throw in the towel, I can't because I have not heard from God, yet."* My emotions were so loud that I could not hear anything that God was saying to me, even if He was speaking. I did not want to look like a fool, but I also wanted to make sure I was obedient to God.

We went through the same thing over and over again. "I have trust issues," I said to myself. Where did this derive from? I do not like the way this feels. "If you're telling me that you don't want to be married anymore, but God didn't give me the approval to give you your wish, I will continue to be the wife," is what I told him. He looked at me like I was crazy, and I understood why. I loved him, but trust was completely different.

"I don't want to be married," he said. I initially thought, really, again? I heard these words before. How many times do I need to hear this before I wash my hands? *Lord, when are you going to give me the approval? Is there an approval? What do I do?* This is where trust and love for God had to be greater than the trust and love for the man. Once trust is broken, it is extremely hard to gain it back. I loved hard, but the trust had just dwindled.

Hearing those words was traumatic and I was left confused, but I stood to hear God clearly. As long as I didn't hear God give a direction, I stood right there. I had to learn that trusting the Creator of this man was my best bet. There was no way I could trust what I saw. It took more than love. I needed to feel secure that he was sure that he wanted to fight for us.

Constantly being in protection mode did not encourage me to trust him. However, that became my new comfort. I was protecting my heart. When I was not intentionally trusting the creator, I automatically defended myself to avoid being hurt by what seemed to be "just words." Just words? I have heard it said that "sticks and stones may break my bones, but words will never hurt me." That was a lie. Some of his words hurt me, and I am sure there were times when my words hurt him. They were not just words. This confirms Policy 1.12, *Speak Life and Not Death*. Words can be deadly to trust in a relationship. These words meant so much more than just words or maybe an emotional rant. For me, it was a life-changing threat.

The Policy:
Trust and Love Your Spouse

Be trusting and trust your spouse to provide love how it was designed to be given. Love was designed to be given with patience, kindness, without envy, it does not boast, it is not proud, it does not dishonor, it is not self-seeking, it is not easily angered, it keeps no record of wrongs, it does not delight in evil, but it rejoices with the truth, it always protects, it always trusts, it always hopes, and it always perseveres.

Everything that you do, commit to doing it with love. Without it, everything is done in vain.

Life Application

- Honesty is the best policy.

There should never be a time when you decide to be dishonest with your spouse. Once trust is broken, it is extremely hard to return to that space in your relationship or marriage when nothing is questioned. Your integrity is questioned when your words are. Remember that you are now becoming one, and when your spouse cannot trust you to be honest other things in the relationship will become questionable.

- Your transparency can be the road to your marriage catapulting to a higher level.

Being open and honest about some of your "isms" may be the answer for your spouse. Give yourself permission to be transparent so that your "why" thoroughly explains your "what." Often, if we know why they do, say, respond, or react in a certain way, the puzzle can be solved because you have all the pieces

- Trust that your spouse will never do anything intentionally to hurt or disappoint you.

You said, "I do" and if you are going into the union without trusting that your spouse has committed to doing marriage the way that it was designed, you have set yourself up for failure. Trust that your spouse spoke those vows and took that commitment because they were ready to fulfill them all. Trust that!

- Trust the process.

Although Policy 1.10 *Do the Work for the Two to Become One*, tells you to do the work, this is confirmation to why it's so important. One thing we cannot get around is that you are still individual beings. You were raised with different dynamics that ultimately molded you to be the individuals that you are today. For example, different parenting styles, homes, belief systems, discipline styles, communities, siblings or maybe being the only child, contribute to molding the person you are today. Bringing two separate cultures together as one will take a lot of work. There is a process that you will have to go through before it can be done. Are you willing to go through the process to bridge any gap that may not be conducive to what your goals are for the union? Trust the process. It will not always be easy but trust the process.

Building YOUR Policy

Who taught you the definition of love and trust, and what was the definition?

Was it the true meaning if what you were taught is different?

From what you have learned in this policy, what will you use?

Do love and trust look the same for you and your spouse?

____

____

____

____

Write a love letter to your spouse that begins with "I trust you because" and end it with, "and that's why I love you."

Every policy section that you have read ultimately connects to this policy, *Love and Trust.* Love and trust are tools that should be used when creating your foundation, and you will add other policies as you continue to build. Love and Trust will get you there but doing the work with the tools from the other policies will keep your going!

Reflect & R.I.S.E.

____

____

____

____

Foundation of a Thriving & Successful Marriage

After reading the policies in this book, I trust that you have given yourself the opportunity to ask yourself questions and find additional ways to enhance your relationship that will result in a thriving and successful marriage. The intent was for you to make the MPP personal and apply it to your daily walk, whether you are DWAP (dating with a purpose) or as a married man or woman. Understand that each day will provide new assignments. I spoke about being a student and a teacher as a husband or wife. Being a student and teacher is what it will take to complete each daily assignment. Some will present themselves as a pop quiz, while others will be from a lesson that you have already learned.

Setting a solid foundation, one that you both agree on, is what you should refer to as the assignments present themselves. Your foundation will be the glue to your relationship. Your foundation must be able to hold up even when the biggest storms hit, and the umbrella is possibly blown apart or ripped up while fighting to hold it down becomes a bit challenging. There will be things that present itself in your marriage, and you will not always have the correct answer immediately. There will be things that you may need to take to wise counsel. There will be things that will require trust and love to recover. There will be things that only effective communication will ease the pain from. There will be things that sex cannot fix. There will be things that money cannot buy. Your family or outside influences may not be the best support during some of the storms. Remembering why you said "I do" can be the start of your healing process but doing the work will have to complete the process. Your desire to be intentional and strategic during the assignment will lighten the weight if you are doing it as a team. Remember that "two becoming one" provides power and strength in the union. Become one in the spirit, mindset, and the flesh. The assignments are inevitable, why not be prepared for the task.

Often, we think that a successful and thriving marriage is one that shows financial stability, children that are in a prestigious college, a beautiful home, nice cars, and all the fixings that come with "the look" of success. These things are great to have, but a successful and thriving marriage, as a result of having acquired these things, is far from the truth. Success is an accomplishment of an aim or purpose. If you write the vision, make it understandable, and do the work to attain it, you are on your way to having a successful and thriving marriage. Not giving up or throwing in the towel when it does not feel like you are going to reach it, is not a success. Although others may not know what the goal was and can only judge success from what they see with the physical eye, you will see what you did not complete nor push yourself to complete. Working through the hiccups as a team is success. Attaining the "two becoming one" is a success. Serving the need of your spouse is a success. Being supportive as a spouse is a success. Working on the marriage, with more intent and purpose than you did the wedding, is a success.

Choose your solid foundation and begin to build on top of it. Design the marriage that you desire. A thriving marriage is in your hand, what will you choose to do with it?

Exclusive Sneak Peek

COMING LATE 2020

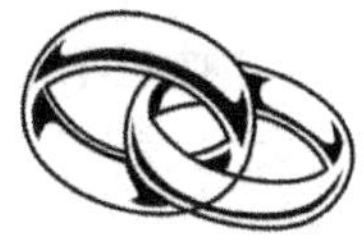

EXCLUSIVE SNEAK PEEK

Journey to the "D"

We were together for 18 years. We were married 14 of the 18. We were separated for 14 months before facing the "D!" For those who do not get it, "D," in this case, is for *divorce*.

I was intentional about fighting for my marriage. I stayed dressed in my war clothes, making sure that I had the proper tools in my marriage toolbox and using them in the correct area. I did all of that just to end up with the "D?!" I thought it was not an option. I thought it was something that we agreed to remove from the table. I just assumed that when we began to do the process of elimination, I would not have the "D" to choose from.

Granted, in the earlier years of the 18, there was a lot of guessing, testing, and flat out just not knowing. Mistakes were made, and bad decisions were agreed upon, but I used it all as experience that assisted in RISE'ing to the next level. Note: Never repeat anything that does not work. Only a fool does that, and as I matured and gained wisdom, strategizing would not allow me to go down the path of familiarity that did not work...so I thought.

On December 8, 2017, the road to 14 months separated began. I knew *her*. She knew me. She and I had discussed our marriages (in detail) with each other...and clearly, so did they.

I remember the first time speaking with her just like it was yesterday. We were at couple's bible study, and neither of our husbands were there with us. After bible study ended and we said our goodbyes, she and I stopped in the parking lot and began to talk. We talked about our daughters going off to college and how proud we were of them. Somehow one of the topics from our bible study came up, and we began to share about our marriages. We were both there because we agreed that we wanted to be better wives, but honestly, we were both pretty fed up with some of the things that we had encountered with our husbands.

Although we did not have similar stories, we were able to relate to each other's frustrations. I remember looking around the parking lot because we were now the last two standing there talking while the deacon waited so that he could lock the gate once we left. I gave her a little insight into what I was dealing with because I wanted her to understand that she is not the only soldier fighting for her marriage. I was there fighting with her. We must extend our hands before others share their hearts, and that is just what I did. Having this conversation was the beginning of getting to know each other, but it did not go beyond our marriages. This was the only subject where we could connect.

On December 8, 2017, when I learned that my husband was stepping outside of our marriage, I never in a million years would have thought it was her. As everyone danced and he asked me to record them (him included) with his phone, I did. Once my arm got tired; I stopped the recording and sat the phone down. His text messages were open, and I saw a photograph of him in the gym that he sent to me earlier, but I was not the only person the picture was sent to. I thought, unless he has me programmed in his phone under KC, I am sure it was for someone else. At that time, I was thinking, he and his boys often send pictures to each other flexing. It was no big deal. I picked up the phone to scroll and see KC, and there was no picture. However, there was a message that was definitely not for one of his buddies.

"Good morning, beautiful," the text read. This was how he addressed me in the morning, but only this time it was not for me. My heart raced, and at some point, I believe it may have stopped just like everyone on the dance floor. I went back and forth, watching him dance, back to reading the messages on the phone. He was doing the cupid shuffle, and it was almost time for the group to "*walk it by yourself*" in my direction. What did I do? I quickly looked at the phone number, memorized it, sat his phone down, picked mine up, and typed it in my notes section on my phone. At this point, I was so lost and unsure of what to do, so the first best thing was to ask God for direction. I did! It was nothing that I expected to hear.

"God, what do I do at this moment?" He quickly replied and said, "Be still!" *What in the...ok, this is God that I am talking to,* is what I thought. *Watch your mouth.* I checked myself.

My husband came back to the table and I said, "Here babe, your phone. I'm going to the restroom; I'll be back." Going downstairs to the restroom felt like the most difficult task I had taken in a while. Like a toddler beginning to walk or a teenager walking in heels for the first time, I wobbled down the stairs, and it was not due to drinking. *If I could just get to the restroom without anyone stopping me*, I thought.

I made it. There was a lady inside of the restroom giving out lotion, candy, perfume, etc. I saw her but never acknowledged anything that she offered me. Like in the movie "Two Can Play That Game," I looked in the mirror and said, "Get it together, Shante, get it together."

Yes, I called myself Shante that night. I took a few deep breaths, asked God again, "What do I do?" and He said again, "Be still! Continue to do everything that you would have done before reading this message." Walking out of the restroom, I was forced to pull it together when I ran into another one of the party attendees. I said, "Hey girl, are they still doing that New Orleans dance?" She said, "Yes, and that was my chance to leave out and use the bathroom because I'm from Kansas City," and we went our separate way.

With the information she gave me it was my cue that he was still inside, and I had more time to try to calm down. I am sure my blood pressure was high. I had to talk to someone that would calm me down. I called my girlfriend and with deep heavy breaths I called her name and then said, "He's cheating"!

With a very calm voice, she told me to relax. She asked if he was near and if I had said anything. I said that I had not because God told me not to. She then removed herself from giving me any advice or her opinion and said, "Well be obedient to what He told you to do." I agreed, we hung up, and it was time to go because he had walked down. The drive home was a bit awkward for me because he was acting normal, and I was forcing normal.

It was not confirmed who *she* was until the next day. I was still doing what God told me and continuing as if nothing had occurred, but the inside of me was broken in a million pieces. We had a funeral to attend, but I needed my car washed, plus I wanted to be away from him as much as possible to avoid saying anything prematurely. I was genuinely depending on God's "go ahead" before mentioning anything.

I went to the car wash. It was a drive-through wash. As I was sitting inside, I decided to remove the number from my notes and put it into my contacts. Just when I thought I had felt the worst from just reading the messages the night before, I was hit, again with another whammy.

As I typed her number in, her name popped up. I thought to myself, "Clearly I typed the wrong number. I deleted the few digits that I had typed and started over. NOPE! I was typing it correctly. God began to bring to my memory as if He were in the passenger seat. He said, "Remember when you walked out of the restroom last night, and she said that she left out because she was from "Kansas City?" I could not allow you to put the name programmed in the phone (KC) and that statement together. I told you to be still because everything must be done decently and in order when I am involved. It happened the way that it was supposed to happen. You would have embarrassed yourself in front of a group of people that would have never seen my glory had you reacted that night."

My car was now out of the wash area and I drove to the vacuum area, held on to the steering wheel and broke down, and said, "Now Lord?" His answer was still, "No, be still." It was a bit easier this time because He just showed me why He said it before, so I was confident that He was totally in control. But I thought, do you really expect me to be able to keep quiet? I said, "God I can't," and He said, "You will."

I went home and surprisingly enough; I could not feel anything. I was numb. I did not feel any emotion. I was not angry; I was not mad, I was not hurt, I was not confused, I was just numb. Not knowing what to do other than think about what God said....*be still.*

I got to the church early in case I needed to help before the family arrived, plus I was on the program. I walked in; there she was. My heart dropped, but I reminded myself of what God told me to do. *Be still.* We spoke and I even hugged her. *God, what are you doing*? I asked Him inside. There was no answer this time. I was afraid because He had been directing me the entire time and this time, I could not hear Him. *Lord, where are you*? He said, "The instruction did not change." I took a seat.

It was pretty full in the church. My husband sat a few rows behind me, but I did not notice until it was my turn to go up and do what I had been asked to do on the program. It was time to view the body, and I did not want to do that, so I walked out of the church into the foyer. Passing her by, I could see her looking at me from the corners of her eye and it was at that point that I could not take it any longer. I did not ask God anything. I made a B-line and went to her, hugged her, and I whispered in her ear, "Hey KC, I'm aware of the affair that you and my husband are having." Her mouth dropped. I leaned back and pointed at her and then looked in the foyer where he was standing and pointed at him. This is where it all began.

I went to him and told him that I could not believe what he had done. Before I made a scene, we went outside, and he admitted to where their relationship was headed! Life had changed just that fast.

My emotions were all over the place. I blamed my husband, the other women and myself at some point in this emotional roller coaster. I was not the blame and honestly, I can't blame her. Truthfully, it is not a finger-pointing game because in the end, with disappointment, a broken heart, and embarrassment, it led to gained wisdom and a closer relationship with God. He ultimately got the glory in it all.

Although if I had to say which knife cut me the deepest, it was the knife of embarrassment and disappointment. All I could hear in my torn spirit was, "Not Tam, the marriage advocate. Ok, so she's teaching how and what in marriage and hers is going down the drain?! She must have known that they were not solid. How hypocritical." I felt that my character had been tarnished and my brand no longer held value at all.

Having my brand and character tarnished tore me up, yet God told me to hold my head up, move forward with ***Make It R.I.S.E.***, and allow Him to fight the battle. It was not easy, but I trusted Him. Blindly, I walked and realized that some folks follow the "purpose" and others follow the "person." Those believing the purpose take a hit with you, and those believing in the person.... hit you!

****

Although I was kept (by God), I was broken. I could not understand why He was allowing me to experience this, though I trusted Him. I "knew" that on the other side of through He had something great in store for me. I just did not "feel" it.

I said, "Lord, are you giving me the approval? Are you releasing me from this marriage?" I never believed that divorce was ok, but in this process, the struggle, the questioning and the studying of the Word, I learned that God will keep you while in it, or release you from it. I recalled hearing God in previous situations in my marriage when my ex-husband said he wanted a divorce. God told me very clearly, "Continue to be the wife." That meant, do not deviate from the plan because of what you see and hear him say. I stood. I was the wife. I did not move. It was hard and unsettling, but I trusted God.

I learned at that time, that during tough situations when it is common to quit, listening and obeying God's instructions were imperative. I read 1 Corinthians 7:14 over and over again because I couldn't believe that I was hearing God correctly. I read it in multiple versions. I asked ministers and Pastors and it all lead back to what God had previously told me. It was only confirmation. I came to the conclusion that God had a message for me that wasn't for everyone and listing to the stories of others who had similar experiences wasn't making what God was saying to me any clearer. In fact, the more I listened to others the further away His voice began to sound. I had to shut everyone out, pray and fast to get clarity about what He was saying to Tamora. I was being prepared for "Life After the D."

The journey of being at peace taught me to not only believe God but to trust God. You ask, what is the difference? There is a BIG difference. I can believe that you can do something, but do I trust that you will do it for me? That is where fear is born. Knowing that fear is paralysis, I attempted to stay away from it, but of course, it was inevitable.

So, what did that do? I was encouraged to talk to God even more, hence the closer relationship. The more you talk to someone, the better you get to know them. So here I am, receiving from God, about not only my husband, but He was showing me things about myself that I ignored previously. It is funny how we can hear so much clearer when we give ourselves permission to shut out "the noise." Boy was this a roller coaster, but when I got to the end of that ride, I understood the loops, drops, turns, and abrupt stops. It just made sense. I stepped off this roller coaster with every hair intact, my heart rate had gone back to normal, my smile was brighter, and you could not tell that I had been on this loopy roller coaster.... I can smile and laugh now. Just like God, to keep you!

Acknowledgements

To my Pastor Rafer Owens and First Lady Natalie Owens, I am grateful to have been under your leadership and tutelage during the hardest time of my life. Your guidance, unbiased, and unwavering counsel was a true example of what it looks like to follow God even in the midst of the stuff. I can't say how I would have handled things, had I not been equipped with the tools that I used to walk with my head held high, trusting God, and doing the work (on self) as I waited (on the shift). Thank you both.

To all my girlfriends who chose to stand by my side during this season of my life, thank you. I don't have the words to express my gratitude. God truly blessed me when He gifted you to me.

To Erika and Maurice, you have no idea how much I appreciate you. There were nights that I could not allow my daughter to see me so broken and you opened your home to me. You saw the side of me that no one else saw. You allowed me to be me without any judgment. I became a part of your beautiful family. Thank you, and I love you so much.

To Bridget, my buddy, your special donation was one of the biggest blessings at the time that you offered. I was caught a bit off guard, but I know that it was God who sent you to sow the seed and I say thank you. I love you, friend, and I thank you for being obedient to Gods instruction.

Tina Tate, thanks for answering the call. I must say that if you had responded any way other than how you did on that night; the prologue would read much different. Thank you for knowing when to remove your emotions and opinions so that I could continue to hear God.

To my Diva Diary chics (Quiana & Herlette), you played a major part in my healing process and I appreciate every meetup, late night/early morning text messages, prayer calls and sisterhood that we now have. You ladies rock!

Angel Brown, you have been my calm in the storm in so many cases and none of it was in vain. I listened to our messages over and over again when I didn't feel like being bothered with anyone but needed to be fed. You were a major part in my healing process and still today you are one of the best chics that I rock with. I love you.

To "that guy" that I never knew that I was "Wade'n" on, thank you for your unconditional love and support during this writing process. Your love and support have truly required me to stretch in areas that I have never tapped into. You were an ear and a shoulder every time things got a little heavy for me. I love you, handsome.

Tasharee, I love you and thank you for hanging in there with me…. still! Nothing will ever change that! You are stuck with me, daughter…you have my heart!

Last, but not least... my girls - Mom, Simone, and Imari. I spent many days and nights locked in the room, going out to Starbucks, and trying to stay on task with writing and balancing out being mom and daughter. It was not always easy, but you never made me feel like I was slacking in any area. I love you, ladies. You are my heart!

About the Author

Tamora K. Johnson's passion lies within providing tools for couples to continue to build or rebuild the relationship or marriage that they are designing. Tamora believes that her transparency can be someone's road to recovery, and therefore is known for sharing her story. Tamora often states that she is what she needed before she said, "I Do."

Tamora was married for 14 years before she and her husband separated, then divorced. She believes the bulk of her knowledge is from God's word, her experience and journey from being a girlfriend, fiancé, wife, separated, and eventually divorced. Tamora has 3 beautiful daughters and prides herself in being an exceptional example for them as a mother, wife, and leader. It is her life's mission to mentor, advocate and help improve the state of the marriage entity, as a whole, on a global level. It is in this realm where she can assist the women and men who have decided to take such a huge leap of faith to love another human being in a Christ-like manner, unconditionally.

Tamora began ***Make It R.I.S.E. (Rebuild Intentionally & Strategically for Effectiveness)*** in 2014, however, she did not completely commit (mind body and soul) until 2015. Workshops, couples events, and one-on-one meetings with couples are a few ways that she has given tools to add into the toolbox of marriage and/or relationships, which encourage the R.I.S.E. Ultimately, Tamora hopes to inspire and motivate all couples to be true to their divine purpose and serve their spouse with that same energy to create the relationship of their dreams.

www.tamorajohnson.com

Make it R.I.S.E. (MIR) was established, by Tamora K. Johnson, in 2014. The organization was created to serve as a vehicle to advocate for healthy marriages and remind couples of the tools they currently possess to create their ideal relationship experience. It functions as an accessible resource to design a healthy marriage that will help to consistently catapult the union to new levels of love and commitment. MIR occasionally hosts interactive workshops, memorable events, and intimate one-on-one sessions with couples, to assist them in their mission to love each other in a Christ-like, unconditional manner.

We are on social media. Search Make It R.I.S.E.

www.ingramcontent.com/pod-product-compliance
Lightning Source LLC
LaVergne TN
LVHW050647100826
845148LV00011B/2026

* 9 7 8 0 5 7 8 5 8 4 1 1 9 *